Adobe® Photoshop® CS2

Level 1 (Second Edition)

Roopa Thomas
Priya Ranjith
Yamini Gopalakrishnan

Adobe® Photoshop® CS2: Level 1 (Second Edition)

Part Number: 084563
Course Edition: 1.0

Acknowledgments

Project Team

Content Developer: Yamini Gopalakrishnan, Roopa Thomas and Priya Ranjith • **Content Manager:** Adrian B K • **Graphic Designer:** Anita Esther Jebakumari • **Project Coordinator:** Anil Kumar Singh • **Media Instructional Designer:** Yamini Gopalakrishnan, Roopa Thomas and Priya Ranjith • **Content Editor:** Sindhu Sreekumar • **Materials Editor:** Anbuselvan A • **Project Technical Support:** Mike Toscano

NOTICES

Your comments are important to us. Please contact us at Element K Press LLC, 1-800-478-7788, 500 Canal View Boulevard, Rochester, NY 14623, Attention: Product Planning, or through our Web site at **http://support.elementkcourseware.com.**

Adobe® Photoshop® CS2: Level 1 (Second Edition)

Lesson 1: Exploring Photoshop Environment

Contents

Lesson 4: Creating Image Composites

Contents

Lesson 7: Applying Colors

Lesson 8: Enhancing Images with Text and Special Effects

Contents

Notes

About This Course

As a graphic designer, you are starting to familiarize yourself with image creation and editing using Photoshop. Understanding the different tools and features available in Photoshop CS2 will help you to maximize your creative potential. In this course, you'll work with several tools and features to edit images using Photoshop CS2.

Photoshop CS2 offers you tools and techniques, including editing, coloring, painting and retouching tools that helps you to create and edit images. By working with these features you will be able to design, create and enhance images with ease.

Course Description

Target Student

This course is intended for new users of Photoshop.

Course Prerequisites

Before taking this course, students should be familiar with the basic functions of their computer's operating system such as creating folders, launching programs, and working with Windows. Students should also have basic Windows application skills, such as copying and pasting objects, formatting text, and saving files.

How to Use This Book

As a Learning Guide

Each lesson covers one broad topic or set of related topics. Lessons are arranged in order of increasing proficiency with *Adobe® Photoshop® CS2 Level 1 Second Edition*; skills you acquire in one lesson are used and developed in subsequent lessons. For this reason, you should work through the lessons in sequence.

We organized each lesson into results-oriented topics. Topics include all the relevant and supporting information you need to master *Adobe® Photoshop® CS2 Level 1 Second Edition*, and activities allow you to apply this information to practical hands-on examples.

You get to try out each new skill on a specially prepared sample file. This saves you typing time and allows you to concentrate on the skill at hand. Through the use of sample files, hands-on activities, illustrations that give you feedback at crucial steps, and supporting background information, this book provides you with the foundation and structure to learn *Adobe® Photoshop CS2 Level 1 Second Edition* quickly and easily.

As a Review Tool

Any method of instruction is only as effective as the time and effort you are willing to invest in it. In addition, some of the information that you learn in class may not be important to you immediately, but it may become important later on. For this reason, we encourage you to spend some time reviewing the topics and activities after the course. For additional challenge when reviewing activities, try the "What You Do" column before looking at the "How You Do It" column.

As a Reference

The organization and layout of the book make it easy to use as a learning tool and as an after-class reference. You can use this book as a first source for definitions of terms, background information on given topics, and summaries of procedures.

Course Objectives

In this course, you will explore the Photoshop interface and use several tools for selecting parts of images, and will move, duplicate, and resize images. You will learn to use layers, and to apply layer effects and filters to create special effects. Additionally, you will use painting tools and blending modes to create shading effects, and will perform adjustments to contrast and color balance. Finally, you will save images in formats for print and web use.

You will:

- explore the Photoshop CS2 environment.
- ensure that images have an appropriate balance between file size and print or display quality and also crop images to remove unnecessary areas.
- use the different selection tools in Photoshop to select parts of images and also save selections for future use.
- create image composites and use several techniques for creating and manipulating layers and use the techniques in Photoshop for undoing the previous steps.
- apply blending effects to composite images so that they appear more realistic.
- identity the various image modes characteristics and select the appropriate image mode for specific purposes.
- select colors and paint image using the various color and painting tools in Photoshop and duplicate parts of an image using the Clone Stamp tool.
- add type to an image, format it, and create special effects by applying filters.
- adjust an image's brightness, contrast, hue, and saturation.

- save completed images for printed applications and for the web and also save the images as PDF documents.

Course Requirements

Hardware

- Intel® Xeon, Xeon Dual, Centrino, or Pentium® class III or 4 processor.
- At least 512 MB of RAM.
- At least 1GB of free hard-disk space to install software, and an additional 500 MB to run the course.
- A color monitor with 16-bit or greater video card; 24 bit color recommended.
- A mouse or compatible tracking device.
- 1024 x 768 or greater monitor resolution.
- A CD-ROM drive.
- A display system to project the instructor's computer screen.

Software

- Microsoft® Windows 2000 with Service Pack 3, or Windows XP with Service Pack 1 or 2
- Adobe® Photoshop® CS2
- Adobe® Reader® 7.0

Class Setup

1. On the course CD-ROM, run the 084563dd.exe self-extracting file located within. This will install a folder named 084563Data on your C drive. This folder contains all the data files that you will use to complete this course. Solution files are also provided in this folder. These files may help you find a possible solution if you get stuck at any point during the course. If you would like to view the final output or solution of an activity, navigate to the respective lesson\topic\activity\solution folder.
2. In order to ensure that all features of Photoshop will be available for this course, run a standard installation from the software installation CD.
3. This course will run best if you remove the Photoshop preferences files. If these preferences are not removed, some of the options chosen during previous sessions may affect your work in Photoshop throughout this course. Navigate to the C:\Documents and Settings\[User]\Application Data\Adobe\ Photoshop\9.0 folder. Delete the Adobe® Photoshop® CS2 Settings folder, or drag it to another location on your computer's hard disk so you can reinstate it after the class to continue using the settings it specifies.
4. This course will run most smoothly if your monitor resolution is set to at least 1024 x 768.

5. In addition to the specific setup procedures needed for this class to run properly, you should also check the Element K Press product support website at **http://support.elementkcourseware.com** for more information. Any updates about this course will be posted there.

List of Additional Files

Printed with each activity is a list of files students open to complete that activity. Many activities also require additional files that students do not open, but are needed to support the file(s) students are working with. These supporting files are included with the student data files on the course CD-ROM or data disk. Do not delete these files.

LESSON 1

Exploring Photoshop Environment

Lesson Time
1 hour(s), 15 minutes

Lesson Objectives:

In this lesson, you will explore the Photoshop CS2 environment.

You will:

- Identify raster and vector images.
- Explore the Photoshop environment.
- Customize the Photoshop environment.
- Work with the navigation tools in Photoshop.
- Customize menus by selecting options in the Menus dialog box.
- Explore the functions of assets in Adobe Bridge.
- Apply metadata and keywords to assets in Adobe Bridge.

Introduction

You are ready to start using Photoshop to edit images. Before you jump into a project, you want to customize the Photoshop environment to suit the way you work. In this lesson, you will explore and customize the Photoshop user interface.

By familiarizing yourself with basic imaging terminology and customizing the Photoshop environment, you can enhance your productivity and tailor the workspace to suit common work tasks.

TOPIC A

Differentiate Raster and Vector Graphics

You have to create an image with scanned photographs and hand-drawn artwork, or by painting and creating artwork from within an application. But before you begin the project, you will need to decide on the type of graphics to use, to create your desired final output. In this topic, you will examine and work with raster and vector graphics.

Photoshop is an invaluable tool for creating graphics, and the results can include retouched and color-corrected photographs, photo-illustrations, realistic simulations of traditional painting and drawing media, and computer effects. But before you create images, you must realize that these graphic images are created by pixels or geometric shapes.

Raster Graphics

Raster graphics are graphics comprised of a grid or raster, which is an array of small squares called pixels. Each of these pixels allows for a wide variation of color. Because raster images contain many pixels, they also require more memory and storage to manipulate them. Photoshop images are raster graphics.

Vector Graphics

Vector graphics are composed of lines, curves, and geometric shapes that are defined by a set of mathematical instructions. They are not pixelated. Graphics applications such as Adobe Illustrator create vector graphics.

 A pixel is a colored, black, white, or transparent square within an image; an array of pixels comprises the raster image as a whole.

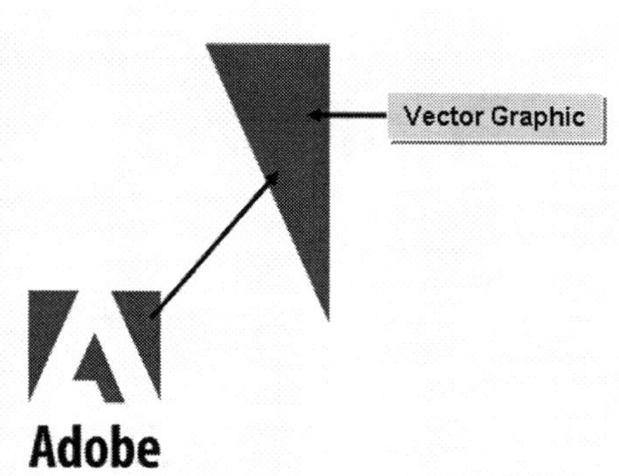

ACTIVITY 1-1

Identifying the Types of Graphics

Scenario:

You have attended a training session on the different types of graphics and would like to test your knowledge at the end of the session.

What You Do	How You Do It

1. **True or False? Raster graphics require less memory and storage to manipulate them.**

   __ True

   __ False

2. **Which statements about raster graphics are true?**

   a) Raster graphics are composed of a grid of pixels.

   b) Raster graphics are composed of lines defined by a set of mathematical instructions.

   c) Raster graphics can be created using the Photoshop application.

   d) Raster graphics are composed of curves and geometrical shapes.

3. **True or False? Vector graphics are composed of mathematically defined shapes.**

   __ True

   __ False

TOPIC B

Explore the Photoshop Environment

You are preparing to explore how to create and edit images using Photoshop CS2. Before you can do that, you will need to recognize the Photoshop environment and the tools you can use. In this topic, you will explore the Photoshop environment.

The Photoshop environment consists of several elements. Familiarizing yourself with the Photoshop environment before starting a project will help you through the tasks of creating and editing an image with less effort.

The Photoshop Window

The Photoshop window contains many of the same features as a window in any other program, such as command menus at the top of the window, but with additional tools and palettes for creating, editing, and enhancing images.

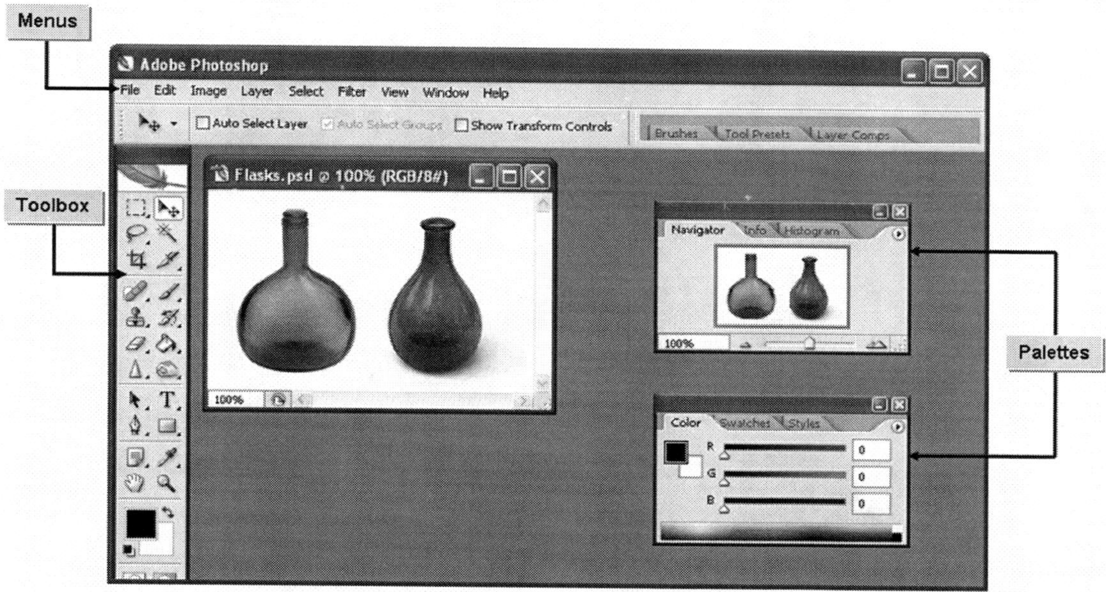

The Status Bar

The status bar at the bottom of the window displays the current magnification of the image, and the File Information box. The *File Information box*, which contains the document size in kilo bytes or mega bytes, is where you get information on the physical and storage size of the displayed Photoshop image.

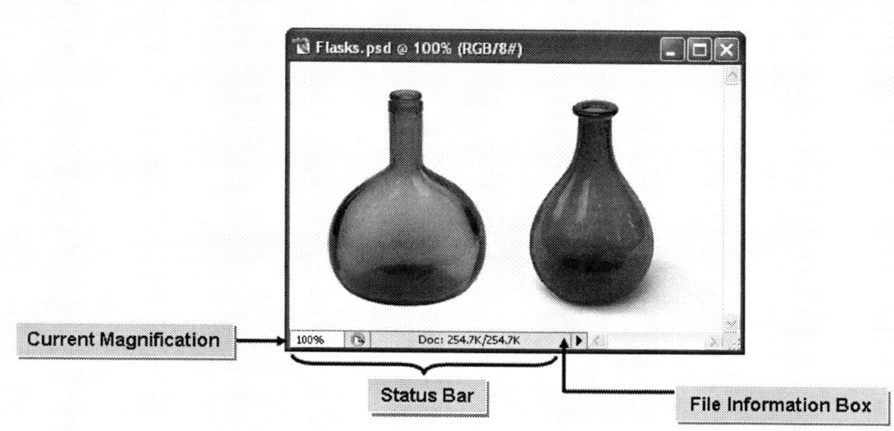

The Floating Palettes

Photoshop employs several floating palettes that help you navigate through an image, choose colors, layer objects, and set other options. Although you can close the palettes individually to hide them, pressing Tab is the quickest way of completely clearing the screen of palettes. You can bring the palettes back by pressing Tab again, or by opening the palettes one at a time. Pressing Shift+Tab hides all palettes except the toolbox and the Tool Options bar.

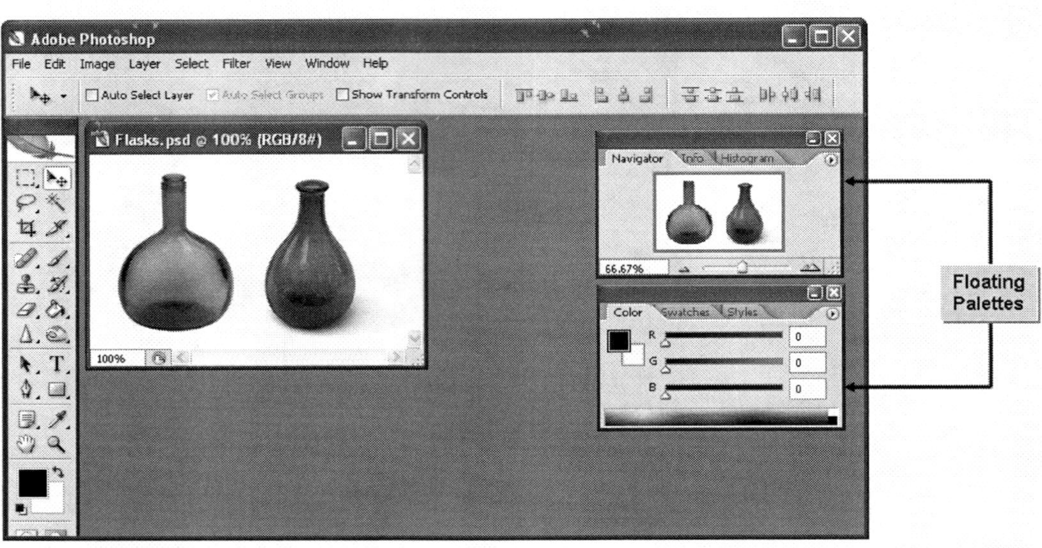

The Tool Options Bar

The Tool Options bar at the top of the screen displays various options for the currently selected tool. In addition, it contains a palette well in which you can store other palettes to free more screen space.

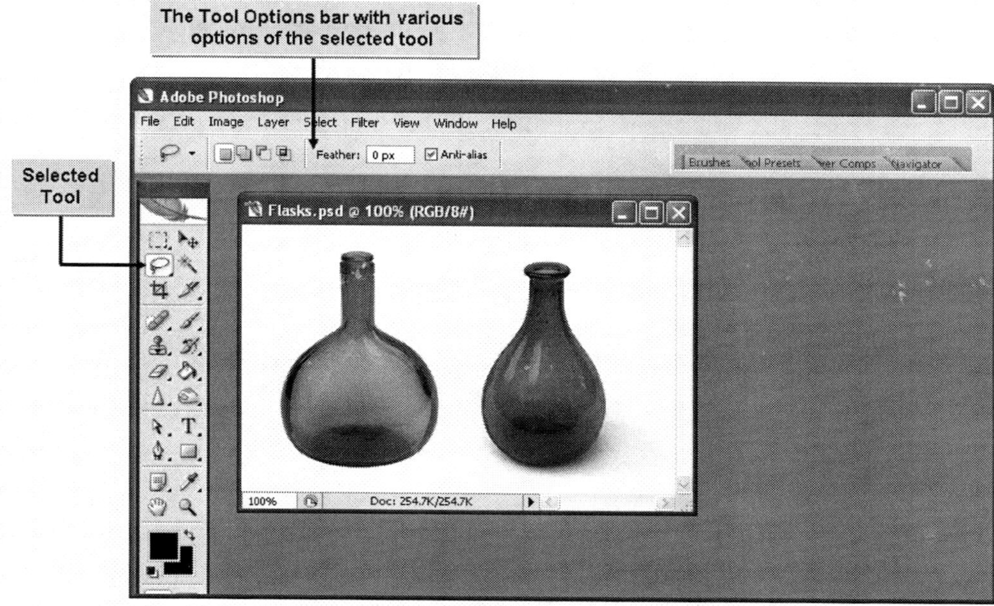

The Toolbox

The Photoshop's *toolbox* is used to select, move, edit, paint, and view images. The toolbox contains seven major sections such as the selection and manipulation tools; painting tools; type, path, and shape tools; utility tools; color controls; mode controls; and window controls. The toolbox also contains a button at the top for navigating to Adobe's website, and a button at the bottom for launching ImageReady. When you position the mouse pointer over a tool, a rectangular tool tip appears, displaying the tool's name and the key that can be pressed to select the tool.

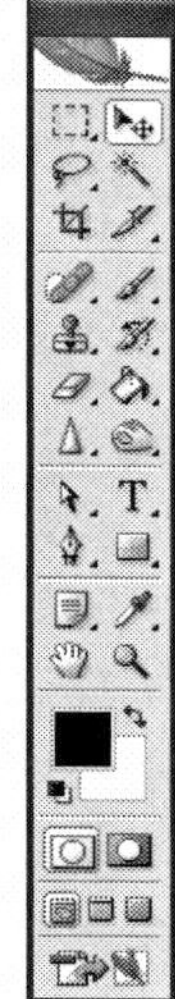

The toolbox contains tools to select, move, edit, paint, and view images

You can access each tool by several methods. You can simply click the tool itself. Otherwise, you can click the tool and hold down the mouse button on the tools that display a small triangle at the bottom-right corner to access additional tools in a group. Similarly, you can hold down Alt and click a tool group to move to the next tool in the group. You can also access the tools by pressing the letter displayed to the right of the tool's tool tip, on the keyboard. Holding down Shift and typing the letter helps you to toggle between tools in a group.

The Selection and Manipulation Tools

The Selection and Manipulation tools help you make selections in an image, move selected areas, edit out specific parts of an image, and select rectangular areas to create links.

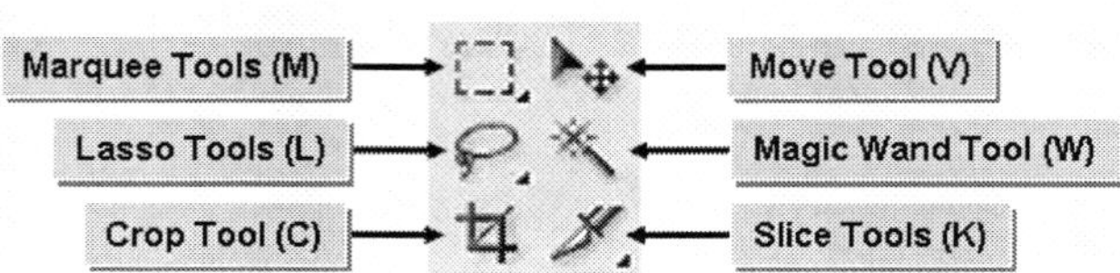

Selection and Manipulation Tool	Description
Marquee tools (M)	These tools allow you to make selections. They consist of Rectangular, Elliptical, Single Row, and Single Column tool. The tool group shortcut, M, functions only to select the Rectangular and Elliptical Marquee tools.
Move tool (V)	This tool allows you to move selected areas or layers within the image, or to another image.
Lasso tools (L)	These tools, which consist of Lasso, Polygonal, and Magnetic lasso, allow you to make selections of any shape by manually dragging the shape of the selection.
Magic Wand tool (W)	This tool allows you to make automatic selections of similarly colored areas.
Crop tool (C)	This tool allows you to select part of an image and discard the remainder.

Selection and Manipulation Tool	Description
Slice tools (K)	These tools, which consist of the Slice and Slice Select tools, allow you to create and select rectangular areas of an image so that each of these areas, or slices, can be used to create links, rollovers, or animations in a web page containing the image.

The Painting Tools

The Painting tools help you correct and repair imperfections in images; paint; take samples of images and paint copies of them elsewhere; paint over images; erase pixels; create gradient files; and sharpen or blur images.

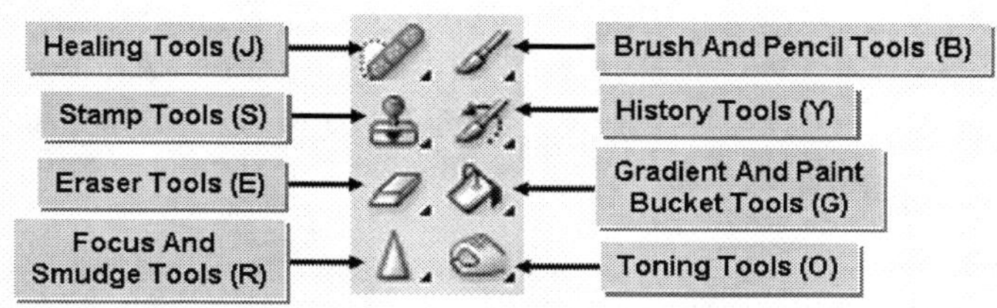

Painting Tool	Description
Healing tools (J)	These tools consist of the Healing Brush and Patch tools, and they let you correct and repair imperfections by sampling an image or a pattern and also paint copies of it elsewhere, like the Stamp tools. In addition, the tools let you match the texture, lighting, and shading of pixels in an image or pattern to the source pixels. The Color Replacement tool replaces color with the foreground color, but maintains the texture, lighting, and shading of the original pixels.
Brush and Pencil tools (B)	These tools allow you to paint with the foreground color using standard or custom brushes, as well as simulate airbrush capabilities.

Painting Tool	Description
Stamp tools (S)	These tools allow you to take a sample of an image or a pattern and paint copies of it elsewhere. The Stamp tools consist of the Clone and Pattern.
History tools (Y)	These tools comprise of the History Brush tool and the Art History Brush tool. The History Brush tool allows you to paint over an image with a previous state that you have specified in order to correct mistakes. The Art History Brush tool allows you to paint over an image with a stylized version of a previous state that you have specified.
Eraser tools (E)	These tools allow you to erase pixels, and revert parts of an image to a previous state. You can use the other eraser tools such as the Background Eraser and Magic Eraser tools to erase to transparency.
Gradient and Paint Bucket tools (G)	These tools allow you to create gradient fills that transition between two or more colors. The Paint Bucket tool fills areas of an image that are similar in color to the color of the pixel on which you click.
Focus and Smudge tools (R)	These tools such as the Blur and Sharpen tools allow you to blur or sharpen part of an image. The Smudge tool simulates dragging a finger through wet paint.
Toning tools (O)	These tools lighten, darken, saturate, or desaturate parts of images. The Toning tools consist of the Dodge, Burn, and Sponge tools.

The Type, Path and Shape Tools

The Type, Path, and Shape tools help select, create, and edit vector path segments, add text to an image; and create shapes.

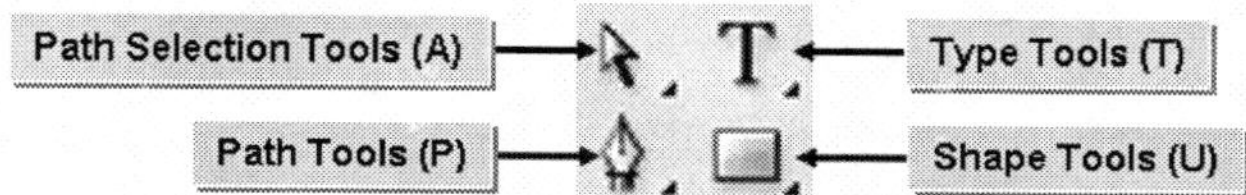

Type, Path and Shape Tool	Description
Path Selection tools (A)	These tools consist of the Path Selection and Direct Selection tools. They select vector path segments and components. Vector paths are composed of connect-the-dots-like segments and points, and allow you to select and paint image areas, and to create clipping paths for the EPS and TIFF file formats.
Type tools (T)	These tools consist of the Horizontal, Vertical, Horizontal Type Mask, and the Vertical Type Mask tools. The Type tools allow you add text to an image. The Type Mask tools create a selection in the shape of the type.
Path tools (P)	These tools consist of the Pen, Freeform Pen, Add Anchor Point, Delete Anchor Point, and Convert Point tools. They allow you to create and edit vector paths. The tool group shortcut, P, functions only to select the Pen and Freeform Pen tools.
Shape tools (U)	These tools consist of the Rectangle, Rounded Rectangle, Ellipse, Polygon, Line, and Custom Shape tools. With the Shape tools, you can draw rectangles, ellipses, polygons, lines, and custom shapes.

The Utility Tools

The Utility tools allow you to make notes and voice annotations, select background and foreground colors, scroll through an image, and reduce or increase image magnification.

Utility Tool	Description
Annotation tools (N)	These tools allow you to make notes and voice annotations that can be attached to an image.
Color Sampling and Measure tools (I)	These tools comprise of the Eyedropper tool, Color Sampler tool, and Measure tool. The Eyedropper tool is used to select foreground or background colors from existing colors in an image. You can use the Color Sampler tool to click up to four positions in an image, and the Info palette will display color information for those positions. The Measure tool is used to measure distances, locations, and angles within images.
Hand tool (H)	This tool can be used instead of the scroll bars to scroll an image within the window.
Zoom tool (Z)	This tool is used to increase or decrease the on-screen magnification of an image.

The Color Control Tools

The Color Control tools display the current foreground and background colors, and enable you to switch between them.

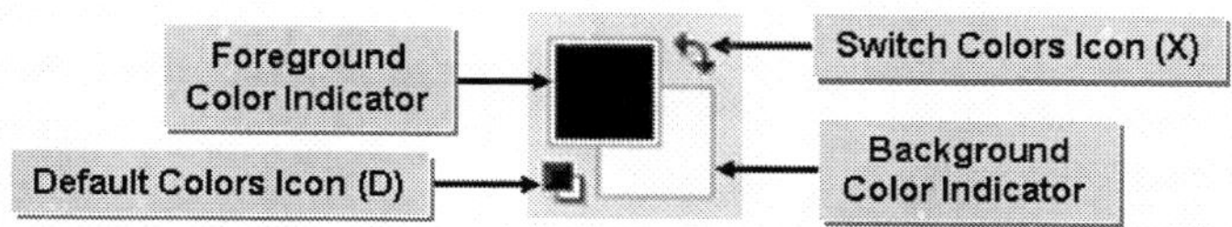

Color Control Tool	Description
Foreground color indicator	Shows the current foreground color. The foreground color is the color you paint with when you use most painting tools.
Background color indicator	Shows the current background color. The background color appears when pixels are erased or moved, and can be used in gradients.
Default colors icon (D)	Resets the foreground color to black and the background color to white.
Switch colors icon (X)	Switches the current foreground and background colors.

The Mode Control Tools

Mode Control tools are used to make selections before editing or painting and to create temporary selection marks.

Mode Control Tool	Description
Standard Mode icon (Q)	Used to make selections and perform standard painting and editing.
Quick Mask Mode icon (Q)	Used to create and edit a temporary selection mask.

The Window Control Tools

The Window Control tools are used for different methods of displaying an image.

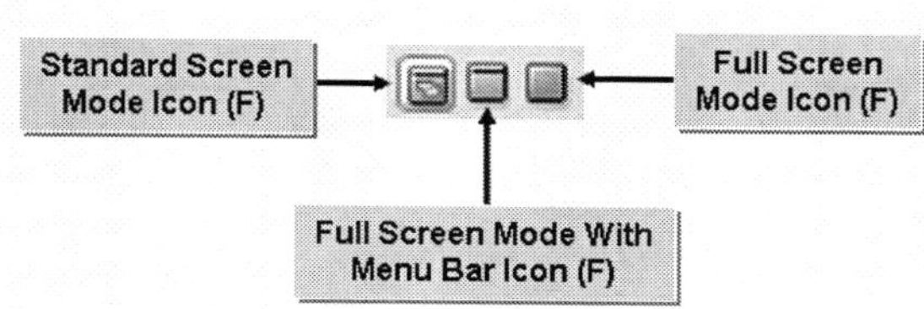

Window Control Tool	Description
Standard Screen Mode icon (F)	Displays an image in a full window with scroll bars and menus at the top of the screen.
Full Screen Mode with Menu Bar icon (F)	Displays an image in a window without scroll bars, window controls, or a title bar. However, the menu bar will still be apparent.
Full Screen Mode icon (F)	Displays the image in a window with no window controls. The rest of the screen is covered with a black background and the menu bar disappears.

How to Explore the Photoshop Environment

Procedure Reference: Set the Photoshop Window Display

To set the Photoshop window display:

1. Choose Start→All Programs→Adobe Photoshop CS2 to launch the application.
2. On the Welcome screen, click Close.
3. Choose File→Open.
4. In the Open dialog box, navigate to the desired folder, select the file and click Open to open an already existing file.
5. Set the window display by selecting the desired mode.

- At the bottom of the toolbox, click the Full Screen Mode With Menu Bar icon to view the image with a gray background at the center of the screen.
- At the bottom of the toolbox, click the Full Screen Mode icon to hide the window controls and menu bar. Only the image appears on your monitor along with the floating palettes.
- Press Tab to hide the palettes.
- At the bottom of the toolbox, click the Standard Screen Mode icon to once again view the image in a window with window controls and the menu bar.

Procedure Reference: Create a New Document

To create a new document:

1. Launch the Adobe Photoshop CS2 application.
2. Choose File→New.
3. In the New dialog box, specify the desired settings.
   - In the Name text box, type a name for the file.
   - In the Width text box, specify the width.
   - From the Background Contents drop-down list, select White, Background Color, or Transparent as the background for the image.
4. Click OK.

ACTIVITY 1-2

Exploring the Photoshop Environment

Data Files:

- Kid Stuff.psd

Scenario:

As a novice user of Photoshop CS2, you would like to explore the Photoshop environment. You also want to set the window display mode for the Photoshop environment to view the image as intended.

What You Do	How You Do It
1. **Open the Kid Stuff.psd file.**	a. **Choose Start→All Programs→Adobe Photoshop CS2** to launch the application.

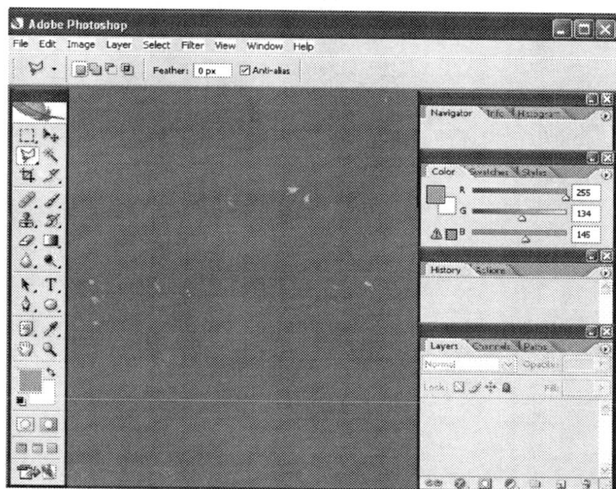

b. On the Welcome screen, **click Close.**

c. In the Adobe Photoshop window, **choose File→Open.**

d. In the Open dialog box, **navigate to the Local Disk (C:)\084563Data\Photoshop Environment\Activity 2\Starter folder.**

e. **Select the Kid Stuff.psd file.**

f. **Click Open.**

2. **Compare the window display modes.**

a. At the bottom of the toolbox, **click the Full Screen Mode With Menu Bar icon** to view the image at the center of the screen.

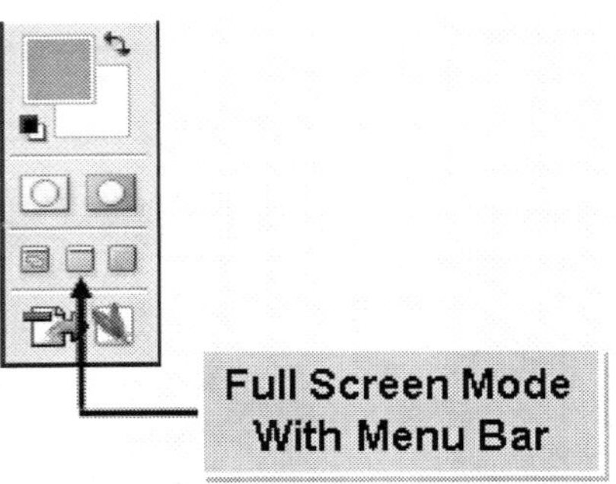

b. At the bottom of the toolbox, **click the Full Screen Mode icon** to hide the window controls and menu bar.

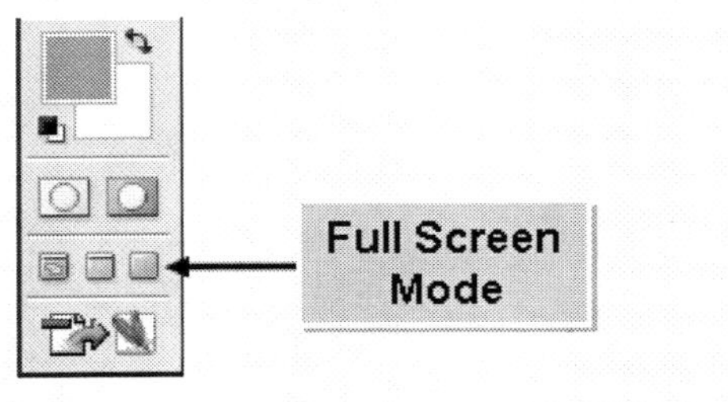

c. **Press Tab** to hide the palettes and view only the image.

d. **Press Tab** to return to view the palettes.

e. At the bottom of the toolbox, **click the Standard Screen Mode icon** to view the image along with the window controls and the menu bar.

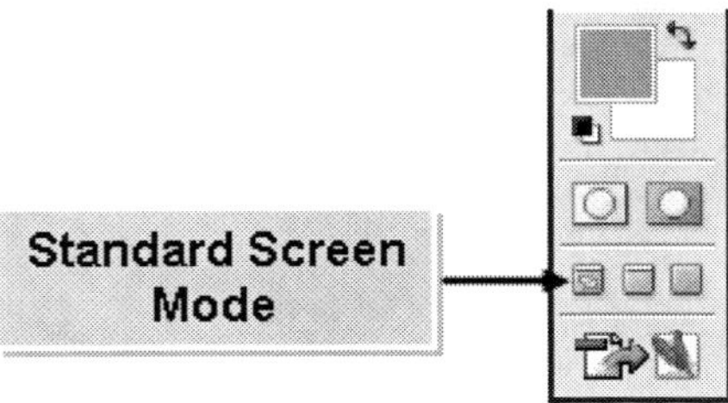

f. **Choose File→Close and click No when prompted to save.**

TOPIC C

Customize the Photoshop Environment

You have explored the Photoshop environment. It is possible to customize your workspace for easy access to tools and menus. In this topic, you will use workspace presets to customize the Photoshop environment.

Using Photoshop may make editing your images easy. But imagine a workspace cluttered with different tools and palettes. You would have a tough time navigating and locating the tools you want. Using workspace presets can make the task even easier, giving you all the specific tools you need, right at your fingertips.

Workspace

Photoshop workspace is the work area that contains the Photoshop environment elements. You can customize the palette locations, keyboard shortcuts and menus and save it as a workspace.

You can save workspaces for specific tasks such as painting or photo restoration, and pull them up quickly.

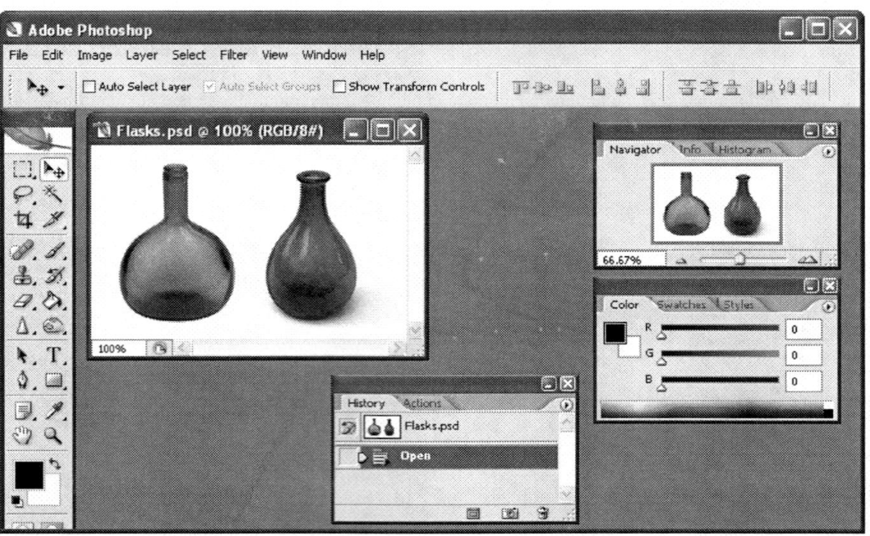

Palettes

By default, the Color, Swatches, and Styles palettes are part of a palette group. Each palette, within a group is represented by a tab at the top of the group, and only one palette is visible at a time. To make a palette visible, click its tab. As you work with images in Photoshop, you may want to rearrange Photoshop's palettes so that they are organized in a way that allows you to work most efficiently.

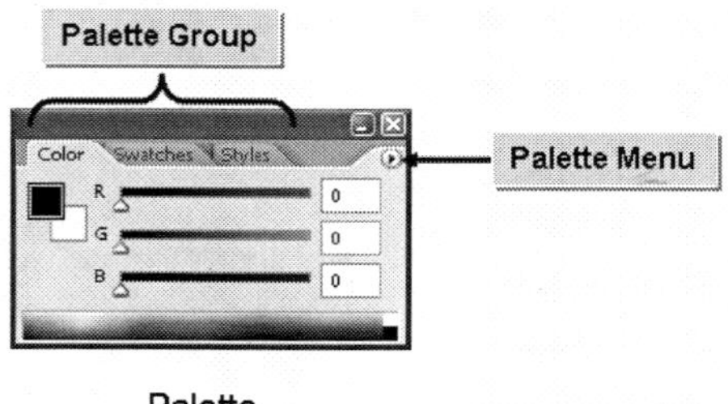

Palette

You can dock palettes together so that they can be moved or collapsed as a unit. To dock a palette to another palette or group, drag the palette by its tab to the top or bottom of the palette group until a horizontal line appears. Releasing the mouse button then docks the palette to the group's top or bottom making it part of the group. However, it continues to remain visible above or below the other palettes in the group. This doesn't save space on the screen, but it allows you to manipulate the docked palette along with the group. To undock a palette, drag its tab away from the palettes to which it is docked.

 Double-clicking the group's title bar collapses the group along with any palettes that are docked to it.

The Info Palette

The Info palette displays color values, document status information such as document size, document profile, document dimensions, scratch sizes, efficiency, timing, current tool, and 8-bit, 16-bit, or 32-bit values.

While specifying CMYK values, an exclamation point appears next to them if the color is unprintable. If a marquee tool is being used, the X and Y coordinates of the pointer position along with the width and height of the marquee will be displayed as you drag it, on the Info Palette. Similarly if the Crop tool or Zoom tool is being used, the Info palette displays the width and height of the marquee as you drag it. Then the palette also shows the angle of rotation of the crop marquee. If you are using the Line tool, the Pen tool, or Gradient tool, and if a selection is being moved, the Info palette will contain the X and Y coordinates of the position where you started.

Using the Info palette is one of the most useful ways of determining the color in your image. The Info palette indicates the actual color of the pixel at the mouse pointer's current location in accordance with the color model used, and shows the same color using an alternative color model. The color values for the current color mode appear on the left side of the Info palette, and CMYK values appear to the right.

The Palette Well

Palettes are added to the palette well on the Tool Options bar. Adding palettes to the palette well is useful when you need to refer to palettes such as the Info palette, while you are working. You can remove a palette from the palette well by dragging the palette tab away from the well. The palette well is only available when your monitor's resolution is set to at least 1024 x 768.

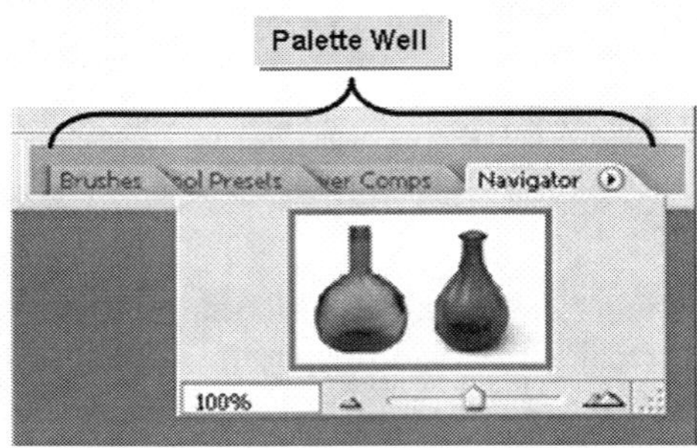

Workspace Presets

To accommodate specific tasks, Photoshop CS2 allows you to set *Workspace presets* to customize and organize menu items. You can select from nine preset options:

- Automation
- Basic
- Color and Tonal Correction
- Image Analysis
- Painting and Retouching
- Printing and Proofing
- Web Design
- What's New in CS2
- And, Working with Type

 When you start a new Photoshop project, a good idea is to customize your workspace for easy access to the menus and tools you will need.

The Preset Manager

The *Preset Manager* lets you choose your own workspace customizations from the library of preset palettes. The Preset Type drop-down list, located at the top of the Preset Manager dialog box, allows you to select from eight palettes to adjust appearances of the tool. The eight palettes are:

- Brushes
- Swatches
- Gradients

- Styles
- Patterns
- Contours
- Custom Shapes
- And, Tools

 In general, after a library is loaded and selected, you are able to access your presets in such places as the Options bar or palettes.

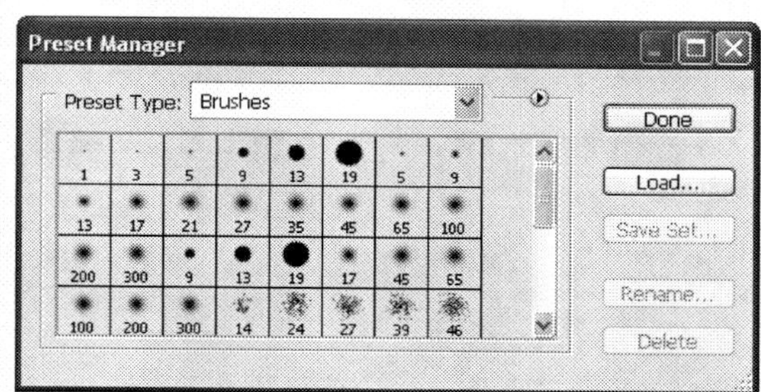

The Preset Manager dialog box

The Preset Manager Menu

Clicking the triangle button next to the Preset Type drop-down list accesses the Preset Manager menu and allows you to change the way items in the palette well are displayed. The following table lists the Preset Manager menu options.

Preset Manager Menu Option	Description
Text Only, Small Thumbnail, Large Thumbnail, Small List, Large List, Stroke Thumbnail	Allows you to choose from a list of categories to decide how your preset type will be displayed on the Options bar, palettes, or dialog boxes.
Reset Brushes, Replace Brushes	Allows you to reset the palette to its default or replace the palette with one from the directory.
Assorted Brushes, Basic Brushes, Calligraphic Brushes, Drop Shadow Brushes, Dry Media Brushes, Faux Finish Brushes, Natural Brushes 2, Natural Brushes, Special Effect Brushes, Square Brushes, Thick Heavy Brushes, Wet Media Brushes	Allows you to choose from libraries of preset brushes. that can be accessed in the Tool Options bar and Brushes palette.

How to Customize the Photoshop Environment

Procedure Reference: Customize the Palette Arrangement

To customize the palette arrangement:

1. Arrange the palettes as desired.
    - From the Window menu, choose the name of the palette to show or hide a palette.
    - Click a palette tab and drag it next to the tabs already within the group to group the palettes.
    - In a palette group, click a palette tab and drag the tab away from the group to ungroup a palette from it.
    - Click a palette tab, drag it to the top or bottom of the palette group until a horizontal line appears, and release the mouse button to dock a palette with another palette or group.
    - Click and drag a palette tab away from the palettes to which it is docked to undock a palette.
    - Double-click a palette tab to collapse or expand the palette.
2. Choose Window→Workspace→Save Workspace.
3. In the Save Workspace dialog box, in the Name text box, type a name for your new workspace.
4. Check the Capture options you want to save.
5. Click Save.

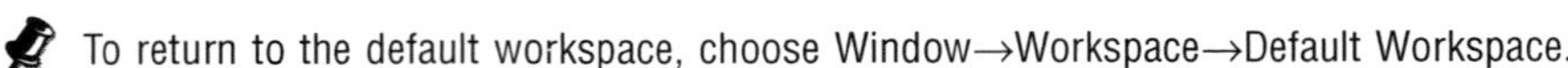

Procedure Reference: Apply a Workspace Preset

To apply a Workspace preset:

1. Choose Window→Workspace.
2. Select the desired Workspace preset.
3. Click Yes to modify and apply the selected Workspace.

Procedure Reference: Load Preset Options Using the Preset Manager

To load preset options using the Preset Manager:

1. Choose Edit→Preset Manager.
2. In the Preset Manager dialog box, click the triangle at the right the Preset Type drop-down list to display the Preset Type list.
3. Select the desired preset type.
4. In the Preset Manager dialog box, click Load.
5. In the Load dialog box, from the Custom Shapes list, select a library file you want to load and click Load.
6. In the Preset Manager, click Done.

Procedure Reference: Replace Preset Options Using the Preset Manager

To replace preset options using the Preset Manager:

1. Choose Edit→Preset Manager.
2. At the upper-right corner of the Preset Manager dialog box, click the triangle.
3. Select the Preset Type option and click OK.
4. In the Preset Manager, click Done.

 When you load a workspace, you add to the current options. When you select a workspace from the Preset Manager list (accessed by clicking the triangle), you replace any current options with only those you select.

Procedure Reference: Reset the Preset Options to Photoshop Defaults

To reset the preset options to Photoshop defaults:

1. Choose Edit→Preset Manager.
2. From the Preset Type drop-down list, select the preset that needs to be reset with default options.
3. Click the triangle at the right of the Preset Type drop-down list to display the Preset list for the selected preset.
4. From the Preset list, select Reset <Preset Type>.
5. In the Preset Manager message box, click OK.
6. In the Preset Manager dialog box, click Done.

Procedure Reference: Delete a Workspace

To delete a workspace you created:

1. Choose Window→Workspace→Delete Workspace.
2. From the Delete Workspace drop-down list, select the Workspace you want to delete and click Delete.
3. In the Delete Workspace message box, click Yes.

ACTIVITY 1-3

Customizing the Photoshop Environment

Data Files:

- Kid Stuff.psd

Before You Begin

Open the Kid Stuff.psd file from the C:\084563Data\Photoshop Environment\Activity 3\Starter folder.

Scenario:

You feel that the Photoshop environment is cluttered. Before starting your work in Photoshop, you would like to arrange the palettes so that they are best organized to suit your needs.

What You Do	How You Do It
1. **Rearrange the palette locations.**	a. In the Color palette group, **click the Styles palette tab** to view the styles.  b. **Click the Color palette tab, drag it and position it to the right of the Histogram palette tab.** c. **Click the Info palette tab and drag it to the palette well at the right end of the Tool Options bar.** 
2. **Save the current position and grouping of the palettes as a workspace.**	a. **Choose Window→Workspace→Save Workspace.** b. In the Save Workspace dialog box, in the Name text box, **type *Class Workspace* and click Save.**

3. **Retrieve the saved workspace.**

a. On the Layers palette, at the top-right corner, **click the Close button.**

b. **Choose Window→Workspace→Class Workspace.**

c. **Notice that the workspace is retrieved and the palettes appear in the locations specified in the saved workspace.**

d. **Choose Window→Workspace→Reset Palette Locations** to reset the palettes in their original locations.

e. **Choose File→Close and click No when prompted to save.**

ACTIVITY 1-4

Applying a Workspace Preset

Data Files:

- Kid Stuff.psd

Before You Begin

Open the Kid Stuff.psd file from the C:\084563Data\Photoshop Environment\Activity 4\Starter folder.

Scenario:

You have recently installed Adobe Photoshop CS2 and want to have easy access to the tools that you use frequently. You know that setting a workspace preset is an efficient way to accomplish this.

What You Do	How You Do It
1. **Modify the Photoshop Workspace with a preset.**	a. **Choose Window→Workspace→Painting And Retouching** to apply the modified Workspace preset.
	b. In the Adobe Photoshop message box, **click Yes** to apply the modified menu options.

2. **Save Workspace preset menu modifications.**

a. **Click Window.**

Presets offer a convenient way for working with tools specifically applicable to your current Photoshop project.

b. **Verify that painting and retouching tools are highlighted.**

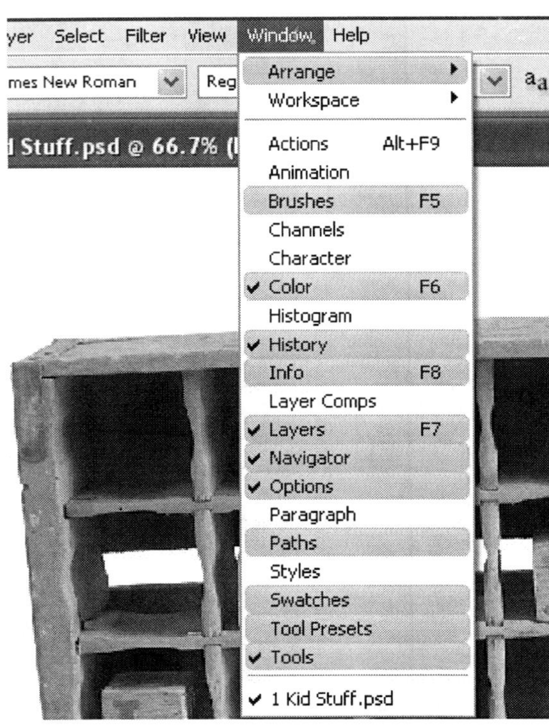

c. From the Window menu, **choose Workspace→Save Workspace.**

d. In the Save Workspace dialog box, in the Name text box, **type *My Workspace***

e. Verify whether the Menus check box is checked to capture the modified Workspace menus and **click Save.**

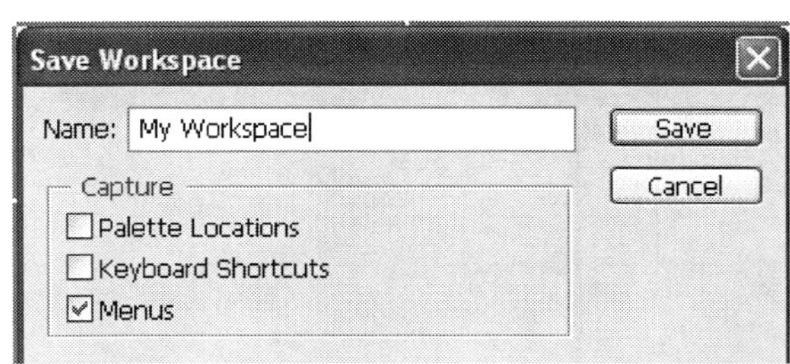

3. **Modify the Photoshop Workspace with the Preset Manager.**

   a. **Choose Edit→Preset Manager.**

   b. In the Preset Manager dialog box, from the Preset Type drop-down list, **select Custom Shapes.**

4. **Add custom shapes to the preset options.**

   a. In the Preset Manager dialog box, **click Load.**

   b. In the Load dialog box, from the Custom Shapes list, **select Nature.csh and click Load.**

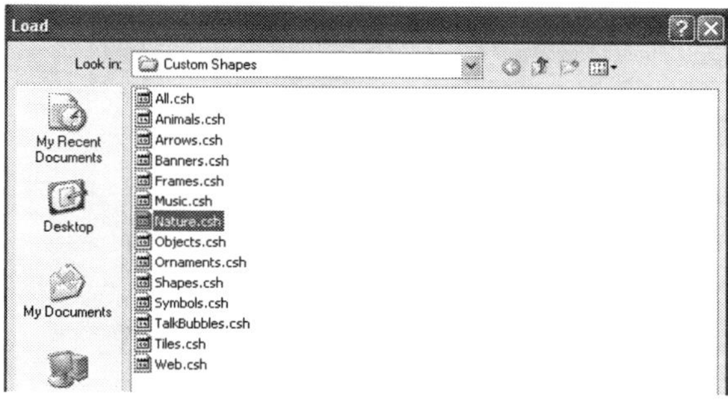

5. **Replace the current selection of custom shapes.**

a. In the Preset Manager dialog box, to the right of the Preset Type drop-down list, **click the triangle** to display the Custom Shapes list.

 Unlike the Load button option, this list enables you to select one category. You can also change the Thumbnail and List views.

b. From the Custom Shapes list, **select Web.**

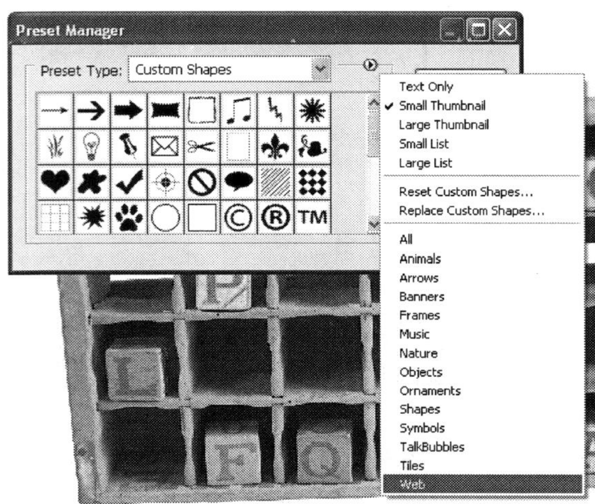

c. In the Preset Manager message box, **click OK.**

d. Verify that only Web shapes are displayed and **click Done.**

---

6. **Reset Custom Shapes to Photoshop defaults.**

a. **Choose Edit→Preset Manager.**

b. From the Preset Type drop-down list, **select Custom Shapes.**

c. **Click the triangle** to display the Custom Shapes list.

d. From the Custom Shapes list, **select Reset Custom Shapes.**

e. **Click OK.**

f. **Click Done.**

---

7. **Delete My Paint And Retouch Workspace and return to the Default Workspace.**

   a. **Choose Window→Workspace.**

   b. **Verify that My Workspace is checked.**

   c. **Select Delete Workspace.**

   d. In the Delete Workspace dialog box, from the Workspace drop-down list, **verify that My Workspace is selected and click Delete.**

   e. In the Delete Workspace message box, **click Yes.**

   f. **Choose Window→Workspace→Default Workspace.**

   g. **Choose File→Close and click No when prompted to save.**

TOPIC D

Work with Navigation Tools

You are now familiar with the Photoshop interface elements. It will be helpful to know how to move and resize the image within the window so you can easily see the area of the image you are editing. In this topic, you will navigate through an image using several techniques and shortcuts for zooming, scrolling, and selecting.

It is necessary to get a closer look at an image frequently to precisely select or edit a part of it. You can save time by zooming out, or switching between documents without scrolling or switching palettes. Photoshop offers tools, commands, keyboard shortcuts, and a floating palette to view images easily.

The Zoom Tool

You can click within an image to zoom in using the Zoom tool. Each time you use the *Zoom tool* to change the image magnification, the size of the image window will not change. You can check the Resize Windows To Fit check box on the Tool Options bar, to resize to the best display of the image, as you adjust magnification. You can also use the Zoom tool to reduce the magnification of an image by holding down Alt while clicking. In addition, you can zoom in closely to a specific portion of an image by dragging the Zoom tool to draw a zoom marquee.

The Zoom Tool Shortcuts

You can use commands in the View menu to change the magnification of an image. By default, the zoom commands do not change the size of the window, irrespective of whether or not the Resize Windows To Fit check box is checked. The Resize Windows To Fit check box affects only the Zoom tool, and not other zoom commands and options.

You will need to change the magnification for an image frequently as you work, so Photoshop has many navigation shortcuts that can save time. Some shortcuts are a combination of keystrokes. For example, to zoom in, hold down Ctrl and press the + key. Some shortcuts are a combination of keystrokes and the mouse. For example to zoom in, hold down Ctrl+Spacebar and click the image to zoom in.

The following table lists the shortcut commands for using the Zoom tool.

Command	Keyboard Shortcut	Shortcut Using Mouse
Zoom in	Ctrl++	Ctrl+Spacebar click
Zoom out	Ctrl+-	Ctrl+Alt+Spacebar click
Fit on screen	Ctrl+0	Double-click Hand tool
Actual size	Ctrl+Alt+0	Double-click Zoom tool
Hand tool		Spacebar drag

The Navigator Palette

The Navigator palette is used to quickly navigate through a document. The Navigator shows a miniature preview of the entire image. You can use the slider at the bottom to quickly choose a magnification; and the zoom icons on the left or right of the slider to change to the nearest preset zoom level. You can also type a percentage in the Magnification text box.

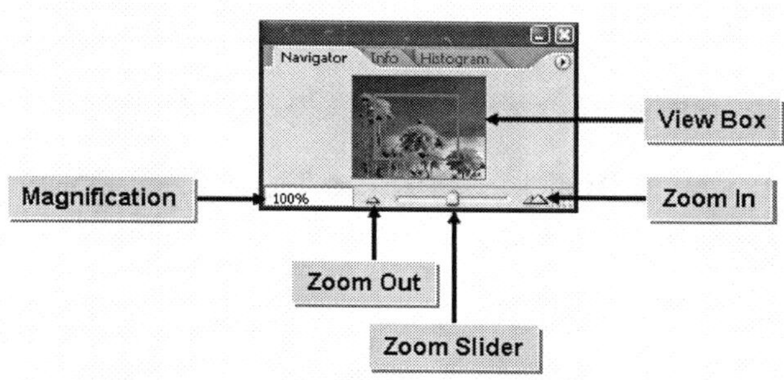

You can drag within the Navigator palette's preview to scroll and zoom in or out. Drag the view box within the preview to scroll the image. The part of the image within the view box appears on the screen also. You can hold down Ctrl and drag within the Navigator palette preview to adjust the view box to zoom in or out on specific areas of the image. This method of zooming is particularly efficient when you need to zoom in to a part of the image that is not shown in the main image window.

How to Work with Navigation Tools

Procedure Reference: View an Image at Different Magnification Levels

To view an image at different magnification levels:

1. In the toolbox, select the Zoom tool. The mouse pointer changes to a magnifying glass.
2. Increase the zoom percentage of the image.
   - Click within the image to zoom in on the entire image.
   - Position the magnifying glass cursor just above the portion of the image to be zoomed and drag the zoom marquee to enclose the portion.
   - Or, choose View→Zoom In.
3. Decrease the zoom percentage of the image.
   - Hold down Alt and click within the image to zoom out the entire image.
   - Or, choose View→Zoom Out.

4. On the Tool Options bar, check the Resize Window To Fit check box and zoom in or out to resize the window as the image magnification changes.
5. Choose View→Fit On Screen to enlarge or reduce the magnification to fit the image window in the available space on the monitor.
6. Choose View→Actual Pixels. The Actual Pixels command makes the zoom level to 100 percent, where each pixel in the image is represented by one pixel on the monitor.

Procedure Reference: Move an Image Within a Window

To move an image within a window:

1. In the toolbox, select the Hand tool.
2. Click and drag the Hand tool cursor in the direction you want to move the image.

Procedure Reference: Zoom an Image Using the Navigator Palette

To zoom an image using the Navigator palette:

1. If necessary, choose Window→Navigator.
2. On the Navigator palette, change the magnification of the image.
   - Drag the slider to the right or to the left to change the magnification.
   - At the right of the slider, click the Zoom In button to increase the zoom percentage.
   - At the left of the slider, click the Zoom Out button to decrease the zoom percentage.
   - In the Magnification text box, double-click the existing number, specify the magnification level and press Enter.
3. If necessary, zoom to a specific area using the Navigator palette.
   1. Position the mouse pointer within the Navigator palette thumbnail display area.
   2. Hold down Ctrl and drag the red zoom marquee around an area to zoom in on it.

Procedure Reference: Move the View of the Image

To move the view of the image using the Navigator palette :

1. In the Navigator palette thumbnail display area, position the mouse pointer in the red box, which is the proxy preview area. The mouse pointer changes to a hand.
2. Move the view of the image.
   - Drag the proxy preview area to a portion of the image you want to view.
   - Or, click the image thumbnail to move the proxy view area.

ACTIVITY 1-5

Viewing Images at Different Magnification Levels

Data Files:

- Kid Stuff.psd

Before You Begin

Open the Kid Stuff.psd file from the C:\084563Data\Photoshop Environment\Activity 5\Starter folder.

Scenario:

Before you start editing the image, it would be useful if you know how to move and view the image at different magnification levels.

What You Do	How You Do It
1. **Magnify the Kid Stuff image using the Zoom tool.**	a. In the toolbox, **select the Zoom tool.**
	b. **Notice that the mouse pointer changes to a magnifying glass.**  
	c. In the Kid Stuff image, **click the yellow block with the letter E.**
	d. At the bottom-left corner of the window, in the Magnification text box, **notice that the zoom percentage is displayed as 100%.** 
	e. **Click the yellow block with the letter E two times** to increase the zoom percentage to 300%.

2. **View the image at different magnification levels.**

a. **Hold down Alt, notice that the + in the magnifying glass changes to a -, and click the image three times.**

b. At the bottom of the image, **position the magnifying glass cursor just above and to the left of the transparent ball.**

c. **Hold down the left mouse button and drag towards the bottom-right corner of the ball.**

d. The magnification of the ball is increased to a greater extent so that you view its individual pixels. **Hold down Alt and click in the window until the zoom percentage becomes 100%.**

e. On the Tool Options bar, **check the Resize Windows To Fit check box.**

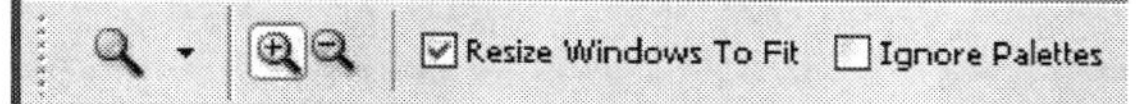

f. **Hold down Alt and click two times** to view the window resize as the image magnification changes.

g. **Click with the Zoom tool two times** to increase the zoom percentage to 100%.

h. On the Tool Options bar, **uncheck the Resize Windows To Fit check box.**

i. **Choose View→Zoom In** to increase the zoom percentage to 200%.

j. **Choose View→Zoom Out** to return to 100% magnification.

k. **Choose View→Fit On Screen** to make the image fill the image window.

3. **Examine the rubber ball's edges for distortion.**
   a. **Choose View→Actual Pixels.**
   b. **Click the ball with the Zoom tool** to zoom it to 200%.
   c. **Scroll to view the rubber ball, to compare the smoothness of the ball's edges with the Fit On Screen view you just examined.**

4. **Drag the image within the window using the Hand tool.**
   a. In the toolbox, **select the Hand tool.**
   b. **Notice that the mouse pointer changes to a hand.**
   c. At the upper-left corner of the image, **position the Hand tool cursor, and click and drag the Hand tool cursor to the bottom-right corner until you view the red block with the letter L.**
   d. In the toolbox, **double-click the Hand tool** to fit the entire image on the screen.
   e. **Choose File→Close and click No when prompted to save.**

ACTIVITY 1-6

Exploring the Navigator Palette Options

Data Files:

- Kid Stuff.psd

Before You Begin

Open the Kid Stuff.psd file from the C:\084563Data\Photoshop Environment\Activity 6\Starter folder.

Scenario:

You would like to explore the options on the Navigator palette to zoom and scroll the images in the window.

What You Do	How You Do It
1. **Zoom an image using the Navigator palette.**	a. If necessary, **choose Window→Navigator.** b. On the Navigator palette, **drag the slider to the right to change the magnification to 450%.** 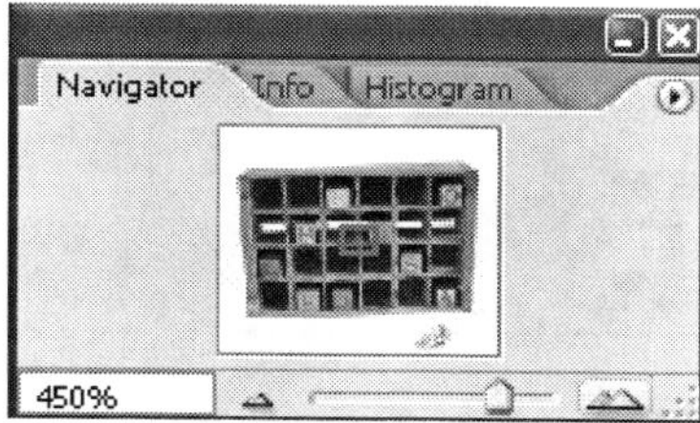 c. **Notice that the zoom percentage of the image is increased to 450%.** d. On the Navigator palette, at the right of the slider, **click the Zoom In button to increase the zoom percentage to 500%.** e. At the left of the slider, **click the Zoom Out button to decrease the zoom percentage to 400%.** f. In the Magnification text box, **double-click the number 400, type *250* and press Enter.**
2. **Scroll through the image using the Navigator palette.**	a. In the Navigator palette preview area, **position the mouse pointer in the red outlined portion and notice that the mouse pointer changes to a hand.**  b. In the Navigator palette preview area, **drag the red outline over the ball.**

3. **Zoom to a specific area with the Navigator palette.**	a. **Hold down Ctrl and drag the red zoom marquee around the first toy block in the first row.**
	b. **Choose File→Close.**

TOPIC E

Customize Menus

You have used workspace presets that helped you become more productive in the Photoshop environment. In addition to these workspace presets, Photoshop menus are also customizable. In this topic, you will use the Menus dialog box to customize Photoshop menus.

Customizing the menus ensures that the commands you need are just a mouse click away.

Menu Customization

Photoshop CS2 introduces menu item customization through the Menus tab in the Keyboard Shortcuts And Menus dialog box.

The Set drop-down list lets you choose the workspace you want to modify. The buttons next to the Set drop-down list let you save current menu sets, create a new set of menu sets, or delete the current set of menus. The Menu For drop-down list allows you to customize the Application or Palette menu. You are then able to choose the menu items that you want visible and/or color coded.

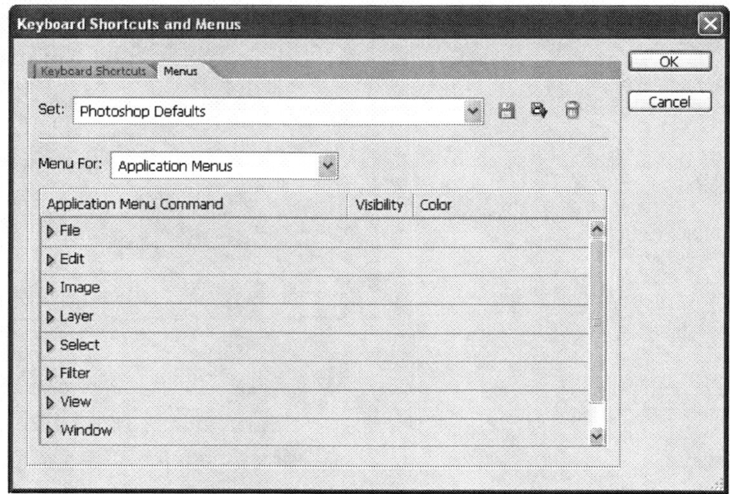

The Keyboard Shortcuts and Menus dialog box

How to Customize Menus

Procedure Reference: Customize Workspace Menus

To customize the workspace keyboard shortcuts and menus:

1. Choose Window→Workspace→Keyboard Shortcuts & Menus.
2. On the Menus tab, from the Set drop-down list, select the Workspace you want to modify.
3. From the Menu For drop-down list, select an option.
   - Select Application Menus to customize the application menus.
   - Or, select Palette Menus to customize the palette menus.
4. In the Menu Command row, expand a menu to view its menu options.

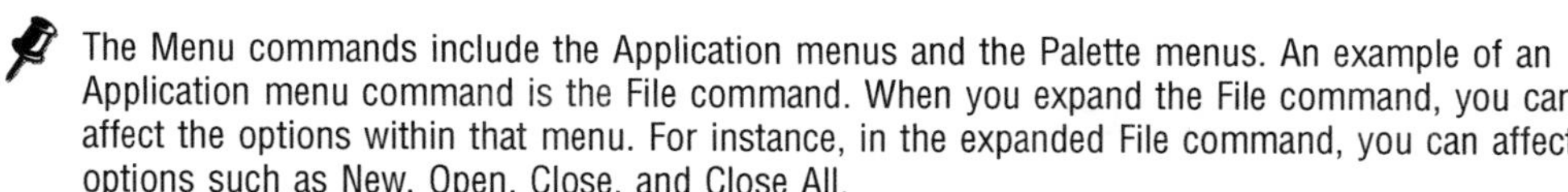

The Menu commands include the Application menus and the Palette menus. An example of an Application menu command is the File command. When you expand the File command, you can affect the options within that menu. For instance, in the expanded File command, you can affect options such as New, Open, Close, and Close All.

5. If necessary, hide a command.
   a. Select a menu option.
   b. In the Visibility list, click the Eye icon of the menu option to hide it.
6. If necessary, add color to a menu option.
   a. Select a menu option.
   b. In the Color list, click None to display the Color drop-down list of the menu option.
   c. Select from the available color options to add color to a menu option.

To make a hidden command visible, click the empty Visibility button.

7. Click the Create A New Set Based On The Current Set Of Menus button.
8. In the File Name text box, type a name for your custom set and click Save.

If you want to modify an existing Photoshop Default set, do not name the new set. Instead, click Save All Changes To The Current Set Of Menus and click OK.

9. Click OK.

Procedure Reference: Delete a Saved Set

To delete a set that you have named and saved:

1. Choose Window→Workspace→Keyboard Shortcuts & Menus.
2. On the Menus tab, from the Set drop-down list, select the set you want to delete.
3. Click the Delete The Current Set Of Menus button.
4. Click Yes and then click OK.

ACTIVITY 1-7

Customizing Workspace Menus

Data Files:

- Kid Stuff.psd

Before You Begin

Open the Kid Stuff.psd file from the C:\084563Data\Photoshop Environment\Activity 7\Starter folder.

Scenario:

Before you start a project, you decide to customize your application File menu for the current workspace. You also want to delete a menu command to prevent it from being used, and highlight another menu command.

What You Do	How You Do It
1. **View the Application Menus for the Photoshop Defaults workspace.**	a. **Choose Window→Workspace→Keyboard Shortcuts & Menus.** b. In the Keyboard Shortcuts And Menus dialog box, **verify that the settings for Photoshop Defaults and Application Menus are displayed.** 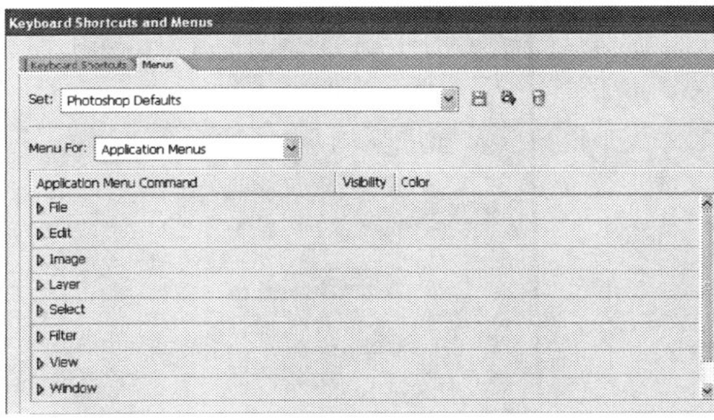 c. In the Application Menu Command list, **expand File.**
2. **Hide a File command option and add color emphasis to another option.**	a. From the File Options list, **select the Open option.**

b. In the Color list for the Open option, **click None** to display the Color drop-down list.

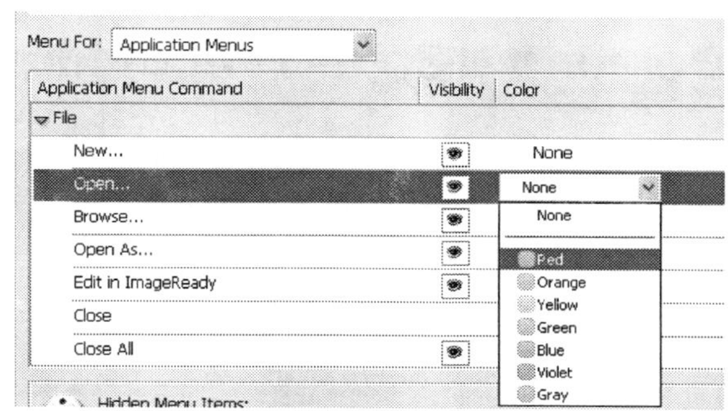

c. From the Color drop-down list, **select Red.**

d. From the File Options list, **select the Close All option and click the Eye icon.**

e. At the top of the Menus tab, **click the Create A New Set Based On The Current Set Of Menus button.**

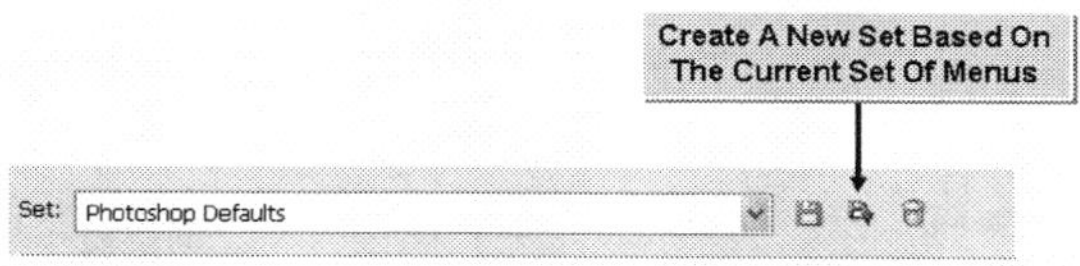

f. In File Name text box, **type *My File Menu,* click Save, and then click OK.**

g. From the File menu, verify that the Open menu is highlighted in red and the Close All menu is hidden, and then **choose Open** to display the Open dialog box.

h. **Click Cancel** to close the Open dialog box.

i. **Choose File→Close and click No when prompted to save.**

ACTIVITY 1-8

Deleting a Saved Set of Menus

Data Files:

- Kid Stuff.psd

Before You Begin

Open the Kid Stuff.psd file from the C:\084563Data\Photoshop Environment\Activity 8\Starter folder.

Scenario:

Just like unused shortcuts on your desktop, you may find unused customized menus in your workspace. It's a good practice to periodically delete custom menus that are rarely or never used.

What You Do	How You Do It
1. **Reset menus to Photoshop defaults.**	a. **Choose Window→Workspace→Reset Menus** to return to default Photoshop menus.
	b. In the Adobe Photoshop message box, **click No.**
	c. In the Photoshop Workspace, **choose File.**
	d. **Verify that the Open menu item is no longer highlighted, and that the Close All menu item is displayed.**

2. **Delete the My File menu.**

a. **Choose Window→Workspace→Keyboard Shortcuts & Menus.**

b. From the Set drop-down list, **select My File Menu, and click the Delete The Current Set Of Menus button.**

c. In the Keyboard Shortcuts And Menu message box, **click Yes** to send the file set to the recycle bin, and **click OK** to close the dialog box and return to the Photoshop Workspace.

d. **Choose File→Close and click No when prompted to save.**

TOPIC F

Explore Adobe Bridge

You have explored the Adobe Photoshop interface. Now, you want to familiarize yourself with the Photoshop file management functionality of Adobe Bridge. In this topic, you will explore asset management through Adobe Bridge.

A well-organized file system is essential for an efficient workflow. If you understand the functions of Adobe Bridge, you will be able to manage assets in Photoshop CS2.

Adobe Bridge

Expanding on the functionality of Adobe Photoshop CS's file browser, *Adobe Bridge* is a next generation file browser that lets you view, sort, and manage both Adobe and non-Adobe application files from a central location. Adobe Bridge allows you to create and manage folders; rename, move, and delete files; and add and edit keywords and metadata. You can also preview, rotate, and rank assets, run batch commands, and preview layouts with the Bridge.

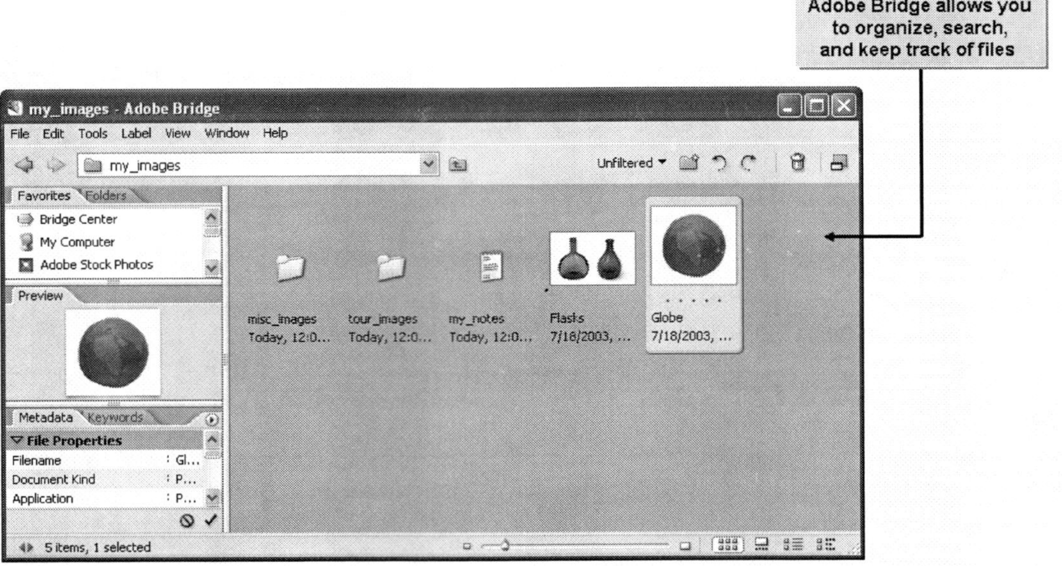

Adobe Version Cue and Adobe Stock Photos

Adobe Bridge allows you direct access to both Adobe Version Cue, Photoshop's project management feature, and Adobe Stock Photos, a new service from CS2 that allows you to search for, test, and purchase stock images.

Views in Adobe Bridge

Adobe Bridge offers several options for viewing files and folders.

Adobe Bridge View	Description
Sort	Selects the order in which files are displayed. Files can be sorted in ascending or descending order, or manually.
Show Thumbnail Only	Displays only a thumbnail of each file.
Show Hidden Files	Displays hidden files, such as cache files and provisionally removed Version Cue files.
Show Folders	Displays folders as well as files.
Show All Files	Displays all files, regardless of type. Includes non-Adobe files.
Show Graphic Files Only	Displays only files in graphic formats, such as JPG, EPS, TIF, PS, GIF, and BMP.
Show Camera Raw Files Only	Displays only Camera Raw files.
Show Vector Files Only	Displays only files created with drawing programs, such as Illustrator, Photoshop, and EPS files.
Refresh	Updates the content window. This is useful for handling Version Cue files that do not update automatically.

Sort Options

Files can be sorted by Filename, Document Kind, Date Created, Date File Modified, File Size, Dimensions, Resolution, Color Profile, Copyright, Label, Rating, Purchase State, or Version Cue Status.

View As Options

Adobe Bridge offers the following four options for viewing the workspace.

View As Option	Description
As Thumbnails	Displays items in a grid.
As Filmstrip	Displays the selected item in an extra-large thumbnail; the other thumbnails are displayed in a scrolling list at the bottom of the screen.
As Details	Displays a list of thumbnails and information about each file, such as creation and modification dates, and file size and type.
As Versions And Alternates	Displays a list of thumbnails and thumbnails of any Version Cue alternative files.

ACTIVITY 1-9

Exploring Adobe Bridge

Scenario:

As the creative director for a design firm, you would like to train your team of graphic designers using Adobe Bridge. You would like to test your knowledge before the training session begins.

What You Do	How You Do It

1. **True or False? Adobe Bridge allows you to create and edit images from one central location.**

   __ True

   __ False

2. **Which tasks can be performed using Adobe Bridge?**

   a) Browse non-Adobe application files.

   b) Color correct Adobe Photoshop files.

   c) Run batch commands.

   d) Apply Photoshop filters to only flattened images.

3. **True or False? Adobe Bridge can be used to add and edit keywords and metadata to files.**

   __ True

   __ False

TOPIC G

Apply Metadata and Keywords

You have used Adobe Bridge to organize and manage your files. You can add metadata and keywords to your assets in order to preform a search task. In this topic, you will add metadata and keywords to your assets.

During the course of a project, it may be necessary to work with numerous images. The ability to search for a specific asset or group of images by using keywords and metadata in Adobe Bridge can help you find the assets more efficiently.

Metadata

Adobe Bridge allows you to organize, search, and keep track of files through the use of metadata. *Metadata* is text that describes a file using keywords, author, resolution, color space, and other file properties.

eXtensible Metadata Platform

Adobe Bridge, Adobe Creative Suite, and metadata are all stored using eXtensible Metadata Platform (XMP). XMP is based on XML, and a lot of the time, the information is stored right in the file to prevent it from getting lost. Depending on what application you are using, custom panels for a variety of properties may appear on the metadata panel as well.

The following table lists the different types of metadata.

Type of Metadata	Description
File Properties	Describes file characteristics such as size, creation date, and modification date.
IPTC Core	Displays any metadata that you can edit. You can add captions and copyright information to your file.
Fonts	Lists fonts used in Adobe InDesign.
Swatches	Lists swatches used in Adobe InDesign.
Camera Data (Exif)	Displays digital camera information, including camera settings when images were taken.

Type of Metadata	Description
GPS	In some digital cameras, navigational information in global positioning systems will be displayed. Photos without GPS information will not have metadata.
Camera Raw	Displays settings from the Camera Raw plug-in.
Edit History	Logs image changes in Photoshop.
Adobe Stock Photos	Lists image information from Adobe Stock Photos.
Version Cue	Lists version information for the file.

Keywords

Keywords are words that allow you to identify files from content. The Keyword panel in Adobe Bridge lets you apply keywords to a file. Categories called keyword sets can be made from a group of keywords.

How to Apply Metadata and Keywords

Procedure Reference: Apply Metadata and Keywords to Assets in Adobe Bridge

To apply metadata and keywords to assets in Adobe Bridge:

1. Open Adobe Bridge.
   - In the Adobe Photoshop window, choose File→Browse.
   - At the right end of the Tool Options bar, click the Go To Bridge icon.
   - Or, choose Start→All Programs→Adobe Bridge.
2. Select the desired file.
3. Select the Keywords tab.
4. At the bottom of the Keywords tab, click the New Keyword button and type the keyword text to create a new keyword.
5. Check the newly created keyword to assign the keyword to the file.
6. On the Metadata tab, click the Pencil icon of the metadata item you want to add or change.
7. Type the text to be added for the metadata item.
8. Click the Apply button to add metadata to the file.
9. If necessary, verify if the keywords and metadata are added to the file.
   a. Select the file.
   b. Choose File→File Info.
   c. Verify if the keywords are displayed.
   d. From the list on the left side of the dialog box, select the option and verify if the relevant metadata is displayed.

Procedure Reference: Perform a Metadata Search

To perform a metadata search:

1. Choose Edit→Find.
2. In the Find dialog box, specify the source of the file.
3. Specify the search criteria.
4. From the Match drop-down list, select If Any Criteria Are Met.
5. Click Find to perform a metadata search.

After performing a metadata search, you can view the information about the file by choosing File→File Info.

ACTIVITY 1-10

Applying Metadata and Keywords to Assets in Adobe Bridge

Data Files:

- Building.jpg

Scenario:

As a graphic designer for a web design firm, you have been asked to find an easy way to locate the images used in your project. You want to find an easy way to search for images on your computer.

What You Do	How You Do It
1. **Open Adobe Bridge and select the appropriate file.**	a. On the Photoshop Options bar, **click the Go To Bridge icon.**  b. In the Adobe Bridge window, on the Folders tab, **browse to the Local Disk (C:)\084563Data\Photoshop Environment\Activity 10\Starter folder and click Building.jpg.**

2. **Add a keyword to the file.**

a. **Select the Keywords tab.**

b. On the Keywords tab, **scroll down to view the San Francisco keyword.**

c. On the Keywords tab, **check the San Francisco keyword.**

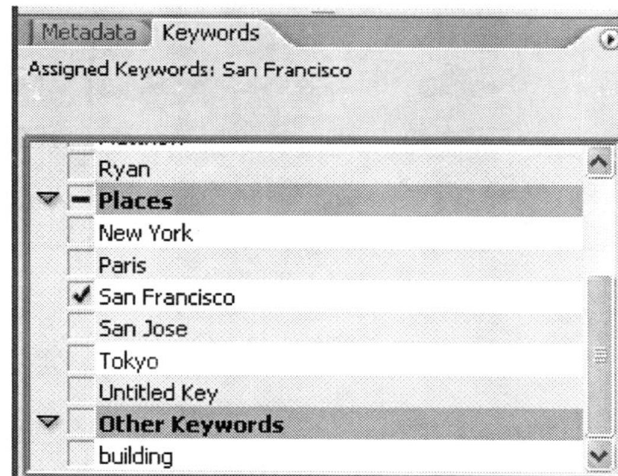

d. On the Keywords tab, **click the New Keyword button.**

e. In the highlighted text box, **type *Building* and press Enter.**

f. On the Keywords tab, **scroll down and check the Building check box.**

g. **Select the Metadata tab and scroll down to the Keywords item.**

h. **Verify that the keywords have been added.**

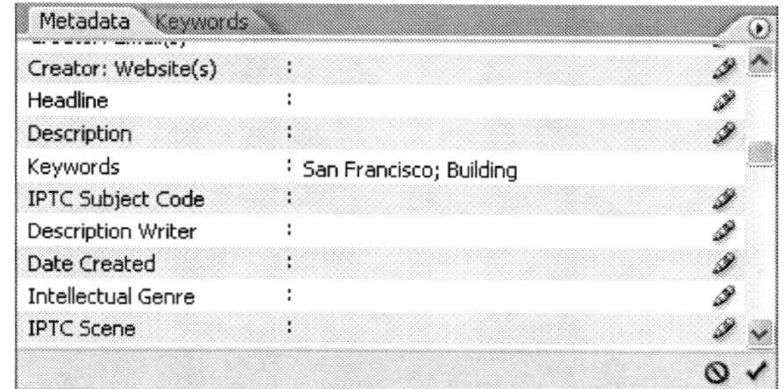

3.	**Add metadata to the file.**	a. On the Metadata tab, **scroll up to view the Creator: Country item.** b. **In the Creator: Country item, click the Pencil icon** to display the Country text box. c. In the Country text box, **type *USA*** d. On the Metadata tab, **click the Apply button.**
4.	**Perform a metadata search.**	a. **Choose Edit→Find.** b. In the Find dialog box, in the Criteria section, from the Filename drop-down list, **select All Metadata.** c. **Press Tab two times and type *San Francisco*** d. **Click the plus (+) sign button.** e. In the Criteria section, in the second row, from the Filename drop-down list, **select Keywords.** f. **Press Tab two times and type *Building*** g. **Click Find.**
5.	**View the information about the file.**	a. In Find Results - Adobe Bridge window, **select the Building.jpg file.** b. In Find Results - Adobe Bridge window, **choose File→File Info.** c. **Verify if the keywords are displayed.** d. **Select IPTC Contact.**

e. **Verify if the country metadata is displayed and click OK.**

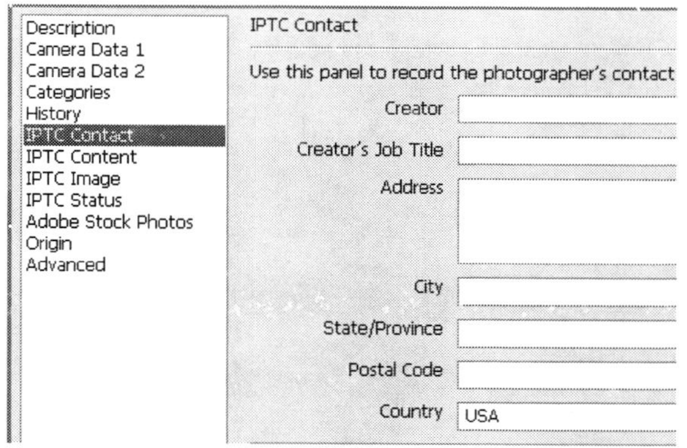

f. **Close the Find Results - Adobe Bridge window.**

g. **Close the Starter - Adobe Bridge window.**

Lesson 1 Follow-up

In this lesson, you explored and customized the Photoshop user interface. You used several techniques for editing, zooming and scrolling, which will enable you to quickly move through the images as you edit them.

1. **Which menus do you customize to enhance productivity in your environment?**

2. **How do you use Adobe Bridge in your work environment?**

Notes

LESSON 2

Sizing Images

Lesson Time
25 minutes

Lesson Objectives:

In this lesson, you will ensure that images have an appropriate balance between file size and print or display quality and also crop images to remove unnecessary areas.

You will:

- Adjust the resolution and size of an image to optimize its quality.
- Crop images to remove the unwanted portions.

Introduction

Now that you have learned to navigate within Photoshop, you will learn several techniques to modify images. In this lesson, you will adjust image size and resolution for printing, and crop images to remove unnecessary areas.

You are working on a project with different images. To ensure that the images have a balance between file size and print or display quality, you must set the image resolution and remove the unwanted portions from them.

TOPIC A

Determine Display and Print Resolution

You have become familiar with the Photoshop environment. Before creating an image, you must understand that the quality of an image depends on its size and resolution. In this topic, you will ensure that your images have an appropriate balance between file size and print or display quality.

While working on images, you need to ensure that the images looks good when they are used for commercial printing. By optimizing resolution and size, you can create visually appealing images for printing.

Image Resolution

Pixels or picture elements are square shaped, and they are positioned adjacent to each other vertically and horizontally. The resolution of a Photoshop image is measured in pixels per inch (ppi). Although you may see image resolution measured in dots per inch (dpi), it is better to use pixels per inch to avoid confusing pixels with printed dots.

The quality of a Photoshop image depends greatly on its size and resolution. The finer the resolution, the sharper the image looks both on the screen, and when it is printed. However, a sharp image may appear grainy when significantly enlarged.

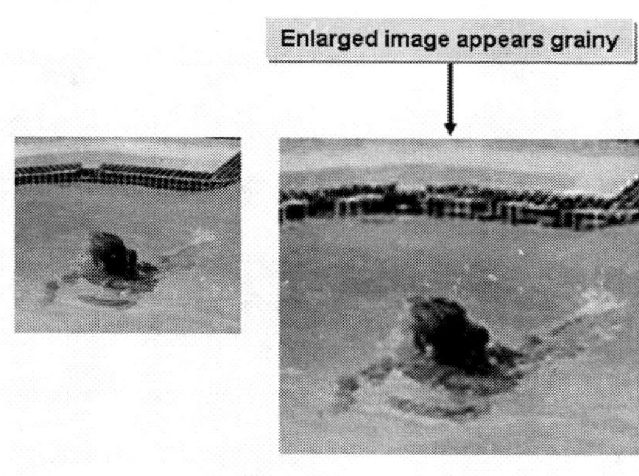

Each square dot that you see on a screen image when you zoom in to high magnification is a pixel. Each pixel within an image can be of a different color or shade of gray.

Halftone Screen

Though pixels make up the screen image, they do not directly correlate with the dots you see in printed output material. For example, each pixel within an on-screen grayscale image is one of 256 levels of gray, varying from white to black. However, the use of 256 different gray inks to print this image is impossible. Therefore, a halftone screen is used to simulate the gray levels.

A *halftone screen* is a dot pattern used to print varying brightness levels of a base ink color. For example, a halftone screen of black ink produces varying gray levels. A traditional halftone screen pattern consists of differently sized dots equidistant from each other.

 A grayscale image is an image that contains up to 256 levels of grays instead of other colors.

PostScript® Printing

When printed using a PostScript® printer, the halftone screen uses rows of dots of varying size, to trick the viewer's eyes into perceiving gray levels. For example, clusters of large dots create the appearance of dark areas, whereas areas of smaller dots appear lighter.

Linescreen

The number of rows of dots in one inch is called the *linescreen*, screen ruling, or screen frequency, and it is measured in lines per inch (lpi). In Photoshop, the linescreen for an image when set, is independent of the image resolution.

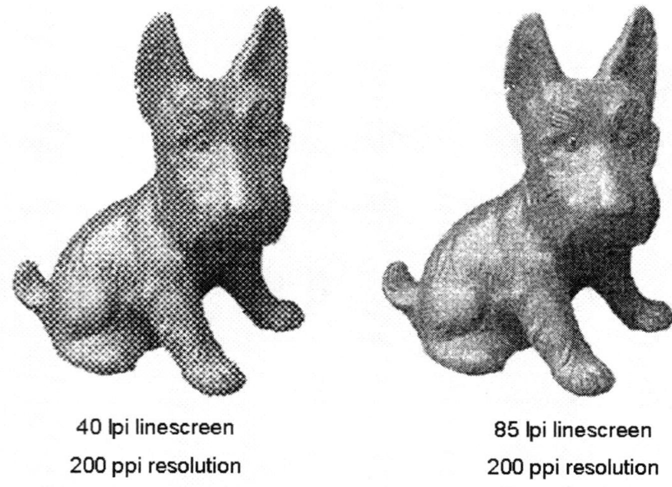

Print Using Inkjet Printer

Inkjet printers typically do not deploy a traditional halftone screen, in which the dots are equally spaced, and differently sized. Instead, inkjets print patterns of equally sized tiny dots, with varying distances between them, creating lighter and darker areas. Although a halftone screen is not measured in lpi, you can determine an approximate equivalent screen value corresponding to the printer's resolution. For example, a 1440 dpi printer would have an equivalent linescreen of up to 150 lpi, so you should not set the image resolution greater than 300 ppi.

 Halftone screen frequency is the number of rows of halftone dots in a given distance in a traditionally printed halftone screen; typically measured in lines per inch (lpi).

Set the Halftone Screen Ruling in Photoshop

You can set the halftone screen ruling in Photoshop. If you plan to print the image from within Photoshop, you can choose the Print With Preview command in the File menu and click Screen. You might need to check Show More Options, and select Output from the drop-down list before you see the Screen button. However, if you print the Photoshop image from another program, such as a page layout application or web browser, its screen settings override the Photoshop screen settings, unless you save the file in EPS format and check the Include Halftone Screen check box in the EPS Options dialog box.

Printer Resolution

Each printed halftone dot is composed of one or more printer dots. *Printer resolution* is the number of dots produced by a printing device; usually measured in dots per inch (dpi). The term dots is used to distinguish the printer's resolution from the image resolution in pixels, which is usually much lower. Most laser printers are 300 or 600 dpi, whereas high resolution imagesetters typically print at 1270 or 2540 dpi.

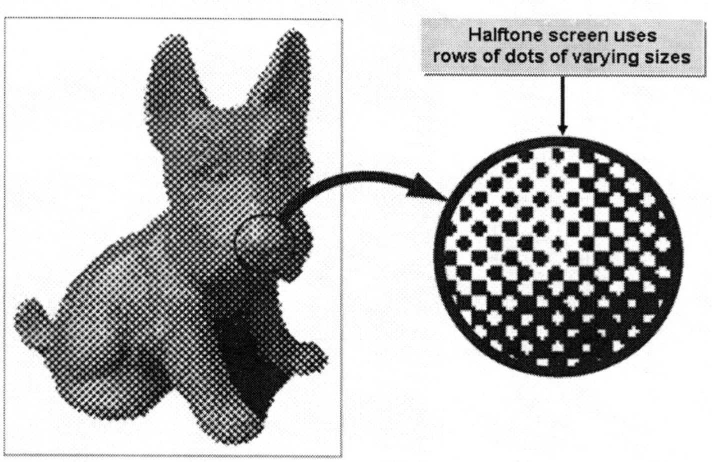

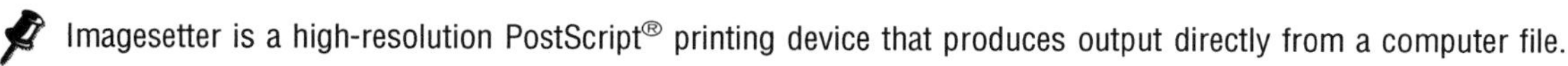
Imagesetter is a high-resolution PostScript® printing device that produces output directly from a computer file.

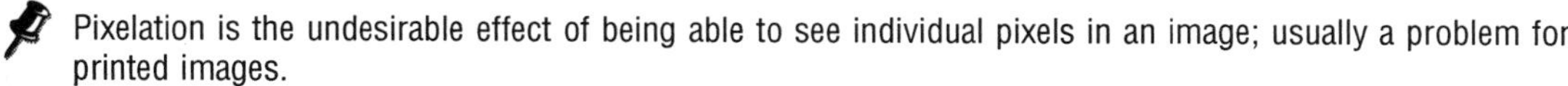
Pixelation is the undesirable effect of being able to see individual pixels in an image; usually a problem for printed images.

Image Resolution vs. Printer Resolution

Image resolution is the number of pixels in the horizontal or vertical direction within an image when printed, and it is typically measured in pixels per inch (ppi). It is part of the image itself, and is independent of the device used to print it. However, printer resolution is the number of dots in a given distance produced by a printing device. It is usually measured in dots per inch (dpi). Each dot referred to in this definition is the smallest dot the printer can produce, not the halftone dots, each of which is composed of several printer dots.

Linescreen and Printer Resolution

The linescreen you specify for printed output should be set according to the printer resolution. The higher the resolution of the printer, the smaller halftone screen dots it can produce. Therefore, low resolution printers cannot use a fine linescreen, since all of the dots would appear to bleed together, resulting in too dark an image. As an example, you typically set a 53 lpi or 60 lpi linescreen for a 300 dpi laser printer, whereas a much finer linescreen of 150 lpi is acceptable for a 2540 dpi imagesetter. There is no fixed mathematical formula for calculating the linescreen from printer resolution, but it does go up as the printer resolution is increased.

Resolution Settings for Images

It is important to set the image resolution based on the printer resolution and halftone screen. If the image resolution is too low, you will see pixelation, or individual dots of color within the image.

A resolution of 40 ppi is too low, and therefore causes pixelation.

If the image resolution is too high, the printed output may not improve. Instead, the file size will become unnecessarily large, thereby occupying more disk space. In addition, it will also slow down editing.

The way to ensure the best image quality is to set the image resolution in ppi between one and a half to two times the linescreen in lpi. This creates pixels that are about half as big as the gap between the centers of printed halftone dots. Since the pixels are small in comparison to the linescreen, they will be indistinguishable to the viewer.

Print Black and White Images

The exception to the rule of setting the image resolution in ppi between 1½ and 2 times the linescreen in lpi is observed while printing black and white line art images. Since only black and white, and not grayscale images are printed with solid areas of ink, no halftone screen of dots will be created. This thereby makes the pixels more easily visible. Therefore, for line art, you should set the image resolution to match the printer resolution, to approximately 800 ppi.

The following graphic summarizes resolution values for several printing conditions.

Type	Appearance	Measurement	Laser Printer	Newspaper	Magazine
Image Resolution		Pixels/inch (ppi)	110-170 ppi	130-200 ppi	200-300 ppi
Halftone Screen		lines/inch (lpi)	71, 85 lpi typical	85, 100 lpi typical	135, 150 lpi typical
Printer Resolution		dots/inch (dpi)	600 dpi typical	1270, 2540 dpi typical	1270, 2540 dpi typical

When creating images for the Internet, you must consider a few issues. Unlike printed images, the resolution of images appearing on the web depends on the viewer's monitor resolution, which is usually between 72 and 96 ppi. The image size in inches and resolution in ppi do not determine the size at which an image will appear online. Instead, the width and height as measured in pixels determine this.

For example, if the pixel dimensions of an image exceed 750 pixels in width or 500 pixels in height, the entire image may not fit in a browser window. This will then force the viewer to scroll to be able to see parts of the image. As a convention, many people save images intended for the Internet with a resolution between 72 and 96 ppi. Therefore, if printed from Photoshop or another application, the image will appear in approximately the same size as it did on the screen.

File Information

The File Information box helps display and check document sizes. In the File Information box, the number on the left represents the size of the document with only one layer of information, as it would be when sent to the printer. The number on the right shows the size of the image as Photoshop saves it, with all the extra layers and channels affecting file size.

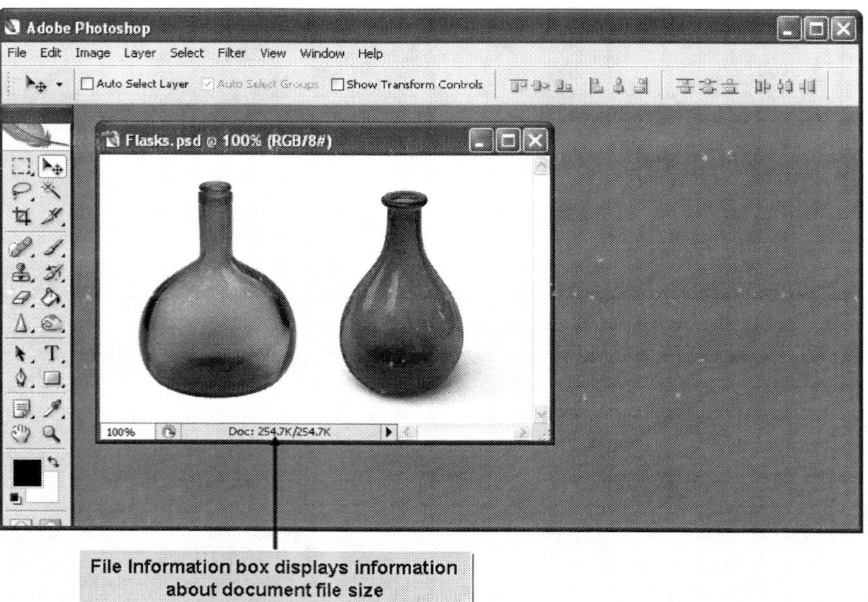

Image Size

It is sometimes necessary to determine the image size in inches so that the printed output fits space requirements. Similarly, since some large Photoshop images require a great deal of storage space, you may need to check its document details.

Exploring Document Details

Using the File Information box, you can view the height and width of the image. Document Dimensions displays the height and width of the image using the same units as the ruler. The unit is inch by default. Scratch sizes show the memory consumption. The number on the left shows the memory consumed by all open images. The number on the right shows the amount of memory (RAM) available to Photoshop. When the number on the left exceeds the number on the right, it indicates that there is no memory available. Photoshop must then employ virtual memory to write additional data to disk. Another way of expressing this is the efficiency value. If the efficiency value is less than 100 percent, Photoshop is using virtual memory, and you will experience a drop in performance. You can choose Timing to see the amount of time Photoshop took to complete the actions since the timer was reset. This value is most useful for time-consuming tasks such as resizing the image or applying effects filters. You can choose the Current tool to display the name of the currently selected tool.

You can also select the Document Profile option in the File Information box drop-down list to display the name of the image's color profile.

Rulers can help you gauge the size of an image as you are editing it. Since the rulers change their apparent size when you zoom in or out in an image, you can tell the actual size of objects in the image at a glance.

When you view the image at 100 percent magnification, one monitor pixel is used to draw one image pixel. Therefore, if the print resolution of an image does not match the monitor's resolution, the 100 percent view will not reflect the printed size of the image. Instead it will only allow you to see each pixel in the image. Photoshop must enlarge any higher resolution image to prevent skipping over pixels within the image. For example, a 192 ppi image must be displayed at twice the actual size on a 96 ppi monitor to enable you to see each pixel. Since the 100 percent size on the monitor typically does not reflect the printed size of the image, you can use the File Information box drop-down list to see the size of the printed image relative to the page. Or else you can also use the Print Size command in the View menu.

 A layer is an overlay consisting of any combination of colored, transparent, and semitransparent pixels, which float above the background of an image.

 A channel is a container of image information in Photoshop. Color channels hold information about each component of the image; alpha channels hold extra data.

The Image Size Command

Image size is determined by pixel dimensions. Pixel dimensions are the amount of pixels that make up the height and width of an image.

There are five ways to check the size of an image. You can use the File Information box, the Adobe Bridge, the Rulers, the Print Size command, or the Image Size command. The Image Size command in the Image menu allows you to modify the size and resolution of an image. This is useful for fitting the image into an output area having a different size. The Image Size dialog box displays the pixel dimensions and the printed size of an image. It can be used to resize an image with or without changing the pixel dimensions and file size.

 Since a web page usually has several graphics, it is a good practice to keep any specific graphic to 5K or lower.

Factors Affecting File Size

One of the main objectives when creating web graphics is to keep the file size as small as possible. The larger the file size, the longer it takes for the viewer to download the file. Some of the main factors that contribute to the file size are the number of pixels, number of colors used, image compression, and the extra information stored in the file.

Number of Pixels in an Image

It is sometimes necessary to change the image size so that the printed output fits within space requirements. Similarly, since some large Photoshop images require a great deal of storage space, you may need to check the storage space needed for an image. It is important to recognize that the file size is closely related to resolution and image size. Large, high resolution images take up much more storage space than low resolution images. However, the most important thing to keep in mind is that file size depends directly on the total number of pixels in an image.

For example, the following two images have the same number of pixels, and therefore the same file size. The first image is at very low resolution, causing visible pixelation. The second image is the same image as the first, but with higher resolution, and therefore smaller printed size. Since the pixels are much smaller, it appears smoother when printed.

Resampling

Resampling determines whether or not to change the pixel dimensions of the image. If you choose to resample the image, the pixel dimensions and file size will change, and Photoshop must recreate the same image appearance using a different set of pixels. In general, if an image has too few or too many pixels, you should rescan, rather than resample.

Original image –
8 pixels/inch

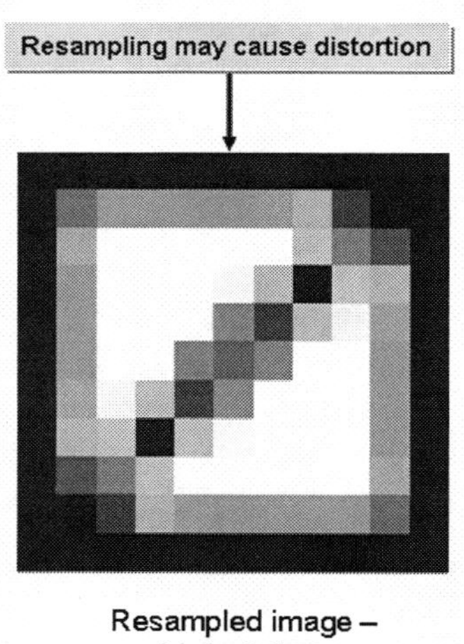

Resampled image –
11pixels/inch

Resampling and Distortion

Resampling causes distortion whether you use it to increase or decrease the file size. But if the original image contains enough pixels, the distortion may be negligible. However, you should avoid repeated resampling of an image, because each successive resampling causes the image to lose more details. Transforming an image by rotating, skewing, and so on, also resamples the image. Therefore repeated transformations should also be avoided. Also, you will not add detail to a low resolution image by resampling it. For example, if small text in an image is fuzzy, increasing the resolution by resampling it will not make the text more legible.

When to Resample an Image

If you can resize an image to the final size you desire while keeping the ratio of image resolution to linescreen between 1½ and 3, you should do so. However, as, the original scan has fewer or many more pixels than are necessary, you will usually achieve the best quality by rescanning the original rather than by resampling it. However, since this is not always practical, you may need to resample some images even when they exhibit some distortion. If you choose to resample an image, you can change the resolution while maintaining the printed size, or change the printed size while maintaining a fixed resolution. For example, you can make an image print larger while maintaining its original resolution. This will increase file size, since you will be adding pixels in order to make the image larger.

How to Determine Display and Print Resolution

Procedure Reference: Determine the Image Size in Photoshop

To determine the image size in Photoshop:

1. In the Status bar, in the File Information area, click the triangle.
2. From the File Information menu, choose Show→Document Dimensions to view the size of the image in the Status bar.

Procedure Reference: Determine the Printed Size of a Photoshop Image

To determine the printed size of a Photoshop image:

1. In the Status bar, in the File Information area, click and hold the mouse button to view the printed size of the image. The physical size of the image as it would print on an 8½ inch by 11 inch page is displayed.
2. Choose File→Page Setup.
3. In the Page Setup dialog box, in the Orientation section, specify the desired options.
    - In the Size drop-down list, specify the paper size.
    - In the Orientation section, select Landscape to turn the page sideways so that the image fits better on the paper.
4. If necessary, view the printed image size again in the File Information area to verify how the image fits on the paper.
5. Choose View→Rulers to view the top and left rulers.
6. View the image at 100% magnification.
    - Choose View→Actual Pixels.

- In the toolbox, double-click the Zoom tool.
- Or, in the Status bar, in the Magnification text box, type 100 and press Enter.

7. View the printing resolution of the image in the Photoshop window.
   - Choose View→Print Size to view the image at the size it would be printed.
   - Or, select the Hand tool or Zoom tool and on the Tool Options bar, click Print Size.

Procedure Reference: Change the Print Dimensions and Resolution of an Image

To change the print dimensions and resolution of an image:

1. Open the desired image.
2. Choose Image→Image Size.
3. In the Image Size dialog box, specify the desired settings.
   - Verify that the Constrain Proportions check box is checked to maintain the width in proportion to the height of the image. This option will automatically update the width of the image as you change its height, and vice versa.
   - If necessary, set the resampling option.
     - Check the Resample Image check box, if you want to change the print dimensions or the resolution of the image and adjust the total number of pixels in the image proportionately.
     - Uncheck the Resample Image check box, if you want to change the print dimensions and the resolution of the image without changing the total number of pixels in the image.
   - In the Document Size section, in the Width and Height text boxes, type the width and height values, respectively.
   - In the Document Size section, in the Resolution text box, type a value to set the resolution of the image.
4. Choose View→Print Size to verify the print size of the image after specifying the settings.
5. If necessary, view the image at 100% magnification and notice the change in its resolution.
6. If necessary, choose Edit→Undo Image Size to remove the image adjustments, incase the results are not satisfactory.

ACTIVITY 2-1

Determining the Image Size

Data Files:

- Kid Stuff.psd

Before You Begin

Open the Kid Stuff.psd file from the C:\084563Data\Sizing Images\Activity 1\Starter folder.

Scenario:

You want to take a print out of the Kid Stuff image. Before you go ahead with printing the image, you would like to determine whether the image would fit within the printable area.

What You Do	How You Do It
1. **Determine the size of the Kid Stuff.psd file.**	a. In the Status bar, in the File Information area, **notice that the printing size and the file's approximate size are displayed.** b. In the File Information area, **click the triangle and choose Show→Document Dimensions.** c. In the Status bar, in the File Information area, **notice that the document dimensions are displayed in inches.** 66.67% 6.333 inches x 5.333 inches (150 ppi)

2. **Determine the print size of the image.**

a. In the Status bar, in the File Information area, **click and hold the left mouse button** to view the thumbnail print preview of your image.

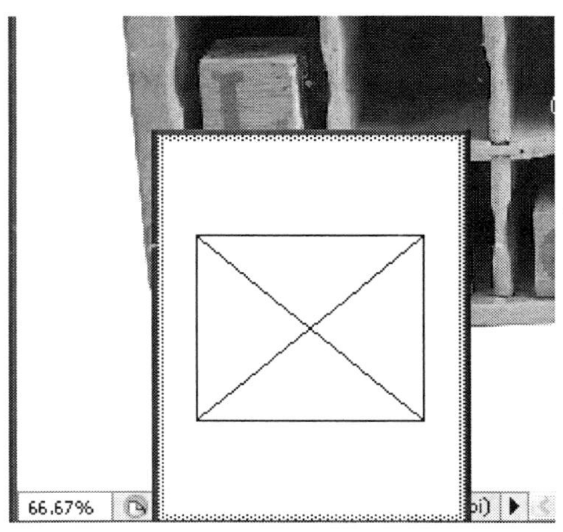

b. **Choose File→Page Setup.**

c. In the Page Setup dialog box, in the Orientation section, **select Landscape and click OK.**

d. In the Status bar, in the File Information area, **click and hold the left mouse button** to view the thumbnail print preview of the image after setting the page orientation.

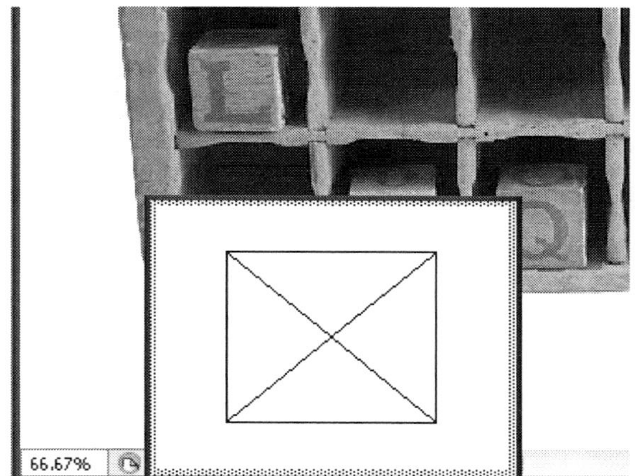

e. In the File Information area, **press Alt and hold the left mouse button** to view the image size in inches, as well as the type and resolution of the image.

f. **Choose View→Rulers** to display the rulers.

g. **Choose View→Actual Pixels** to view the image at 100% magnification.

h. **Choose View→Print Size** to zoom the current window to the printing resolution.

i. **Close the file and click No when prompted to save.**

ACTIVITY 2-2

Adjusting the Image Resolution

Data Files:

- Kid Stuff.psd

Before You Begin

Open the Kid Stuff.psd file from the C:\084563Data\Sizing Images\Activity 2\Starter folder.

Scenario:

You are planning to use the image in the Kid Stuff.psd file for the magazine you are preparing for your organization. Before printing the image, you want to adjust its resolution and dimensions to suit the print requirement.

What You Do	How You Do It
1. **Modify the image resolution and size for printing.**	a. **Choose Image→Image Size.**
	b. In the Image Size dialog box, **verify that the Constrain Proportions check box is checked.**

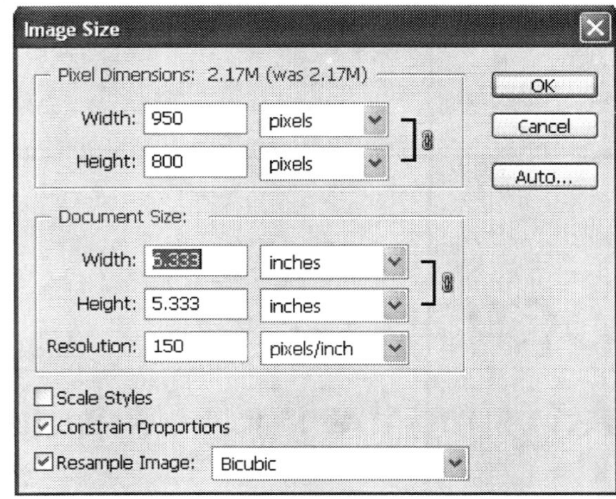

c. **Uncheck the Resample Image check box** to resize the image without sampling.

d. In the Resolution field, **double-click and type *300*** to print the image using a half-tone screen of 150 ppi that is suitable for magazines.

e. **Click OK.**

f. Notice that the image on the screen appears to be of the same size as it was before, but the inches in the ruler appear larger, and instead of being about 6 inches across, it is now about 3 inches across.

g. **Choose View→Print Size** to verify the print size of the image.

2. **Resample the image using the Image Size dialog box.**

   a. **Choose Image→Image Size.**

   b. **Check the Resample Image check box** to resample the image.

   c. In the Document Size section, in the Width text box, **double-click and type *6*** to increase the printed size of the image.

   d. Notice that the height also increases proportionally, since the Constrain Proportions check box is checked. **Click OK.**

   e. **Notice that the image appears larger than the original. The printed resolution is still at 300 ppi and the magnification of 24% still reflects the actual print size of the image.**

   f. **Double-click the Zoom tool** to view the image at 100% magnification.

   g. The resulting image is a bit more blurred than the original image due to resampling error. **Choose Edit→Undo Image Size** to remove the image size adjustment and view the image with its original pixel dimensions.

   h. **Close the file and click No when prompted to save.**

TOPIC B

Crop an Image

You know how to set the optimal print and display resolution. Sometimes you may need to work on a specific part of a scanned image. In this topic, you will crop images to remove unwanted portions.

You may not need to use the entire image as it was originally scanned. For example, you may only want to show a person's head instead of his or her entire body. Photoshop allows you to crop an image, removing parts of the image that you do not need.

Cropping

Cropping is the process of removing parts of the image that you do not need. In addition, it reduces the amount of storage space and memory that an image requires.

You can crop an image by dragging the Crop tool to designate a cropping border. The area outside the cropping border appears gray, indicating that when you perform the crop, this area will be eliminated from the image. This area is called the cropping shield. You can then move the cropping border by dragging from within it, resize it by dragging its corner handles, or rotate it by dragging from outside the cropping border.

The cropping shield appears as a black area at 75 percent opacity by default. If you do not wish to view the shield, uncheck the Shield check box on the Tool Options bar. You can also use the Color and Opacity options on the Tool Options bar to control the color and opacity of the shield.

The Crop And Straighten Photos Command

You can scan multiple photos on a scanner, and then use the Crop And Straighten Photos command to create separate files for each photo. The Crop And Straighten Photos command finds rectangular areas in a file and extracts each region into its own Photoshop file. You can also use this command to automatically straighten single images.

Rotate a Cropped Image

Rotating the crop area is useful for straightening images that were scanned at a slight angle, or for rotating the image as you crop it. Before rotating the crop area, you can choose the center of rotation, which appears at the center of the image. Although this is a simple way of rotating an image, remember that Photoshop will have to resample the image by recreating it with a different number of pixels. Like in resampling, rotating the crop area distorts the image slightly during resizing. If an image needs straightening, it may be better to rescan the image as opposed to rotating it. Finally, press Enter to crop the content outside the crop area, leaving only the content that was inside the crop area. It is useful to display the Info palette as you resize and rotate a crop marquee, so you can adjust the marquee with precision.

Delete or Hide a Cropped Area

When the Crop tool is selected, you can use the fields on the Tool Options bar to force the cropped area to certain dimensions with a specific resolution. This is useful when you need an image to fit within a space of specific size in a finished document.

After you establish a cropping area, the Tool Options bar displays the Cropped Area option. This option allows you to delete or hide the image area that is cropped away. The Delete option removes the cropped area from the image. The Hide option hides the cropped area. So if you increase the canvas size with the Image→Canvas Size command or the Image→Reveal All command, the data you cropped will appear again. However, the Cropped Area options are not available for the Background layer, in which cropped areas are always deleted.

You can also save the settings for the Crop tool to any tool to reuse. To save the settings defined on the Tool Options bar for a tool, click the drop-down arrow next to the Tool Presets Picker on the Tool Options bar. Click the triangle at the top-right corner, and choose New Tool Preset. The settings are saved and can be accessed from the Tool Presets Picker drop-down list.

How to Crop an Image

Procedure Reference: Crop an Image

To crop an image:

1. In the toolbox, select the Crop tool.
2. Position the Crop tool cursor at the point from which you need to create the cropping marquee.
3. Click and drag the Crop tool cursor over the portion of the image that needs to be cropped.
4. If necessary, adjust the cropping marquee.
   - Scale the marquee.
     a. Position the mouse pointer at the corners of the cropping marquee and notice that the mouse pointer changes to a double-headed arrow.

b. Drag the handle to scale the marquee.

- Rotate the marquee.
  a. Position the mouse pointer outside the cropping marquee and notice that the mouse pointer changes to a curved arrow.
  b. Click and drag the handle to rotate it. You can use the Info palette to view the angle of rotation.
- Move the marquee to a different position.
  a. Position the mouse pointer inside the cropping marquee.
  b. Click and drag to move the marquee to a different position.

5. Press Enter to crop the image.
6. If necessary, save the image.

ACTIVITY 2-3

Cropping an Image

Data Files:

- Kid Stuff.psd

Before You Begin

Open the Kid Stuff.psd file from the C:\084563Data\Sizing Images\Activity 3\Starter folder.

Scenario:

You do not want to use the entire Kid Stuff image as it was originally scanned. You want to eliminate the unwanted areas of the image.

What You Do	How You Do It
1. **Create a cropping marquee to enclose the crate, excluding the ball.**	a. In the toolbox, **select the Crop tool.** b. **Position the Crop tool cursor in the white space at the upper-left corner of the image, and click and drag the Crop tool cursor towards the bottom-right corner of the image** to create a cropping marquee surrounding the crate containing the toy blocks, while excluding the rubber ball. 
2. **Adjust the cropping marquee.**	a. **Position the mouse pointer at the top-left corner of the cropping marquee and notice that the mouse pointer changes to a double-headed arrow.** b. **Click at the top-left corner of the cropping marquee and drag the handle diagonally down so that the marquee does not cut any portion of the image.**
3. **Crop the image after rotating the marquee.**	a. In the Navigator palette group, **click the Info palette tab** to view the palette. b. **Position the mouse pointer just outside the top-left corner of the cropping marquee and notice that the mouse pointer changes to a curved arrow.**

c. **Click and drag the curved handle to rotate the cropping marquee until the angle of rotation on the Info palette becomes -2.0°.**

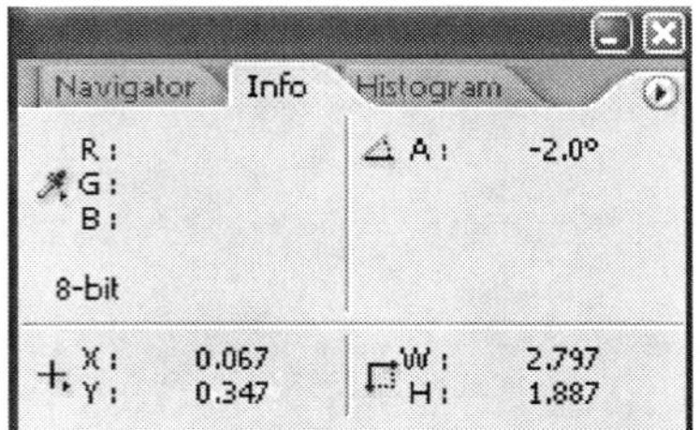

d. **Press Enter** to crop the image.

---

4. **Move the cropping marquee to a different position.**

a. **Click and drag across the block with the gray colored L** to create a cropping marquee.

b. **Position the mouse pointer at the center of the marquee, click and drag it over the block with letter P.**

c. **Press Esc** to cancel the crop.

d. **Choose File→Save As.**

e. In the Save As dialog box, in the File Name text box, **type *My_Kid Stuff* and click Save.**

f. **Close the file.**

Lesson 2 Follow-up

In this lesson, you adjusted image size and resolution for printing. You also ensured that the images have a balance between file size and print or display quality, by setting the image resolution and removing the unwanted portions from them.

1. **While creating Photoshop images for print, what do you do to determine the best print resolution?**

2. **Give examples of situations in which the cropping tool in Photoshop has been helpful to you.**

Notes

LESSON 3
Selecting Image Areas

Lesson Time
1 hour(s)

Lesson Objectives:

In this lesson, you will use the different selection tools in Photoshop to select parts of images and also save selections for future use.

You will:

- Select image areas with the Marquee tools.
- Select image areas with the Lasso tools.
- Save and load selections.
- Select image areas with the Magic Wand tool.
- Select image areas with the Magnetic Lasso tool.
- Modify selections with selection options.

Introduction

Now you know how to size and crop images. Before editing an image, you will often select the part of the image that is to be edited. Once this selection is made, you can move that part, rotate it, copy it, fill it with color, or apply a variety of special effects to it. In this lesson, you will explore several techniques for selecting parts of images.

You want to work with only a part of an image. However, if the selection isn't made accurately, the edited result will look sloppy, grainy, or unrealistic. Therefore, it is important to select areas precisely to add or subtract from existing selections, and to modify the sharpness of the selection border.

TOPIC A

Select Image Areas with the Marquee Tools

You have explored the Photoshop interface and are about to start work on an image. You may want to work with only a specific part of the image. In this topic, you will select specific image areas that you want to work on.

Selecting geometrical areas such as boxes and circles can be quite tricky. Photoshop's Marquee tools enable you to easily select geometrical areas in an image that you are working on.

The Marquee Tools

The Marquee tools enable you to select geometric areas in images.

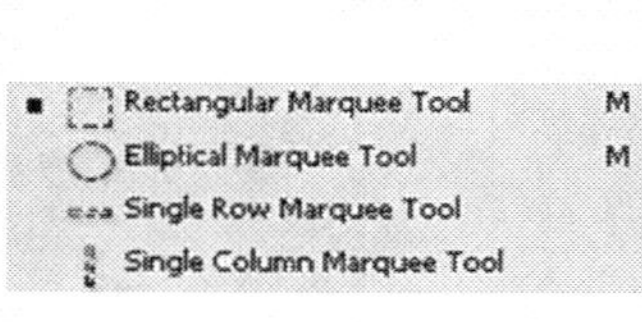

The Marquee Tools

Tool	Description
Rectangular Marquee	This tool is useful for selecting geometric areas like boxes. Drag with this tool to establish a selection marquee in an image.
Elliptical Marquee	This tool is useful for selecting geometric areas such as circles. To draw an elliptical marquee with accuracy, you should position the Elliptical Marquee tool cursor at the upper-left corner of an imaginary bounding box around the area you want to select. Once you have made a selection, you can move and *transform* the selection marquees. While transforming, the values of the angle of rotation will be displayed on the Info palette.
Single Row Marquee	This tool creates a border as a 1-pixel-wide row.
Single Column Marquee	This tool creates a border as a 1-pixel-wide column.

Cropping a Row or Column of Pixels

If you want to crop one extra row or column of pixels from an image that includes just a bit of the background, use the Single Row or Column Marquee tool to select the extra row or column.

The Extras Command

Once an image area is selected, it is recommended that you hide the selection marquee to view the image better. You can hide a selection marquee at any time by disabling the Extras command. You can do so by choosing View→Extras, or pressing Ctrl+H. This merely hides the selection marquee. The Extras command also shows or hides selection marquees, grids, guides, annotations, slices, and target paths. You can also individually show or hide each of these items by choosing the item you want to show or hide from the Show submenu in the View menu.

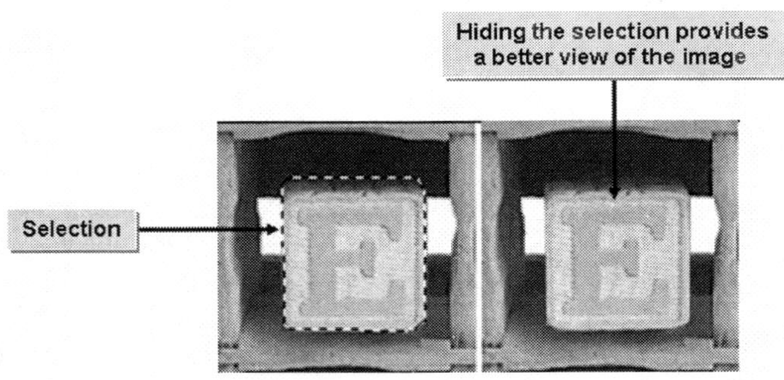

How to Select Image Areas with the Marquee Tools

Procedure Reference: Make a Rectangular Selection

To make a rectangular selection:

1. Select the Rectangular Marquee tool.
2. Position the cross hair cursor at the location where you would like to start the selection.
3. Click and drag to make a rectangular marquee selection.
4. If you are not satisfied with the results, choose Select→Deselect to remove the selection.

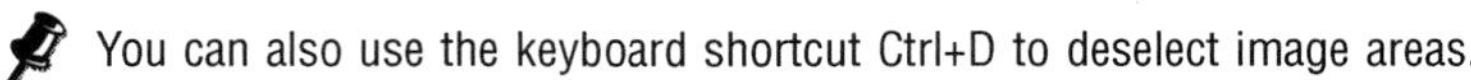
You can also use the keyboard shortcut Ctrl+D to deselect image areas.

Removing Selections

Whenever you want to remove a selection you have made, you should always choose the Deselect command in the Select menu. Unlike with other graphics applications, you should not simply click in a blank space to deselect when using Photoshop. Since the entire image is made up of individual pixels, there is no empty or transparent space in a Photoshop image, unless you add layers. White space in a single-layer image is simply a large area of white pixels.

Procedure Reference: Make an Elliptical Selection

To make an elliptical selection:

1. Select the Elliptical Marquee tool.

2. Position the cross hair cursor at the location where you would like to start the selection.

3. Click and drag to make a elliptical marquee selection.

Constrain Selections

Sometimes it is important that the selection area you create with the Rectangular or Elliptical Marquee tools be a perfect square or circle. You can constrain the marquee tools to create squares or circles by holding down Shift while using the marquee tools.

Procedure Reference: Hide a Selection

To hide a selection:

1. Click the View menu. A check mark appears next to the Extras command.
2. Choose Extras to uncheck the command and hide the selection marquee.

Select from the Center of an Object

It is often difficult to estimate where to begin dragging an elliptical marquee in order to enclose an entire object perfectly. However, you can select from the center of an object toward the edge instead of from the edge to simplify selection.

Procedure Reference: Select from Center Toward the Edges

To select from center toward the edges:

1. Select a marquee tool.
2. Position the mouse pointer at the center of the object to be selected.
3. Click, hold down the Alt and Shift key, and drag to constrain shape and draw a selection from the center toward the edge.
4. When the selection matches the letter, complete the selection by first releasing the mouse button, then releasing the Alt and Shift keys.

Move Selections

If the area you selected is approximately the right size but is not centered over the pixels you wished to select, you may want to move the selection marquee. Photoshop allows you to easily move the selection marquee either as you draw it or afterwards. To move a selection as you draw it, continue to hold down the mouse button, and hold down the Spacebar. You can then drag to move the selection. You can move an existing selection marquee itself without moving any pixels by positioning the selection tool within the marquee and dragging the tool to move it.

Procedure Reference: Transform a Marquee Selection

To transform a marquee selection:

1. Create the selection marquee.
2. If necessary, zoom the image.
3. Choose Select→Transform Selection.
4. Position the mouse pointer on the side or on the corner handles that appear around the selection, and drag to reshape the selection.

5. If necessary, position the mouse pointer inside the selection, except on the reference point at the center, and click and drag the selection marquee to move it to a different location.

6. Press Enter to apply the changes to the selection.

Transform Handles

When you choose the Transform command to modify a selection, a bounding box appears around the selection. The transform handles, which are square shaped, appear at the corners and the sides of the bounding box. You can place the mouse pointer on any of these handles and drag the double-headed arrow to reshape the selection.

ACTIVITY 3-1

Selecting Image Areas

Data Files:

- Kid Stuff.psd

Before You Begin

Open the Kid Stuff.psd file from the C:\084563Data\Selecting Images\Activity 1\Starter folder.

Scenario:

You want to make some changes to a part of the Kid Stuff image. You want to ensure that the selection is accurate to avoid problems while editing the image. Before making the selection, you would like to explore the different methods to make an elliptical selection.

What You Do	How You Do It
1. **Make a rectangular selection.**	a. If necessary, in the toolbox, **double-click the Zoom tool** to view the image at 100 percent magnification.
	b. **Select the Rectangular Marquee tool.**
	c. If necessary, **scroll to view the block with the letter Q at the bottom of the crate.**

d. On the Q block, at the top-left corner of its front face, **position the cross hair cursor, and click and drag the marquee to its bottom-right corner** to create a marquee that selects the block's front face.

e. **Choose Select→Deselect** to remove the selection.

---

2. **Make an elliptical selection.**

a. **Hold down the mouse button on the Rectangular Marquee tool** to display the Rectangular Marquee tool flyout.

b. From the Rectangular Marquee tool flyout, **select the Elliptical Marquee tool.**

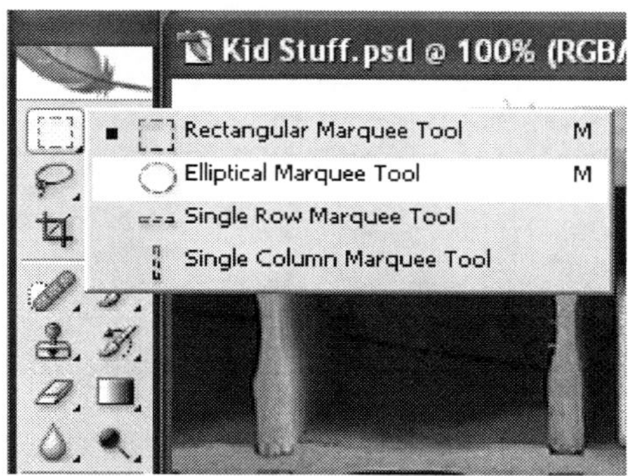

c. **Position the cross hair cursor a bit above and to the left of the letter Q, and click and drag across the letter** to create an elliptical marquee around the letter Q.

d. **Choose Select→Deselect** to remove the selection.

---

3. **Create a circular selection marquee around the letter O.**

a. If necessary, **scroll up and then to the right to view the letter O.**

b. **Position the cross hair mouse pointer just above and to the left of the letter O within the block. Hold down Shift and drag across the letter O** to create a selection marquee around the letter.

---

4. **Hide and reveal a selection marquee.**

a. The Extras command is selected by default. **Choose View→Extras** to uncheck it and hide the selection marquee.

b. **Choose View→Extras** to check it and reveal the selection marquee.

c. **Choose Select→Deselect** to remove the selection.

---

5. **Create a selection marquee around letter O starting from the center toward the outer edge.**

a. **Click at the center of letter O, hold down Alt and Shift, and drag the mouse pointer toward the outer edge of the letter O** to create a marquee and constrain it to a circle.

b. **When the selection matches the letter, complete the selection by first releasing the mouse button, then releasing the Alt and Shift keys.**

c. **Choose Select→Deselect** to remove the selection.

d. **Close the file and click No when prompted to save.**

ACTIVITY 3-2

Transforming Selections

Data Files:

- Kid Stuff.psd

Before You Begin

1. Open the Kid Stuff.psd file from the C:\084563Data\Selecting Images\Activity 2\Starter folder.
2. In the Status bar, double-click in the Magnification text box.
3. Type 50 to view the image at 50 percent magnification.

Scenario:

You have just learnt to use the marquee tools and would like to transform a selection so that the selection marquee accurately fits the image area.

What You Do	How You Do It
1. **Create a selection marquee around the letter O.**	a. **Position the mouse pointer just above and to the left of the letter O within the block. Hold down Shift as you drag to create a circular marquee that is approximately the size of the letter O, but do not release Shift or the mouse button.**
	b. While still holding down Shift and the mouse button, **hold down the Spacebar and drag to move the marquee so that it is centered on the letter O.**

2. **Transform the selection marquee to fit the letter Q accurately.**

a. **Position the mouse pointer at the center of the selection for letter O, and click and drag the selection marquee over the circular area in letter Q.**

b. **Select the Zoom tool.**

c. **Position the mouse pointer on the block with letter Q, and click and drag** to magnify the selection area.

d. **Choose Select→Transform Selection.**

e. **Position the mouse pointer on the side or on the corner handles that now appear around the selection, and drag to reshape the selection to better fit to the letter Q.**

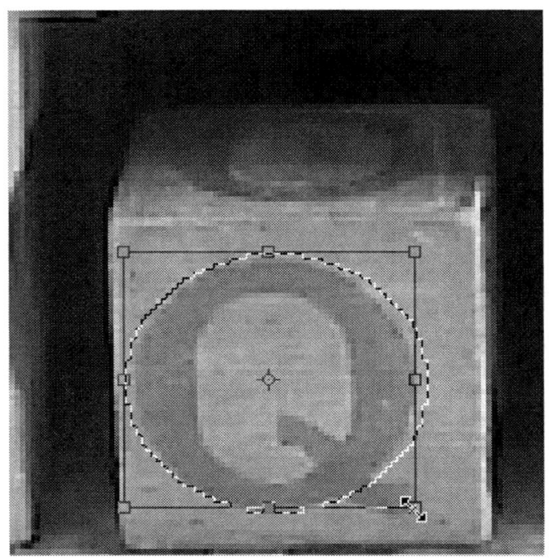

f. **Click anywhere inside the selection,**

except on the reference point at the center, and drag to move the selection to fit it over the letter Q.

g. **Press Enter** to apply the changes to the selection.

h. **Choose Select→Deselect** to remove the selection.

i. **Close the file and click No when prompted to save.**

TOPIC B

Select Image Areas with the Lasso Tools

You have been using the Marquee tools to make selections. But if you want to select more complex areas, you cannot use the Marquee tools, as they are only used to select elliptical and rectangular areas. In this topic, you will use the Lasso tools on images when you require more control over the shape of a selection.

The image you are working on is of animals in a zoo. You want to select a giraffe, and make changes to its texture. But you can't select it using a Marquee tool. For freeform selections that provide you with more control, you can use the Lasso tools.

The Lasso Tools

The Lasso tools are used to select complex areas in an image.

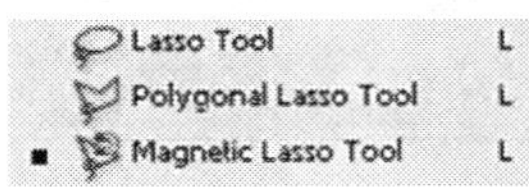

The Lasso Tools

Tool	Description
Lasso	This tool is used to make free form segments of a selection border. To establish a selection using the Lasso tool, drag to create a selection of any shape. If you release the mouse button, without ending the selection at the same location where you began, the Lasso tool will automatically connect the selection's beginning and end points with a straight line.
Polygonal Lasso tool	This tool is used to make straight-edged segments of a section border. You can also use it to select areas that are made up of straight lines. When using the Polygonal Lasso tool, instead of dragging to make a selection, you can click to create selections made up of straight lines. If you added a polygon point in the wrong location, you can remove the previous polygon point added by pressing Backspace. When you position the mouse pointer on the location where you began, a circle will appear next to the mouse pointer, indicating that clicking at that location completes the selection.
Magnetic Lasso tool	This tool is used to select portions of an image with complex edges, that are set against high-contrast background. It is used to accurately select image areas that contain many colors.

Toggling Between Polygonal Lasso Tool and Lasso Tool

When using the Polygonal Lasso tool, you can hold down Alt to temporarily access the Lasso tool. If you continue to hold down Alt, you can still create straight segments by moving the mouse pointer without holding down the mouse button, and clicking to add points.

The Cross Hair Cursor

It is sometimes difficult to use the Lasso tool to create precise selections, because the hot spot or tip of the tool is difficult to locate. Therefore, it becomes difficult to know where the selection marquee will be created as you drag. For more accuracy, you can access a *cross hair cursor* to replace the lasso cursor by pressing Caps Lock. The hot spot of the cross hair cursor is at the dot in the center. If you need to see the cursor of the tool you are using, you can turn off the cross hair cursor by pressing Caps Lock again.

 Most Photoshop tools utilize cross hair cursors for extra accuracy. It is also useful for indicating what tool you are using.

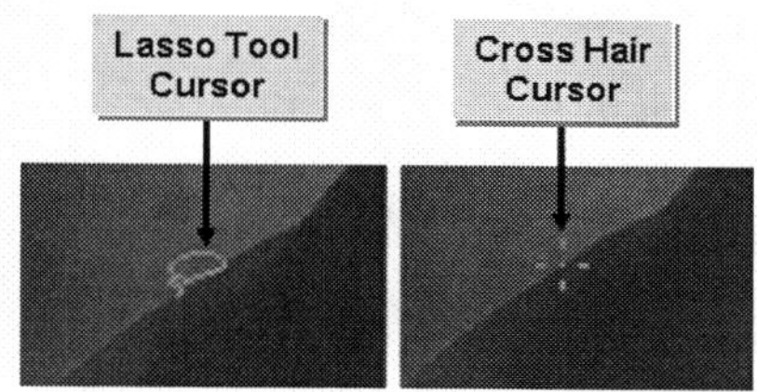

How to Select Image Areas with the Lasso Tools

Procedure Reference: Select an Image Area Using the Lasso Tool

To select an image area using the Lasso tool:

1. Select the Lasso tool.
2. Click at the outer edge of the object or on the portion of the image to be selected.
3. Drag to make a freehand selection.
4. Release the mouse button to end the selection at the same location it began.

5. If necessary, press Caps Lock to display the cross hair cursor instead of the Lasso tool cursor for creating more accurate selections, and then click and drag to make the selection.

Procedure Reference: Select an Image Area Using the Polygon Lasso tool

To select an image area using the Polygonal Lasso tool:

1. If necessary, choose View→Fit On Screen to fit the image in the window.
2. Hold down the mouse button on the Lasso tool to display the Lasso tool flyout.
3. From the Lasso tool flyout, select the Polygonal Lasso tool.
4. Position the Polygonal Lasso tool cursor at the location you would like to start the selection and click.
5. Move the mouse pointer and click to set an endpoint to create a straight line connecting the points.
6. If necessary, use the Lasso tool temporarily to select the rounded edges in the object.
   a. Hold down Alt to temporarily select the Lasso tool.
   b. Keep holding the Alt key, then hold down the mouse button and drag to select the rounded edges.
   c. Release Alt and the mouse button to switch to the Polygonal Lasso tool again.
7. Continue clicking to create the straight line segments that select the object.
8. Complete the selection by clicking at the location you started.

Activity 3-3

Selecting Image Areas Using the Lasso Tool

Data Files:

- Kid Stuff.psd

Before You Begin

Open the Kid Stuff.psd file from the C:\084563Data\Selecting Images\Activity 3\Starter folder.

Scenario:

You would like to edit a specific portion of the image precisely and before you start editing, you want to use the selection tools to quickly select it.

What You Do	How You Do It
1. **Select the letter Q using the Lasso tool.**	a. **Select the Lasso tool.** b. **Click at the outer edge of the letter Q and drag to create a freehand selection around its outer edges.** c. **Choose Select→Deselect** to remove the selection.
2. **Create a more accurate selection of the letter Q using the cross hair cursor.**	a. **Press Caps Lock** to display the cross hair cursor in place of the Lasso tool cursor. b. **Click and drag the cross hair cursor around the outer edge of the letter Q.** The cross hair pointer makes it easier to create accurate selections.  c. **Choose Select→Deselect** to remove the selection. d. **Close the file and click No when prompted to save.**

ACTIVITY 3-4

Selecting Polygon Areas

Data Files:

- Kid Stuff.psd

Before You Begin

Open the Kid Stuff.psd file from the C:\084563Data\Selecting Images\Activity 4\Starter folder.

Scenario:

You want to select areas in the Kid Stuff image that are made up of straight lines using the selection tools. Also, you find that you need to select a specific block that is a combination of straight and rounded edges.

What You Do	How You Do It
1. **Select the crate in the Kid Stuff image.**	a. **Choose View→Fit On Screen.**
	b. **Hold down the mouse button on the Lasso tool** to display the Lasso tool flyout.
	c. From the Lasso tool flyout, **select the Polygonal Lasso tool.**
	d. **Position the Polygonal Lasso tool cursor at the bottom-left corner of the crate and click.**
	e. **Move the Polygonal Lasso tool cursor to the upper-left front corner of the crate and click** to create a straight line selection connecting the points.
	f. **Move the Polygonal Lasso tool cursor to the upper-left back corner of the crate and click.**

g. **Move the mouse pointer to the upper-right back corner of the crate and click.**

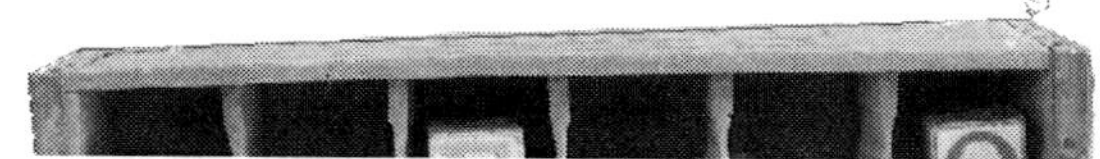

h. **Move the mouse pointer to the upper-right front corner of the box, and click.**

i. **Click at all the other corners of the crate to complete the selection.**

j. **Choose Select→Deselect** to remove the selection.

---

2. **Select the block with gray colored letter L.**

a. **Select the Zoom tool.**

b. **Click and drag over the block with gray colored letter L** to magnify it.

c. **Select the Polygonal Lasso tool.**

d. **Position the mouse pointer at the block's top-left front corner, and click once.**

e. **Move the mouse pointer to the block's bottom left, above the rounded corner, and click again.** A line connects the two locations on which you clicked.

f. **Hold down Alt, then hold down the mouse button and drag along the block's bottom-left corner** to select the slightly rounded bottom-left corner.

g. As you drag with Alt held down, the mouse pointer appears as the Lasso tool cursor. **Release Alt and the mouse button when you finish dragging along the bottom-left corner.** The mouse pointer appears as the Polygonal Lasso again.

h. **Move the mouse pointer to the block's bottom-right corner and click.**

i. **Hold down Alt to temporarily select the Lasso tool, and drag along the block's bottom-right corner.**

j. **Use the Polygonal Lasso tool to select the remaining sides of the block, holding down Alt to access the Lasso tool, if necessary.**

k. **Click again at the location where you began the selection to complete it.**

Topic C

Save Selections

You have made a selection in your image using the Marquee and Lasso tools. Now you want to save your selection for future reference. In this topic, you will save selections made earlier in an image.

Once you have made a selection, Photoshop allows you to save it for future use, so you will not have to select the area again.

Alpha Channel

Selections can be saved in Photoshop for future reference. The selection when saved will appear as an additional channel or alpha channel on the Channels palette. The *alpha channel* consists of additional information stored with an image, in the form of a grayscale image, and is typically used to store selections. These selections are referred to as masks.

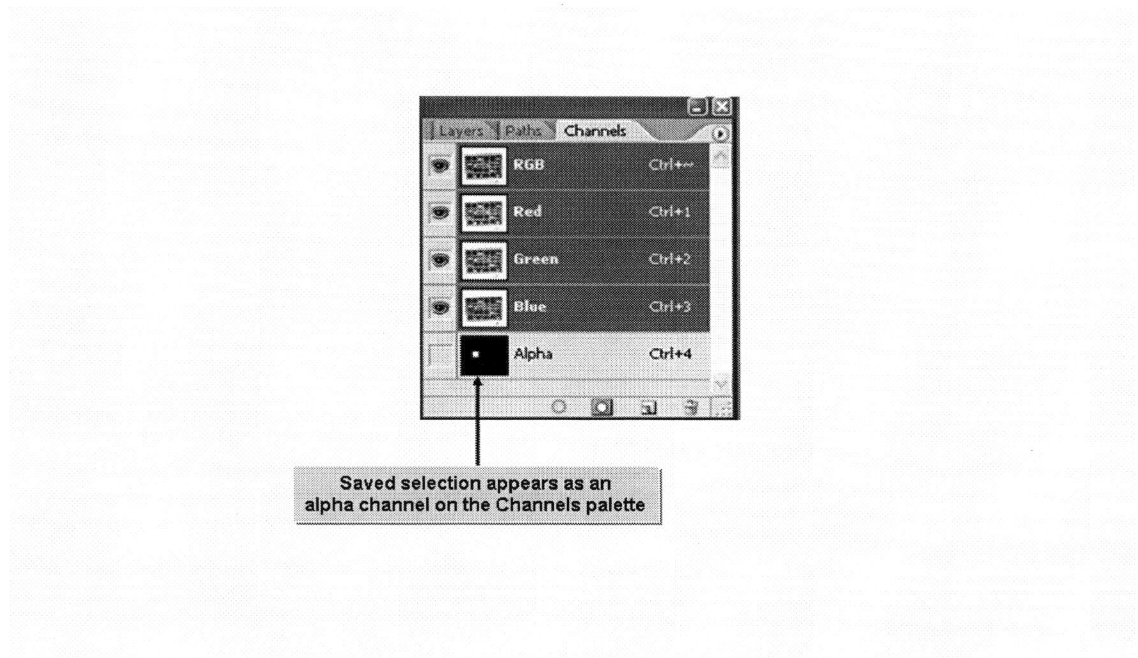

Save Selections

Procedure Reference: Save Selections

To save selections:

1. Create a selection using a Selection tool.
2. Choose Select→Save Selection.
3. In the Save Selection dialog box, specify the desired settings.
   a. From the Document drop-down list, choose the file to be used as the source. By default, the active file is used as the source.

b. If necessary, in the Name text box, specify a name for the selection.

4. If necessary, retrieve the saved selection.
   a. Choose Select→Load Selection.
   b. In the Load Selection dialog box, from the Channel drop-down list, select the channel containing the saved selection.

Procedure Reference: Rename a Saved Selection

To rename a saved selection:

1. In the Layers palette group, click the Channels palette tab to view the alpha channel that was created when you saved the selection.
2. On the Channels palette, double-click the alpha channel.
3. In the Channel Options dialog box, in the Name field, type a name and click OK.
4. If necessary, select the composite channel to display all the colors in the image.
5. If necessary, hold down Ctrl and on the Channels palette, select the alpha channel to load the saved selection again.

ACTIVITY 3-5

Saving Selections

Data Files:

- Kid Stuff.psd

Before You Begin

- The Kid Stuff.psd file the selection made in the previous activity needs to be kept open.
- If you have closed the file and the selection is lost, you need to create the selection of the gray colored L block in the crate all over again by following the steps given in the Activity 3-4—Selecting Polygon Areas.

Scenario:

You want to create a selection around the gray colored letter L. As the selection is quite complicated, you would like to save it and use it later to select the letter instantly.

What You Do	How You Do It
1. **Save the selection.**	a. **Choose Select→Save Selection.**

b. In the Save Selection dialog box, **click OK** to use the default settings.

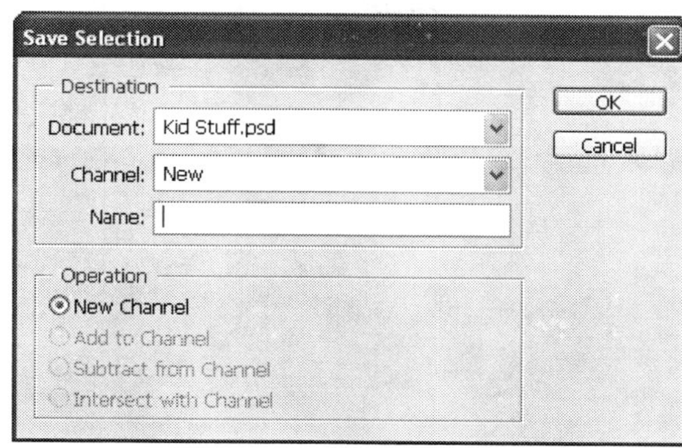

c. **Deselect the image.**

d. **Choose Select→Load Selection** to retrieve the saved selection.

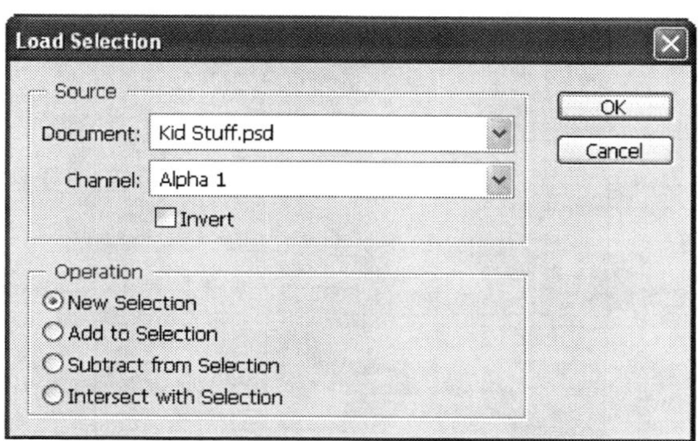

e. **Click OK** to view the selection marquee created around the gray colored L block.

---

2. **Rename a saved selection.**

a. In the Layers palette group, **click the Channels palette tab** to view the alpha channel that was created when you saved the selection.

b. **Double-click in the Alpha 1 channel just away from the Alpha 1 text** to view the Channel Options dialog box.

c. In the Channel Options dialog box, in the Name field, **type *L Selection***

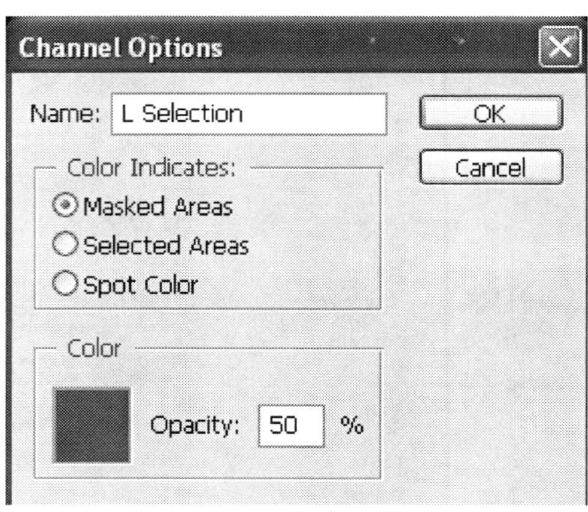

d. **Click OK.**

e. **Notice that the L Selection channel is displayed within the image window.**

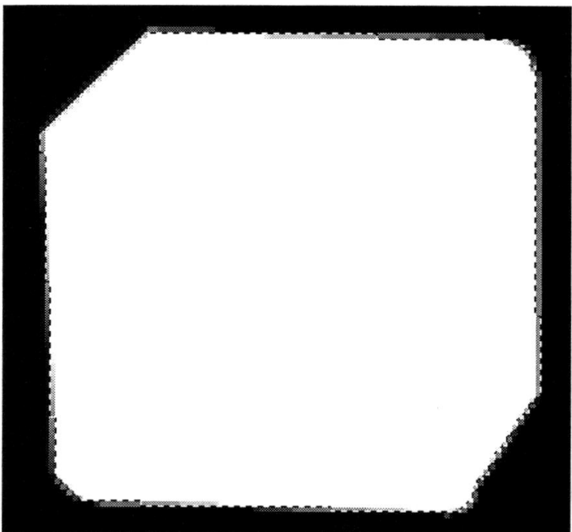

3. **Load the L Selection channel.**

   a. **Select the RGB channel** to make the Red, Green, and Blue channels visible at the same time, displaying all the colors in the image.

   b. **Deselect the image.**

   c. **Hold down Ctrl and on the Channels palette, select the L Selection channel** to load the saved selection again.

   d. **Deselect the image.**

   e. **Save the file as *Kid Stuff_modified*.**

   f. **Close the file.**

TOPIC D

Select Image Areas with the Magic Wand Tool

You made selections in an image using the Marquee and Lasso tools. But it is not always possible to make accurate selections by hand. In this topic, you will learn to select items based on the color similarity of image pixels.

An image you are working on consists of intricately designed patterns in different colors. You want to change the color scheme in one of these patterns, but using the Lasso tools to make your selection might prove to be difficult. In such situations, selections can be made on the basis of colors, using the Magic Wand tool.

The Magic Wand Tool

To use the Magic Wand tool, select it in the toolbox and click any pixel in the image. The *Magic Wand tool* will select the pixel on which you click, and any other pixels that fall within a specified color and brightness range. This makes it a useful tool for selecting areas of an image that are similar in color or brightness. You can specify whether the Magic Wand tool should select contiguous or discontiguous pixels by either checking or unchecking the Contiguous check box on the Tool Options bar.

Tolerance

In Photoshop, each pixel within an image is coded with color and brightness information. While working with the Magic Wand tool, you can specify the range or tolerance of pixels selected, to ensure that only pixels that are similar in color to the one that was clicked are selected. *Tolerance* refers to the Magic Wand tool's sensitivity to color differences. If the tolerance is low, it means that the Magic Wand tool has less tolerance for color differences, and vice versa.

For example, each pixel in a grayscale image is assigned a number from 0 to 255, corresponding to its brightness. Black pixels are assigned a value of 0 and white pixels have a value of 255. Each pixel within RGB or red, green, blue color images has three values ranging from 0 to 255, one each for red, green, and blue.

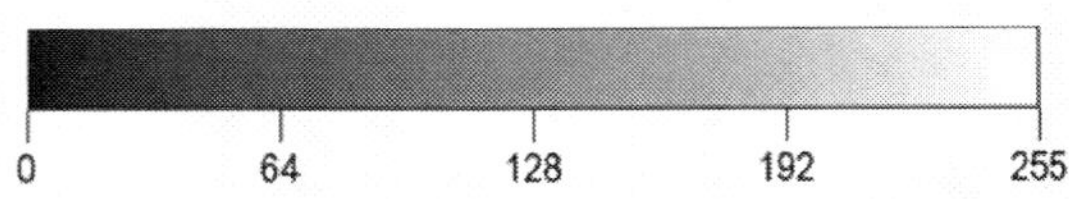

Grayscale pixel brightness value range

The Magic Wand tool works by reading the brightness of the pixel you click, and comparing it to the values of the surrounding pixels. If an adjacent pixel is within the tolerance you have chosen, it will be selected. For color images, the Magic Wand tool compares the red, green, and blue brightness values separately.

Tolerance Levels

The higher the tolerance, the larger the area you will select, and the lower the tolerance the smaller the area. For example, if you choose a tolerance level of 255, all the pixels within an image will be selected, and if you choose zero tolerance, only select pixels of exactly the same brightness value as the pixel you click with the Magic Wand tool will be selected. By default the tolerance is set to 32.

If you click a gray pixel valued at 128 in a grayscale image, while using a tolerance of 40, Photoshop will select all adjacent pixels with values ranging from 40 less than 128 (88) to 40 greater than 128 (168). Your success in using the Magic Wand tool depends partly on where you click. It is often best to click a color that is in the middle of the tonal range you wish to select. This means it is better to select one that is lighter than some colors you wish to select, but darker than others.

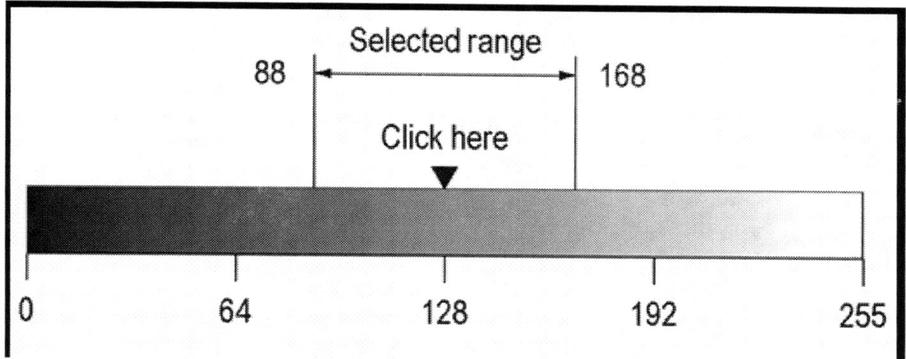

You can expand any selection to include areas with similar color. After making a selection, choose Select→Grow to add adjacent pixels whose brightness and color values fit within the Magic Wand tolerance set on the Tool Options bar. Use Select→ Similar to add pixels throughout the image whose brightness and color values fit within the current Magic Wand tolerance.

The Anti-Aliasing Feature

Anti-aliasing is a feature that enables you to smoothen jagged edges by placing light pixels around a selected object. For example, it is often used on text to create the illusion of smoother curves.

If you choose the Anti-alias option for selecting objects with the Magic Wand tool, any editing you perform on the selection will have slightly blended edges. For example, if you fill the area with a color, the edges will be softened. In addition, creating an anti-aliased selection may leave a halo of the blended color around the selection, if you move it in front of other differently colored objects.

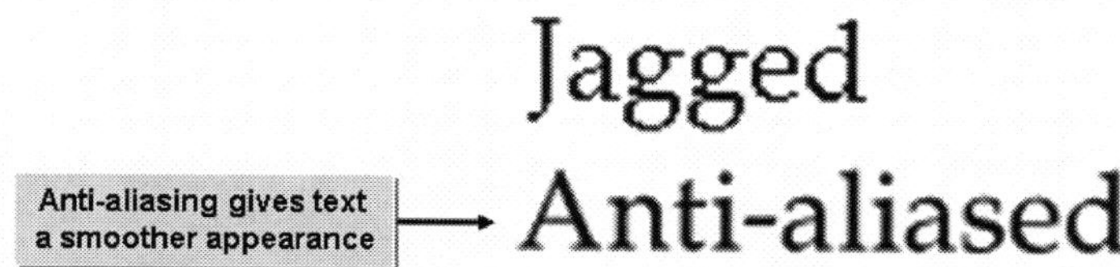

How to Select Image Areas with the Magic Wand Tool

Procedure Reference: Select Image Areas Using Magic Wand Tool

To select image areas using the Magic Wand tool:

1. Select the Magic Wand tool.
2. On the Tool Options bar, specify the desired settings.
   - In the Tolerance text box, type a value in pixels, ranging from 0 to 255.
   - Check the Anti-Alias check box to create blended edges.
   - Check the Contiguous check box to select only the adjacent areas with the same color.
3. In the image, click the color you would like to select.
4. If necessary, save the selection.
5. If necessary, save the file and close it.

ACTIVITY 3-6

Selecting Image Areas with the Magic Wand Tool

Data Files:

- Kid Stuff.psd

Before You Begin

Open the Kid Stuff.psd file from the C:\084563Data\Selecting Images\Activity 6\Starter folder.

Scenario:

You want to make a complex selection and feel that with the freehand selection tools it would be difficult to select precisely. You want to select items based on the color similarity of image pixels.

What You Do	How You Do It
1. **Select image areas with identical color.**	a. **Choose View→Fit On Screen.**
	b. **Select the Magic Wand tool.**
	c. **Click at the top-left corner, within the white background of the block with letter A.**

d. **Notice that the white area in the block is selected but other white pixels outside the dark border are not.**

e. On the Tool Options bar, **uncheck the Contiguous check box.**

f. **Choose Select→Deselect** to remove the selection.

g. **Click at the top-left corner, within the white background of the block with letter A.**

h. **Notice that the Magic Wand tool selects the white pixels throughout the image.**

i. **Deselect the image.**

2. **Select only the bright pixels within the image.**
   a. **Select the Zoom tool.**
   b. **Click and drag over the block with letter A** to magnify it.
   c. **Select the Magic Wand tool.**
   d. On the Tool options bar, in the Tolerance text box, **type *0*** to select only the brightest white pixels within the block.
   e. **Click at the top-left corner, within the white background of the block with letter A.**

---

3. **Save the Selection.**
   a. **Choose Select→Save Selection.**
   b. In the Save Selection dialog box, in the Name text box, **type *Background* and click OK.**
   c. **Deselect the selection.**

---

4. **Select areas of similar but not identical color and create blended edges.**

a. **Double-click the Zoom tool** to magnify the image to 100%.

b. **Select the Magic Wand tool.**

c. **Click at the top-left corner of the gray colored letter L.**

d. **Notice that the pixels with the same brightness as the one you clicked are selected, since the Magic Wand tolerance is set to 0.**

e. **Deselect the selection.**

f. On the Tool options bar, in the Tolerance text box, **type *100*** to use a greater tolerance for selecting the pixels within the letter L.

g. **Click at the top-left corner of the gray colored letter L.**

h. **Notice that many pixels outside the letter L are selected because the tolerance is high.**

i. **Deselect the selection.**

j. On the Tool options bar, in the Tolerance text box, **type *50*** to decrease the tolerance and try to make a more accurate selection of the gray colored letter L.

k. On the Tool Options bar, **check the Contiguous check box** to select the contiguous pixels.

l. On the Tool Options bar, verify that the Anti-aliased check box is checked and **click at the top-left corner of the gray colored L** to create blended edges.

m. **Notice that the selection is fairly accurate.**

n. **Deselect the selection.**

o. **Save the file as *Kid Stuff_selection*.**

p. **Close the file.**

TOPIC E

Select Image Areas with the Magnetic Lasso Tool

You have been using the Magic Wand tool to select areas consisting of similar colors. However, most objects are made up of numerous colors in different shades. These regions cannot be selected using the Magic Wand tool, especially when the object is not on a flat background. In this topic, you will use the Magnetic Lasso tool to make accurate selections of multi-colored objects.

You are working on an image with several colors. You want to select the dark blues and replace them by a lighter shade of blue. You cannot use the Magic Wand tool, as the objects in dark blue are made up of different shades of navy blue. To select the navy blue object accurately, you will have to use the Magnetic Lasso tool.

The Magnetic Lasso Tool

You use the Magnetic Lasso tool in a fashion similar to the standard Lasso tool by dragging it around the contour you wish to select. However, unlike the standard Lasso tool, the Magnetic Lasso tool will snap the selection to a line where it detects high contrast. This will enable you to guide Photoshop to make accurate selections around a multi-colored object quickly.

As the Magnetic Lasso tool detects contrasts, it creates points along a path as you move the mouse pointer. The Magnetic Lasso tool finds the edge of highest contrast within a specified distance from the mouse pointer as you drag. This distance is specified by the Width field on the Tool Options bar, and is set to 10 pixels by default. You can press Caps Lock to display the cursor as a circle whose size reflects the value specified by the Width field.

You can increase or decrease the Magnetic Lasso tool's Width value by pressing the] and [, respectively.

Modify a Selection

Points are added along the path automatically, but you can add points along the path at any time by clicking on it. You can press Backspace to remove the previous point along the path. In addition, you can cancel a selection you have started by pressing Esc.

The Magnetic Lasso Tool Options Bar

The Magnetic Lasso Tool Options bar contains several additional options that affect how the tool functions.

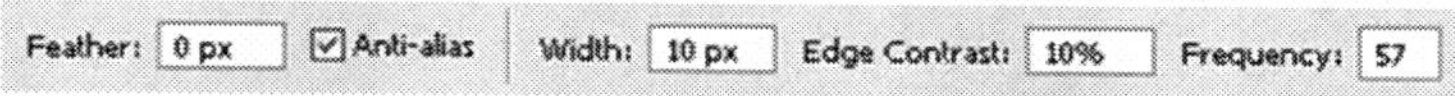

The Magnetic Lasso Tool Options bar

Option	Description
Feather	You can specify how soft the resulting edges will be when a selection is complete, by specifying the Feather value on the Tool Options bar.
Anti-aliased	Checking the Anti-aliased check box specifies whether the selected area will be anti-aliased.
Frequency	Entering a value in the Frequency text box specifies how often Photoshop places points on the path.
Edge Contrast	The percentage value in the Edge Contrast text box specifies how much contrast Photoshop must find to snap the path.

How to Select Image Areas with the Magnetic Lasso Tool

Procedure Reference: Select Image Areas using the Magnetic Lasso tool

To select image areas using the Magnetic Lasso tool:

1. Hold down the mouse button on the Polygonal Lasso tool or the Lasso tool, and from the flyout, select the Magnetic Lasso tool.
2. Click at the edge of the image to set the first fastening point. The fastening points anchor the selection around the edges of the object.
3. Move the mouse pointer along the edge of the image to create the selection. Fastening points are created along the edges of the image you move.
4. If required, click to add more fastening points.
5. If necessary, press Backspace or Delete to remove a point you just added.
6. If necessary, press Caps Lock to display the mouse pointer as a large circle with a cross hair at the center of the circle. Creating selection with this cursor ensures that the mouse pointer is close enough to the edge you want to select.
7. Click at the starting point where you began the selection to close the selection border.

ACTIVITY 3-7

Selecting Image Areas with the Magnetic Lasso Tool

Data Files:

- Dog.psd

Before You Begin

Open the dog.psd file from the C:\084563Data\Selecting Images\Activity 7\Starter folder.

Scenario:

You are creating an advertisement for This and That Collectibles and want to use the dog image in the dog.psd file. Therefore, you want to select the image to isolate it from the background. As the image consists of a wide range of shadows and highlights, some of which are similar to the shadows in the background, you feel it would not be appropriate to use the Magic Wand tool. You would like to use a Photoshop tool that would enable you to make an accurate selection around this object quickly.

What You Do	How You Do It
1. **Make a selection.**	a. From the Polygonal Lasso tool flyout, **select the Magnetic Lasso tool.** b. **Click on the left ear of the dog** to set the first fastening point. c. **Move the mouse pointer along the edge of the dog's left ear.**  d. **Press Backspace** to remove the point you just added. e. **Press Esc** to cancel the selection.

2. **Change the mouse pointer to a cross hair to make a precise selection of the image.**

   a. **Press Caps Lock** to display the mouse pointer as a large circle with a cross hair at the center of the circle.

   b. At the top of the dog's left ear, **position the mouse pointer so that the cross hair at the circle's center is at the tip of the dog's left ear.**

   c. **Click to add a point at the top of the dog's left ear.**

   d. **Move the mouse pointer along the edge of the dog's body.**

   e. **Click the top of the dog's left ear where you began** to complete the path again.

TOPIC F

Modify Selections

You have learnt to make accurate selections around multi-colored objects. You are making selections in an image using the selection tools. However, you cannot make multiple selections as Photoshop selects only one area at a time. In this topic, you will use Photoshop to add to your existing selection, and also delete from an existing selection.

There are times when the original selection is not sufficient. If an area is selected, using another selection tool will eliminate it, thereby creating a new selection elsewhere. You can use Photoshop to add to an existing selection. Similarly, you can eliminate part of a selection before editing the final selected area.

Selection Options

You can use any selection tool to add to or subtract from an existing selection. Four selection option buttons, appear on the Tool Options bar, whenever a selection tool is active.

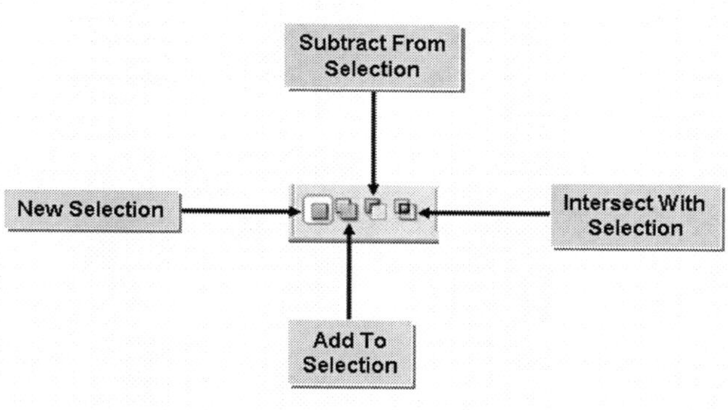

Option	Description
New Selection	When this button is active, you can select new areas within an image.
Add To Selection	When this button is active, you can select new areas within an image while keeping all existing selections.
Subtract From Selection	When this button is active, you can use the current selection tool to deselect part of an existing selection.

Option	Description
Intersect With Selection	When this button is active, you can create a selection that intersects existing selections. Here, the resulting selection is made up of areas where the selections intersect.

Keyboard Shortcuts to Access Selection Options

Each selection option button can be temporarily activated using a keyboard shortcut.

- Hold down Shift to temporarily access the Add To Selection button.
- Hold down Alt to temporarily access the Subtract From Selection button.
- Hold down Shift+Alt to temporarily access the Intersect With Selection button.

How to Modify Selections

Procedure Reference: Modify a Selection

To modify a selection:

1. Select a Lasso tool and make the selection.
2. On the Tool Options bar, select a selection option to modify the selection.
    - Select the New Selection button to select new areas.
    - Select the Add To Selection button to add new areas to an existing selection.
    - Select the Subtract From Selection button to deselect part of an existing selection.
    - Select the Intersect With Selection button to create a selection that intersects the existing selection.
3. Click and drag the mouse pointer over the existing selection to modify the selection.
4. If necessary, save the selection.

ACTIVITY 3-8

Modifying Selections

Data Files:

- Dog.psd
- Flasks.psd

Before You Begin

- The dog.psd file with the selection needs to be kept open.
- If you have closed the file and the selection is lost, you need to create the selection of the dog again by following the steps given in the Activity 3–7—Selecting Image Areas with the Magnetic Lasso Tool.

Scenario:

In the selection you made around the dog image, the Magnetic Lasso tool probably missed part of the dog's front paws, because the dark bottom edge does not contrast much with the shadow beneath it. You would like to add to the existing area of selection instead of selecting it again. Also, you want to eliminate a part of a selection that you have created in the Flasks.psd file before editing it.

What You Do	How You Do It
1. **Add to the selection made around the dog image.**	a. **Select the Zoom tool.**
	b. **Click and drag the Zoom tool cursor over the front right paw** to magnify it.
	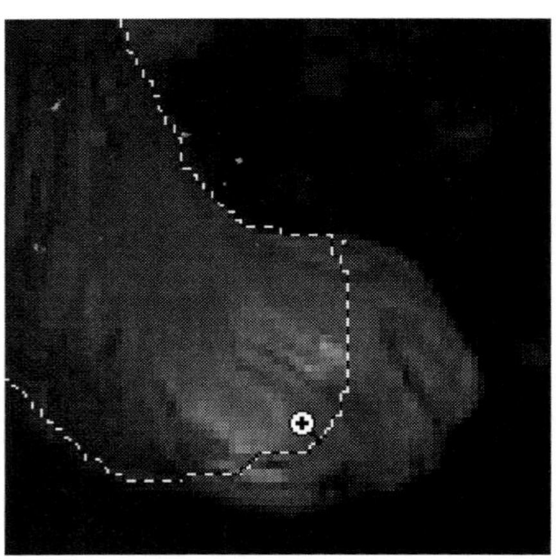
	c. **Hold down the mouse button on the Magnetic Lasso tool and** from the Magnetic Lasso tool flyout, **select the Lasso tool.**
	d. **Press Caps Lock** to switch to the standard Lasso tool cursor.
	e. On the Tool Options bar, **click the Add To Selection button.**
	f. **Position the Lasso tool cursor inside the existing selection near the dog's front right paw, and click and drag around an area of the paw that is currently not included in the selection** to enclose it.
	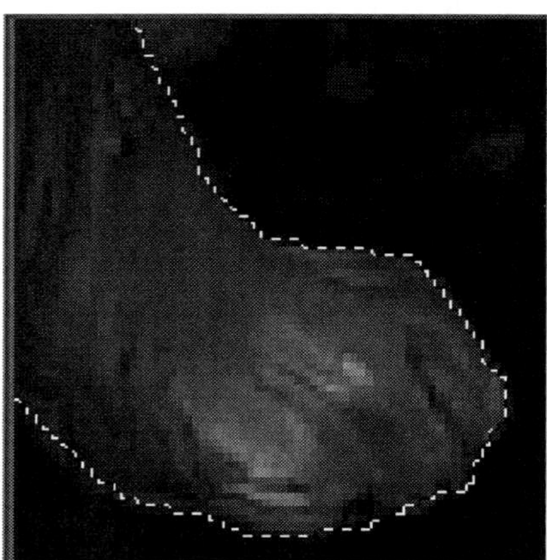

2. **Save the selection.**	a. **Choose Select→Save Selection.**
	b. In the Save Selection dialog box, in the Name text box, **type *Dog* and click OK.**
	c. **Save the file as** *My_Dog*.
	d. **Close the file.**

3. **Select the green flask in the Flasks.psd file.**

a. **Choose File→Open.**

b. From the C:\084563Data\Selecting Images\Activity 8\Starter folder, **open the Flasks.psd file.**

c. On the Tool Options bar, **click the New Selection button.**

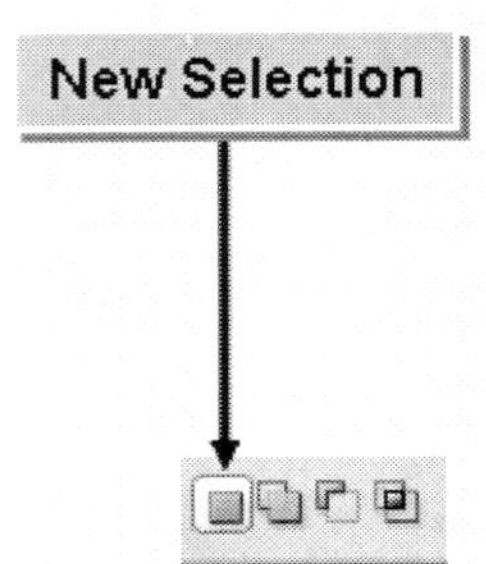

d. **Drag a loose selection around the green flask so that a large part of the white background is included within the selection.**

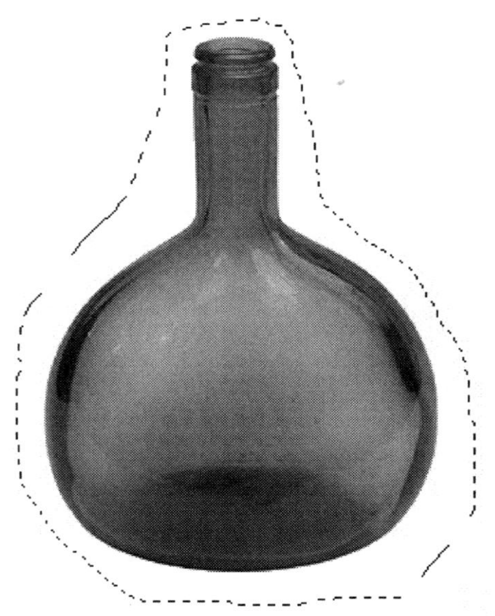

e. **Select the Magic Wand tool.**

f. On the Tool Options bar, **click the Subtract From Selection button.**

g. **Notice that the Magic Wand mouse**

pointer appears with a minus symbol, indicating that clicking will remove pixels from the selection.

h. On the Tool Options bar, in the Tolerance text box, **double-click and type *32*** to deselect only the white and very light pixels around the flask.

i. **Position the mouse pointer over the white area within the selection and click** to exclude the white area and select only the flask.

4. **Save the selection.**

a. On the Tool Options bar, **click the New Selection button.**

b. **Choose Select→Save Selection.**

c. In the Save Selection dialog box, in the Name text box, **type *Green Flask***

d. **Click OK.**

e. **Save the file as *Green Flask*.**

f. **Close the file.**

Lesson 3 Follow-up

In this lesson, you selected image areas using the Rectangular Marquee tool, Elliptical Marquee tool, Lasso tool, Polygonal Lasso tool, Magic Wand tool, and Magnetic Lasso tool. You also saved selections for future use, and added to and subtracted from selections.

1. **You are editing an image of a scene inside a busy office. You are required to change the color scheme of the decor. Which tools would you use to make your selection? Why?**

2. **You have made a selection to perform an edit in the object you have created. Now, you feel that you want to modify the selection to make the edit more accurate. Which tool in Photoshop would you use to modify the selection?**

LESSON 4

Creating Image Composites

Lesson Time
1 hour(s), 40 minutes

Lesson Objectives:

In this lesson, you will create image composites and use several techniques for creating and manipulating layers and use the techniques in Photoshop for undoing the previous steps.

You will:

- Make floating and fixed selection in images.
- Undo the previous steps to correct mistakes.
- Copy selections with the Move tool.
- Create layers.
- Create smart objects.
- Transform selections.
- Copy layers between images.
- Save the images in Photoshop formats.
- Change the stacking order of the layers.

Introduction

You have experimented with selecting images in Photoshop. To quicken the pace of your work, undo errors, and be more effective, you can work with layers. In this lesson, you will use layers to isolate specific parts of an image. You will also use several techniques for creating and manipulating layers, and undoing steps.

Photoshop offers a wide variety of tools and techniques that enable you to create composite images. Creation and manipulation of composite images are made easy by the usage of layers, where every element in an image can be positioned and edited in a separate layer. Layers provide an easy and efficient way of organizing and editing complex images.

TOPIC A

Make Floating Versus Fixed Selections

You know how to make selections in an image. However, while working on the image, you might want to move a selected portion to another area in the same image or in a different image. In this topic, you will identify floating and fixed selections.

When a selected region is moved, its initial position is replaced by the current Photoshop background color. This is usually an undesirable effect. For example, you are combining two photographs, by placing one image over a portion of the second image. If you want to move the image on top, the portion of the image below it, which was previously obscured, will be replaced by a solid area of the background color. Understanding the concepts of floating and fixed selections will help you avoid such problems.

Floating and Fixed Selections

A *floating selection* refers to a selected group of pixels that are moved from its original spot. It indicates that the selected pixels are floating above the background image. If you move the selection again to another spot, the background will remain as it was. However, if you deselect it, it will get fixed at its current position. This is a *fixed selection*, and as a result, the selected image area gets pasted over the old background. If you reselect it and attempt moving it again, its background will be filled with the background color, and not the image area that was previously below it.

Moving Image Areas

If the background layer is made up of a single layer of pixels, moving image areas or painting creates permanent changes that can be difficult to modify. Photoshop provides layers to alleviate these problems. You can put selections of pixels into layers and manipulate them without affecting the underlying pixels. The space surrounding the visible pixels in a layer is transparent space, allowing you to see the rest of the image behind the layer. This differs from an image with only the background layer of pixels, where there is no transparent space in the image.

How to Make Floating Versus Fixed Selections

Procedure Reference: Make Floating and Fixed Selections

To make floating and fixed selections:

1. Select a Lasso tool.
2. Click and drag the mouse pointer along the edges of the image to be selected.
3. Choose File→Save Selection.
4. In the Save Selection dialog box, in the Name text box, type a name.
5. Click OK.
6. Select the Move tool.
7. Click and drag the selected area to the desired target location. When the pixels you drag are cut from the current location, they become a floating selection.
8. Deselect the selected area, so that it becomes a fixed selection in the new location.

You can temporarily access the Zoom tool by holding down Ctrl+Spacebar.

ACTIVITY 4-1

Making Floating and Fixed Selections

Data Files:

- Kid Stuff.psd

Setup:

Open the Kid Stuff.psd file from the C:\084563Data\Image Composites\Activity 1\Starter folder.

Scenario:

You want to move the blocks in the Kid Stuff image to the empty slots to form the word "SPELL". To start with, you want to select and move the block with the letter E to an empty slot below it.

What You Do	How You Do It
1. Select the block E in the top row.	a. **Select the Zoom tool.**
	b. In the top row, **click and drag a zoom marquee around the block with the letter E and the empty slot below it.**
	c. From the Lasso tool flyout, **select the Polygonal Lasso tool.**
	d. At the bottom-left corner of the block with letter E, **click to begin the selection, move the Polygonal Lasso tool cursor up to the top-left corner, and click.**

	e. **Hold down Alt, drag the Lasso tool cursor along the top-left edge's rounded corner, and then release the Alt key.**
	f. **Move the Polygonal Lasso tool cursor along the top-right edge and then click.**
	g. **Continue selecting the outline of the block, while holding Alt for any curved corners.**

	h. **Choose Select→Save Selection.**

i. In the Save Selection dialog box, in the Name text box, **type *E Selection***

j. **Click OK.**

2. **Move the selected block to the empty slot below it.**

a. **Select the Move tool.**

b. **Notice that as you position the Move tool cursor on the selected block, a Scissors icon appears next to the mouse pointer.**

c. **Click and drag the selected block into the empty slot below it.**

d. **Deselect the image.**

e. **Save the file as *Kid Stuff_modified*** and close the file.

TOPIC B

Undo Previous Steps

You have begun working with images in Photoshop. But as you continue working, you might be faced with situations that require you to correct unforeseen errors. In this topic, you will correct errors in your file, by undoing or altering previously performed steps.

Photoshop recognizes only pixels, and not individual objects. Therefore, correcting errors in Photoshop can be more difficult than it is in drawing applications that treat entire shapes as objects. Fortunately, Photoshop offers several approaches to correct mistakes or undo previous steps.

Tools to Undo Previous Steps

Photoshop offers several approaches to correcting mistakes or undoing previous steps.

Tool	Description
Eraser tool	This tool is useful for erasing pixels in the active layer.
Undo command	This command will undo the most recent command or action.
History palette	This palette allows you to undo multiple steps, returning the image to an earlier state.
History Brush tool	This tool offers even more control over undoing steps, by allowing you to return specific areas within an image to a prior state, while the rest of the image remains unchanged.

The Eraser Tool

The *Eraser tool* is used to erase pixels in an image. When working in the default background layer, the Eraser tool doesn't erase pixels. Instead, it changes their color to the background color. However, when you use the Eraser tool in other layers, it replaces pixels with transparent space, thereby erasing them.

 The Eraser tool is mostly used to isolate part of an image on either a white or transparent background.

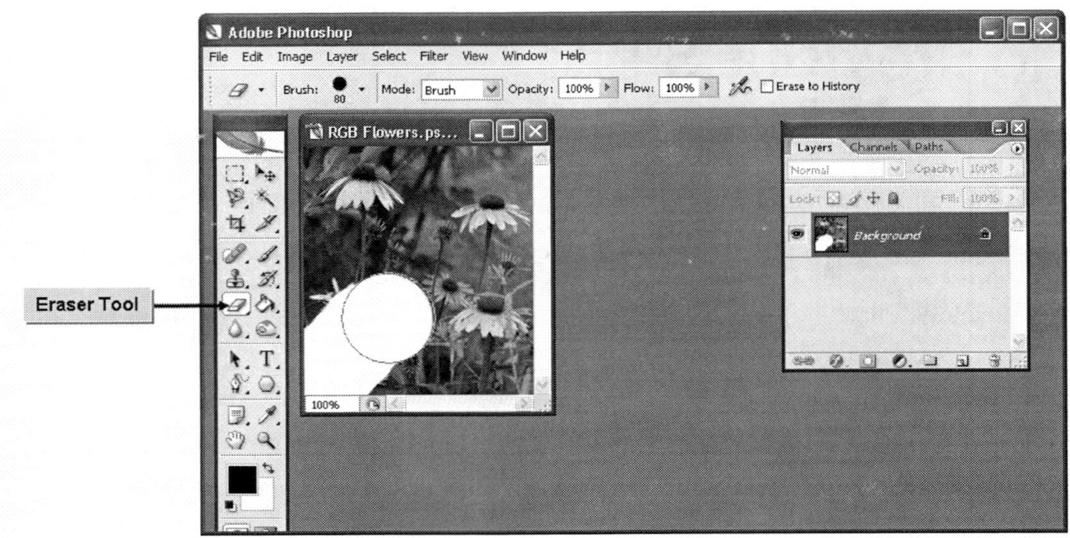

When part of an image is selected, the Eraser tool and the painting tools operate only in the selected area. However, if no areas are selected, the Eraser tool will then operate on any part of the active layer.

The Undo Command

The Undo command is another option used for fixing mistakes. You can use the *Undo command* to undo the most recent change that you have made. However, the limitation to the Undo command is that it only allows you to undo the last action performed. After undoing an action, you can click on the Edit menu, to redo the action that you have just undone, using the Redo command.

The History Palette

As you work, Photoshop keeps track of all the menu choices and mouse movements that affect the status of the image. These steps appear on the *History palette* and you can use it to return the image to an earlier stage during its development. The top state on the History palette is the file as it appeared the last time the image was saved. By default, Photoshop remembers the last twenty image states, in addition to the original image you opened.

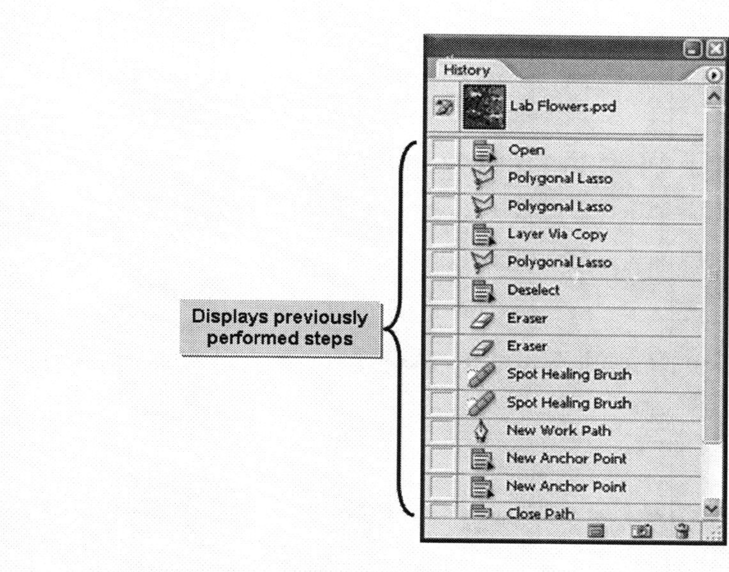

Number of Image States

To change the number of image states remembered by Photoshop's History palette, choose Edit→Preferences→General and enter a new value in the History States field. However, be aware that Photoshop needs memory to retain history states, so entering a large number could diminish performance. If you find performance unacceptable, you can choose Edit→Purge→Histories to clear the History states and free the memory required to retain them.

The History Brush Tool

You can use the *History Brush tool* to revert to part of an image if necessary. This is extremely useful if you want to correct a mistake you made several steps ago, without undoing all of the steps in between. You can erase image areas so that they appear as they did at any state on the History palette. This technique allows you to return specific areas of an image as they appeared at an earlier state, without affecting the rest of the image. You can click in the box to the left of any state on the History palette to designate that state as the source you wish to return to, when using the History Brush tool.

The Revert Command

You use the *Revert command*, if you want to return to the version of the image saved on your hard disk. After using the Revert command, the steps on the History palette remain, enabling you to return to a previous image state.

How to Undo Previous Steps

Procedure Reference: Erase Parts of an Image

To erase parts of an image:

1. Select the Eraser tool.

2. Drag the Eraser cursor over the portion of the image to erase the pixels as you drag.
3. If necessary, choose Edit→Undo Eraser to restore the erased area.
4. If necessary, choose Edit→Redo Eraser to display the erased stroke.

Procedure Reference: Undo Steps with the History Palette

To undo steps with the History palette:

1. If necessary, click the History palette tab to display it.
2. On the History palette, click the name of the state that needs to be reverted.
3. Drag the History state slider at the left of the state up to revert to the previous states.
4. If necessary, drag the History state slider down to redo the steps.

Procedure Reference: Revert to the Previous Image State with the History Brush Tool

To revert to the previous image state with the History Brush tool:

1. Select the History Brush tool.
2. On the Tool Options bar, click the Brush Preset Picker drop-down arrow.
3. From the list box, select a brush tip.
4. Click the Brush Preset Picker drop-down arrow again to collapse the list box.
5. Click and drag the History Brush tool cursor to erase some areas in the image and to return some others to their earlier state.
6. If necessary, choose File→Revert to return to the last saved version of the image.

ACTIVITY 4-2

Undoing Image Editing Tasks

Data Files:

- Kid Stuff.psd

Setup:

Open the Kid Stuff.psd file from the C:\084563Data\Image Composites\Activity 2\Starter folder.

Scenario:

You want to change a part of the Kid Stuff image to the background color. As there is a possibility of committing some mistakes while editing, you want to get familiarized with the Photoshop options that allow you to undo the mistakes.

What You Do	How You Do It
1. **Erase a few pixels above the block with the letter P.**	a. **Select the Rectangular Marquee tool and drag a selection around the slot containing the letter P.**
	b. **Select the Eraser tool.**
	c. At the top edge of the block with the letter E, **drag the mouse pointer from left to right.**
	d. **Notice that the block with the letter E is not erased, because it is not within the selected area.**
	e. In the slot containing the letter P, **drag the mouse pointer from left to right, above the block with the letter P** to erase a few pixels.
2. **Restore the erased area.**	a. **Choose Edit→Undo Eraser** to restore the erased area.
	b. In the slot containing the letter P, **drag the mouse pointer from left to right, above the block with the letter P.**
	c. **Drag the mouse pointer below the erased region from right to left** to erase some more pixels.
	d. **Choose Edit→Undo Eraser** to restore the erased area.
	e. **Notice that the Undo command restored only the last erased area.**
	f. **Choose Edit→Redo Eraser** to display both of the eraser strokes through the slot.

ACTIVITY 4-3

Undoing Steps

Data Files:

- Kid Stuff.psd

Setup:

- The Kid Stuff.psd file with the steps performed in the previous activity needs to be kept open.
- If you have closed the file the history states would be lost. Hence, you need to perform the steps in the Activity 4–3–Undoing Image Editing Tasks before continuing with the activity.

Scenario:

After performing a sequence of actions on the Kid Stuff image, you find that you need to revert the image to its original state.

What You Do	How You Do It
1. **Navigate through the History palette.**	a. If necessary, on the History palette, **scroll down to view the last steps listed.**
	b. On the History palette, **select the Rectangular Marquee state just above the Eraser states.**

	c. **Notice that the eraser strokes disappear from the image.**

2. **Restore the image.**

a. If necessary, **scroll up the History palette.**

b. **Select the Deselect state** to make the image and the selection return to the previous state.

c. **Drag the History state slider down to the bottom of the History palette.** The steps are performed as you drag past them.

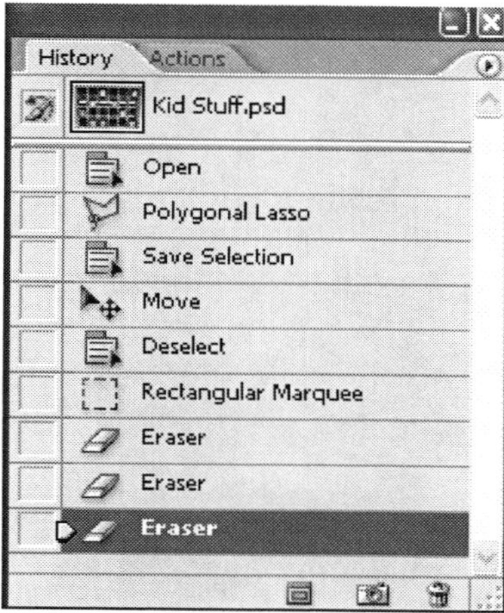

d. **Drag the slider until you reach the Rectangular Marquee step just above the Eraser steps at the bottom of the History palette.**

---

3. **Zoom out the image and select the block L using the Channels palette.**

a. **Deselect the image.**

b. **Double-click the Hand tool.**

c. If necessary, **select the Channels palette tab.**

d. On the Channels palette, **hold down Ctrl and select the L Selection channel.**

4. Move the block L to the empty slot below its current location.

   a. **Select the Move tool.**

   b. **Click and drag the block with the gray colored letter L to the empty slot below it.**

   c. **Deselect the image.**

5. **Restore the blocks to their original location.**

a. **Select the History Brush tool.**

b. **Scroll up the History palette.**

c. On the History palette, **verify that the History Brush icon appears in the square to the left of the Kid Stuff.psd.**

d. On the Tool Options bar, **click the Brush Preset Picker drop-down arrow.**

e. In the list box for selecting brush tips, **scroll down and select the Hard Round 19 Pixels brush tip.**

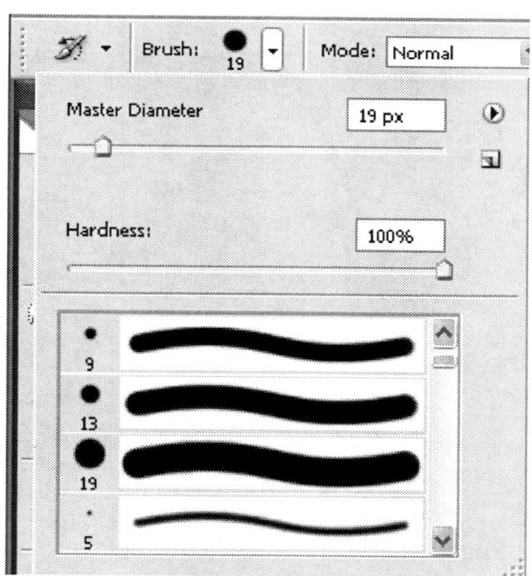

f. **Click the Brush Preset Picker drop-down arrow** to collapse the list box.

g. In the top row of the crate, **drag the History Brush cursor over the white space left by the block with the letter E** to restore the block with the letter E in its original location.

h. **Drag the History Brush cursor over the block with the letter E, which was moved to the second row** to replace the block with the original background.

i. **Drag the History Brush cursor over the white space left by the block with the letter L, which was moved.**

j. **Choose File→Revert** to return to the last saved version of the image.

k. **Close the file and click No when prompted to save.**

TOPIC C

Copy Selections

You can now move selected areas with an image. However, in certain situations you may have to move copies of a selection to other areas in the same image. In this topic, you will use the Move tool to copy as well as move selected image areas.

You are working on the image of a garden. But in the image, only one of the plants has flowers. To fill the others with the same flowers, you can use Photoshop to select and copy the flowers.

Copy a Selection

There may be times when you need to repeat certain areas of the image throughout a composite. You can then move a copy of a selected image area with the Move tool by holding down Alt as you drag. When you hold down Alt, a white arrow gets added to the Move tool cursor, indicating that you are making a copy by dragging the selection.

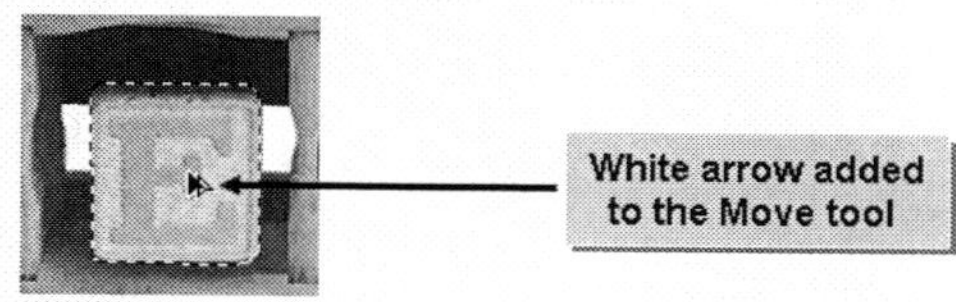

How to Copy Selections

Procedure Reference: Copy Selections

To copy selections:

1. Make a selection.
    - Create a new selection.
    - Or, load an existing selection.
2. Select the Move tool.

3. Hold down the Alt key, and click and drag the selection to move the copy of the selected area to the desired location.
4. If necessary, choose Edit→Undo Duplicate to remove the copy.
5. Deselect the image.

ACTIVITY 4-4

Copying Selections

Data Files:

- Kid Stuff.psd

Before You Begin

Open the Kid Stuff.psd file from the C:\084563Data\Image Composites\Activity 4\Starter folder.

Scenario:

You want to move certain blocks of the Kid Stuff image to the empty slots in the crate. Instead of moving the blocks from the original location, you feel it would be better if you could move a copy of the selected blocks.

What You Do	How You Do It
1. **Load the E Selection channel.**	a. On the Channels palette, **hold down Ctrl and select the E Selection channel.** b. **Notice that the block with the letter E is selected in the image.**

2. Move a copy of the block with the letter E to a new location.

a. Select the Move tool.

b. Hold down Alt, and click and drag the selected block to the empty slot below it.

c. Choose Edit→Undo Duplicate.

d. Deselect the image.

e. Close the file and click No when prompted to save.

TOPIC D

Create Layers

You have created and modified images in Photoshop. However, there are limitations to working with one layer of pixels. Changes or errors made in one layer could result in much rework. In this topic, you will create layers in addition to the background layer.

You are working on an image and you realize you want to make several inclusions in the image. After making them, you realize the inclusions were unnecessary. Photoshop lets you perform each of the steps resulting in these inclusions, in different layers. This renders the base layer unaffected.

Layers

In Photoshop, you are allowed to work on one piece of an image at a time through the use of layers. *Layers* are transparent pieces of an image, stacked on top of one another to create one image. Individual layers of an image can be edited, relocated, or deleted without affecting other layers. In essence, each image is comprised of several transparent layers, and putting them together allows you to see all parts of the image.

Need for Layers

There are certain limitations to working with one layer of pixels in Photoshop. For example, deselecting a floating selection eliminates the underlying pixels. Creating layers in addition to the default Background layer solves this problem. While the Background layer is filled with a single layer of pixels, additional layers you create can contain both pixels and empty areas. Placing only a specific part of an image in its own layer makes it much easier to work with that image area later. In addition, the part of the image you place in its own layer will not replace pixels on the Background layer when it overlaps those pixels. If you want to move the entire contents of the layer, you do not need to select the area first. When no areas are selected, dragging within a layer moves the entire layer.

Use of Layers in Creating Animations

You can create animations in Photoshop from the layers in the files. Animations are created using the Animation palette and the Layers palette options. The content of each layer becomes a frame on the Animation palette. The layers are arranged in a stacking order, with the bottom layer being the first frame. You can make changes to the frame using the Layers palette.

The Layers Palette

The *Layers palette*, is used to create and name layers, and to apply layer effects. When you create a new layer on the Layers palette, it is added above the currently selected layer. You can create a new, empty layer by clicking the New Layer button on the Layers palette, or by choosing the New Layer command in either the Layer menu or the Layers palette menu. The New Layer button creates a new untitled layer without displaying the New Layer dialog box. However, if you hold down Alt when you click the New Layer button, the New Layer dialog box will appear, and you can enter a name for the layer. To make a copy of a layer, you can drag the layer to the New Layer button on the Layers palette.

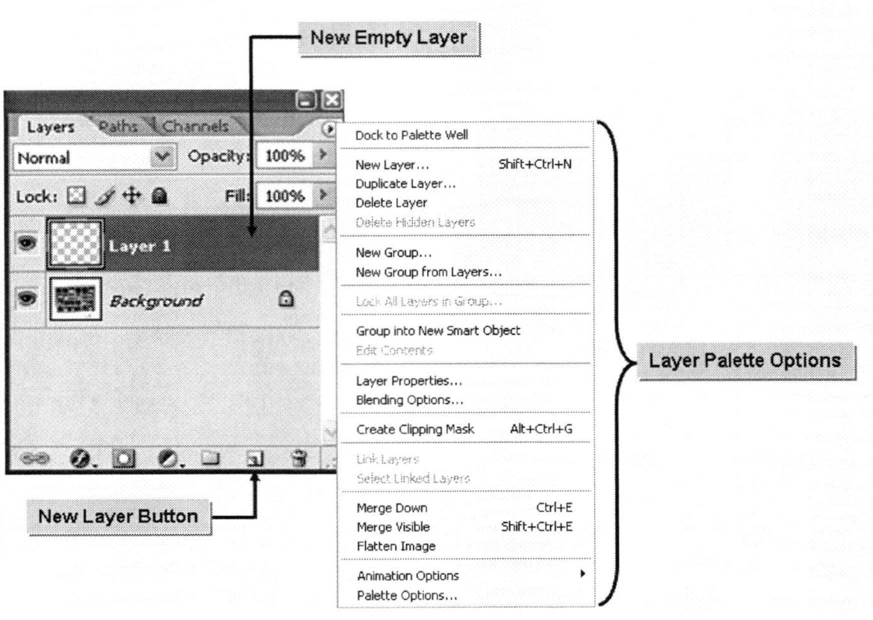

It is helpful to name all of the layers in your image, as it will help you quickly identify the layer you need to use. You can name a layer by selecting the Layer Properties command from the Layer menu, or by using the Layers palette shortcut menu. You can also double-click the layer name on the Layers palette to rename the layer.

The New Layer Via Cut Command

You can create additional layers by selecting an image area, and choosing the *New Layer Via Cut command.* This command removes the selected group of pixels from their original layer, and places them in a new layer. The position occupied by the selected pixels in the original layer will then be filled with pixels in the background color.

You can also use the New Layer Via Copy command to move a copy of the selected image area to a new layer, while leaving the selected pixels in their original location. Once a selected image area is moved to a new layer, you can easily manipulate the pixels in the new layer. You can use either cut or copy pixels in the active layer.

Layer Visibility

The content in a layer can be moved only if the layer is active. Otherwise, you will end up moving the contents of the current active layer instead. When working with several layers, it might be helpful to hide some layers, to focus on areas of the image. You can selectively show and hide the layers. Visible layers are indicated by the Eye icon to the left of each layer on the Layers palette.

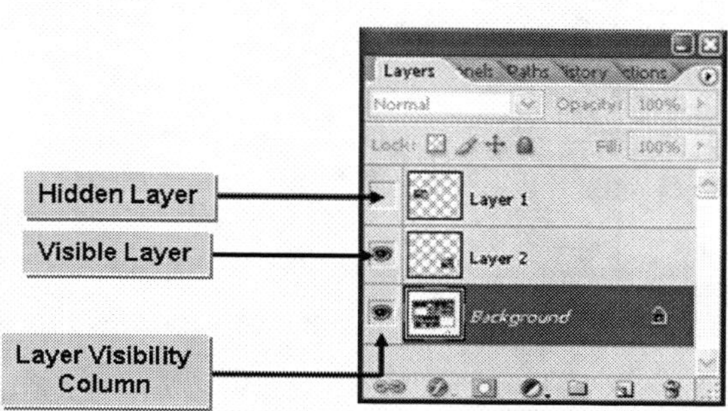

To hide a layer, click the Eye icon in the Layer Visibility column to the left of the layer. To reveal it, click again in the Layer Visibility column. To quickly hide all layers except one, hold down Alt and click the Eye icon in the Layer Visibility column to view only that layer. Hold down Alt and click the Eye icon again, and all layers appear.

How to Create Layers

Procedure Reference: Move Selections to a New Layer

To move selections to a new layer:

1. Make a selection.
   - Create a new selection.
   - Or, load an existing selection.
2. Move the selection to a new layer.
   - Choose Layer→New→Layer Via Cut to cut the selected area and paste it in a new layer. The new layer gets created above the background layer of the image.
   - Choose Layer→New→Layer Via Copy to copy the selected area and paste it in a new layer.

Procedure Reference: Rename a Layer

To rename a layer:

1. Open the Layers palette menu.
   - At the top-right corner of the Layers palette, click the triangle button.
   - Or, on the Layers palette, hold down Ctrl and right-click the layer.
2. From the Layers palette menu, choose Layers Properties.
3. In the Layer Properties dialog box, in the Name text box, type a name and click OK.

Procedure Reference: Move an Image in a Layer

To move a layer:

1. On the Layers palette, select the layer to be moved. The portion of the image added to that layer gets selected.
2. Select the Move tool.
3. Click and drag the selected portion of the image to the desired location.
4. If necessary, on the Layers palette, in the Layer Visibility column, click the Eye icon to the left of the layer to hide or reveal a layer.

ACTIVITY 4-5

Moving Selections to a New Layer

Data Files:

- Kid Stuff.psd

Before You Begin

Open the Kid Stuff.psd file from the C:\084563Data\Image Composites\Activity 5\Starter folder.

Scenario:

You are trying to form the word "SPELL" by moving the blocks in the crate to the empty slots. You feel that it would be better if you could create additional layers to contain the blocks that are moved to form this word.

What You Do	How You Do It
1. **Create a new layer to hold the block with the letter E.**	a. **Choose Select→Load Selection** to load the selection.
	b. In the Load Selection dialog box, from the Channel drop-down list, **select E Selection.**
	c. **Click OK** to display the selection for the block with the letter E.
	d. **Choose Layer→New→Layer Via Cut.**
	e. In the Channels palette group, **select the Layers palette tab.**
	f. **Notice that a new layer, Layer 1, which holds the block with the letter E, is displayed above the Background layer.**

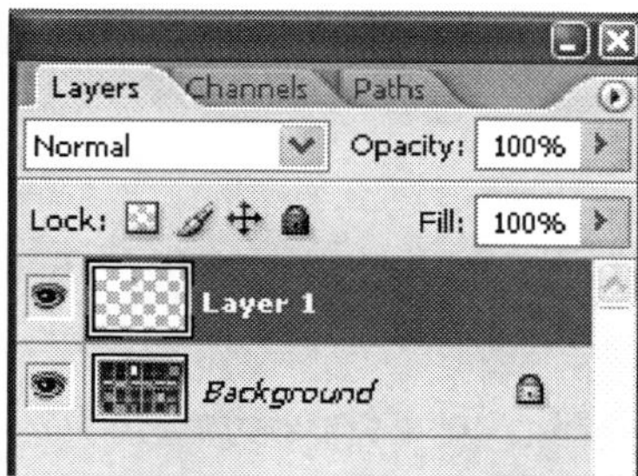

2. **Rename the newly created layer**

   a. At the top-right corner of the Layers palette, **click the triangle button.**

   b. From the Layers palette menu, **choose Layer Properties.**

   c. In the Layer Properties dialog box, in the Name text box, **type *E Block* and click OK.**

---

3. **Move the block with the letter E to the slot below its original location.**

   a. If necessary, **select the Move tool.**

   b. **Click and drag the block with the letter E to the empty slot below it.**

---

4. **Save the selection made over the block with the letter S.**

   a. **Select the Zoom tool.**

   b. **Click and drag the Zoom tool cursor over the block with the letter S.**

   c. On the Layers palette, **select the Background layer.**

   d. **Select the Polygonal Lasso tool.**

   e. **Select the straight edges of the block with the letter S using the Polygonal Lasso tool and hold Alt to temporarily switch to the Lasso tool** to select its rounded corners.

   f. **Choose Select→Save Selection.**

   g. In the Save Selection dialog box, in the Name text box, **type *S* and click OK.**

---

5. **Create a new layer to copy the image.**

   a. **Choose Layer→New→Layer Via Copy.**

b. **Notice that a copy of the block with the letter S is copied to the new layer.**

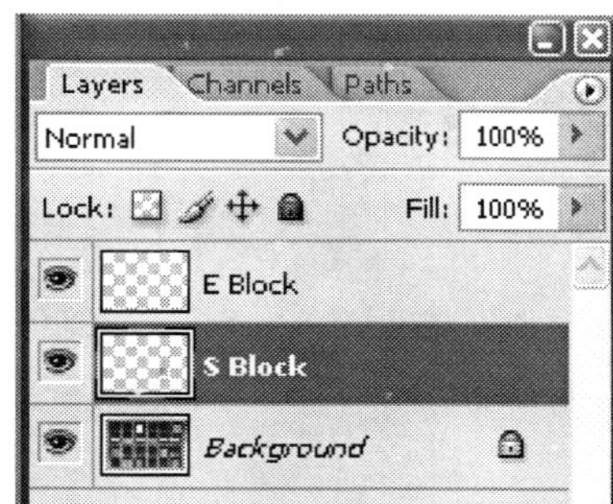

c. On the Layers palette, **double-click Layer 1.**

d. **Type *S Block* and press Enter** to rename the layer.

---

6. **Move the blocks to arrange the blocks to form the word SPELL.**

a. **Choose View→Fit On Screen.**

b. **Select the Move tool.**

c. **Click and drag the block with the letter S to the empty slot at the left of the block with the letter P.**

d. On the Layers palette, **select the Background layer.**

e. **Choose Select→Load Selection.**

f. In the Load Selection dialog box, **click OK.**

g. **Choose Layer→New→Layer Via Copy.**

h. On the Layers palette, **hold down Ctrl and right-click Layer 1.**

i. From the Layers palette menu, **choose Layer Properties.**

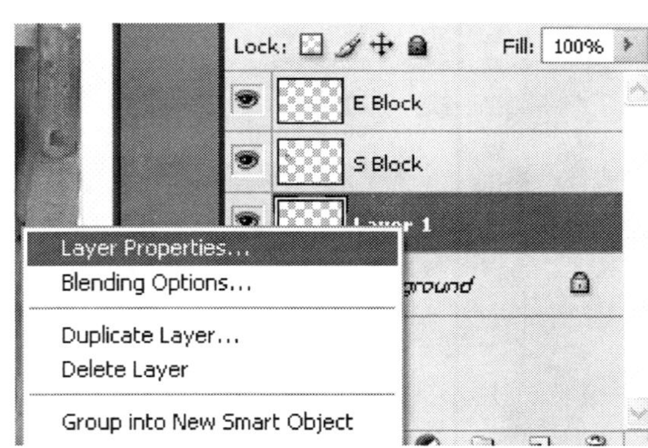

j. In Layer Properties dialog box, in the Name text box, **type *Gray L Block* and click OK.**

k. **Click and drag the block with the gray colored letter L to the empty slot next to the block with the red colored letter L** to form the word SPELL.

l. **Close the file and click No when prompted to save.**

ACTIVITY 4-6

Moving Layers

Data Files:

- Kid Stuff.psd

Before You Begin

Open the Kid Stuff.psd file from the C:\084563Data\Image Composites\Activity 6\Starter folder.

Scenario:

You have moved a few blocks in the crate to new layers and would like to explore the options to view, hide and move these layers on the Layers palette.

What You Do	How You Do It
1. **Move the block with the letter E to a new location.**	a. **Select the Move tool.**
	b. In the second row, **click and drag the block with the letter E to the slot below P.**
	c. **Notice that the block with the letter L is moved instead of the block with the letter E since the Gray L Block is the current layer.**
	d. **Choose Edit→Undo Move.**
	e. On the Layers palette, **select the E Block layer.**
	f. In the second row, **click and drag the block with the letter E to the slot below it.**
	g. **Notice that the block with the letter E in the currently selected layer is moved to the slot below it.**
	h. **Choose Edit→Undo Move** to restore the block to its original layer.

2. **Toggle the visibility of a layer using the Layers palette.**

   a. On the Layers palette, in the Layer Visibility column, **click the Eye icon to the left of the E Block layer** to hide the block.

   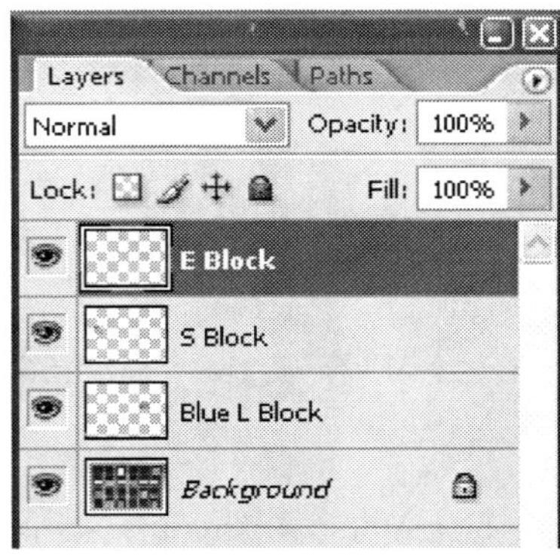

   b. On the Layers palette, in the Layer Visibility column, **click the Eye icon of the E Block layer** to view the block.

   c. **Save the file as *Kid Stuff_layers*** and close the file.

TOPIC E

Create Smart Objects

You've edited imported images in Photoshop. Using Smart Objects makes this task easier. In this topic, you will create a Smart Object in Photoshop.

Using an object created outside of Photoshop can be a real time saver, but editing the object can be difficult. Using Smart Objects, you can store a copy of an object's source data inside your Photoshop projects. This will allow you to work on a composite of the data in an image.

Smart Objects

A *Smart Object* is an object imported into or created within Photoshop, and it stores a copy of the object's source data within a Photoshop project. A Smart Object allows you to manipulate objects imported from other Adobe and third-party applications, and layers within Photoshop, without altering the original file.

For example, you might be working with an image in Adobe® Illustrator®, which you want to modify in Photoshop. When you place the object in Photoshop, it becomes a Smart Object. You can apply any number of edits to the image without altering the original Illustrator file.

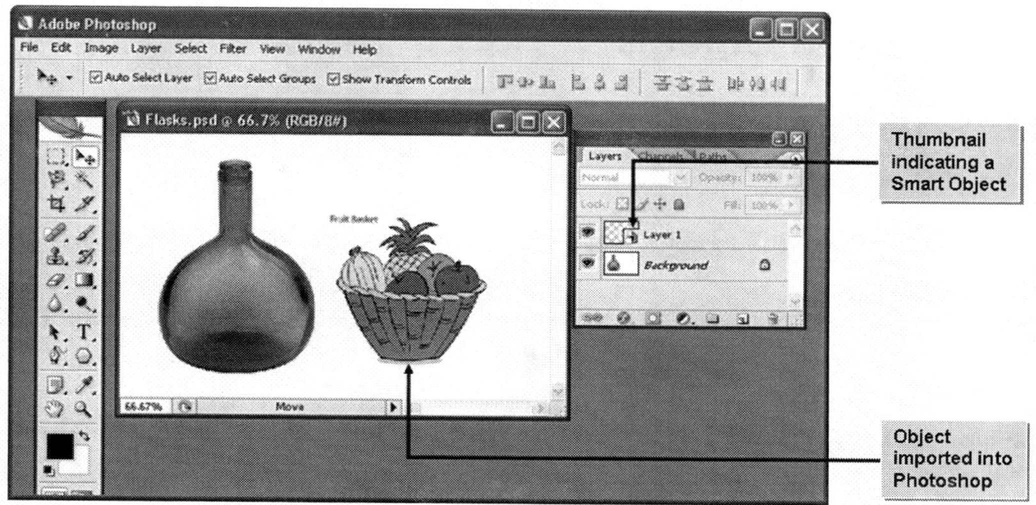

Benefits of Using Smart Objects

Smart Objects allow non-destructive scaling, rotation and warping of layers within Photoshop CS2. Rich vector data pasted or placed from Adobe Illustrator CS2 graphics remain live and scalable, and edits applied in Illustrator CS2 are automatically reflected in Photoshop CS2. Smart Objects can also work much like symbols in Illustrator CS2, as editing one linked copy will update all other linked copies automatically.

How to Create Smart Objects

Procedure Reference: Create Smart Objects

To create Smart Objects:

1. Open the desired image.
2. Place the desired object in Photoshop.
   - Choose File→Place, select your object file and click OK.
   - Copy from the source application and paste the object into Photoshop.
   - Or, open the file directly into Photoshop.
3. Double-click within the boundaries of the object's transform box to convert the object into a Smart Object.

ACTIVITY 4-7

Creating Smart Objects

Data Files:

- Nature.psd
- Travel_logo.ai

Before You Begin

Open the Nature.psd file from the C:\084563Data\Image Composites\Activity 7\Starter folder.

Scenario:

As a graphic designer, you are creating a poster for a travel agency. The client has provided you with the photograph to be used in the poster. You have already created a logo in Adobe Illustrator and would like to place it in your Photoshop document without altering the original object.

What You Do	How You Do It
1. **Create a Smart Object from an Adobe Illustrator file.**	a. **Choose File→Place.**
	b. From the C:\084563Data\Image Composites\Activity 6\Starter folder, **open the Travel_logo.ai.**
	c. In the Place PDF dialog box, **click OK.**

	d. **Double-click in the transform box of the logo** to place the logo.
2. **Transform the Smart Object.**	a. **Choose Edit→Free Transform.**

b. At the bottom-right corner of the transform box, **click and hold the transform handle, and drag the double-headed arrow down to the bottom-right corner of the image.**

c. **Double-click in the transform box of the logo.**

d. **Notice that the imported Adobe Illustrator object maintains its vector properties.**

e. **Drag the logo to the upper-right corner of the image.**

3. **Verify that the object is now a Smart Object.**

   a. On the Layers palette, in the Travel_logo layer, **verify that a thumbnail is visible on the layer icon.**

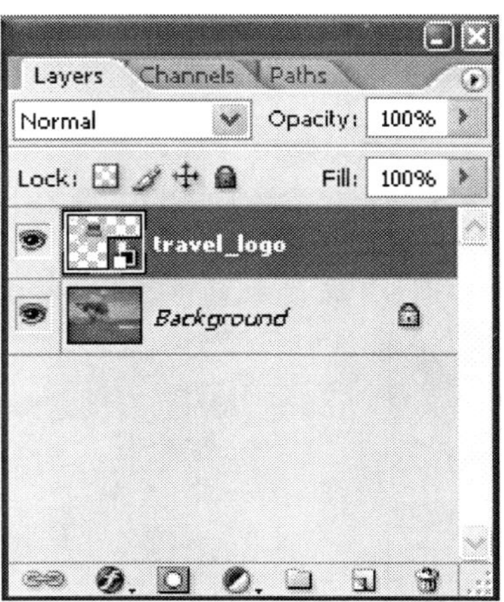

   b. **Right-click the travel_logo layer.**

   c. **Verify that the menu options for a Smart Object are available.**

   d. **Save the file as *Mynature.psd* and close the file.**

TOPIC F

Transform Layers

You have learned to work with layers. It is often useful to resize, rotate, or reshape layers or selected areas in order to straighten these areas, or when you are compositing images. In this topic, you will transform layers.

You have made a selection in the image that you are working on. Now using Photoshop, you can not only transform the selection, but also the pixels within the selection.

The Free Transform Command

A layer or selection can be transformed using the Free Transform command. This command transforms the actual image pixels within the selection marquee rather than the marquee itself. A bounding box is displayed around the selection when the Free Transform command is chosen. The transform handles in the middle of each side are used to drag and resize the image's height or width, or the transform handles at the corners are used to resize the image's height and width together.

Dragging a corner handle and holding Shift can maintain the image's aspect ratio. Dragging from outside the handles will rotate the selected image area. An image can be skewed or warped by holding down Ctrl and dragging a handle. To flip a selected image area horizontally, a transformation handle can be dragged horizontally to the other side. The transformation can be cancelled by pressing Esc, or accepted by pressing Enter. The Tool Options bar displays options for transforming an object numerically.

The Free Transform Tool Options Bar

After you choose the Free Transform command, you can also size, rotate, or skew the selected area using the Tool Options bar. The transformations are based on the selected reference point. By default Photoshop transforms areas based on the center point of the selected area.

The Free Transform Tool Options Bar Options

The elements of the Free Transform Tool Options bar are given in the following figure.

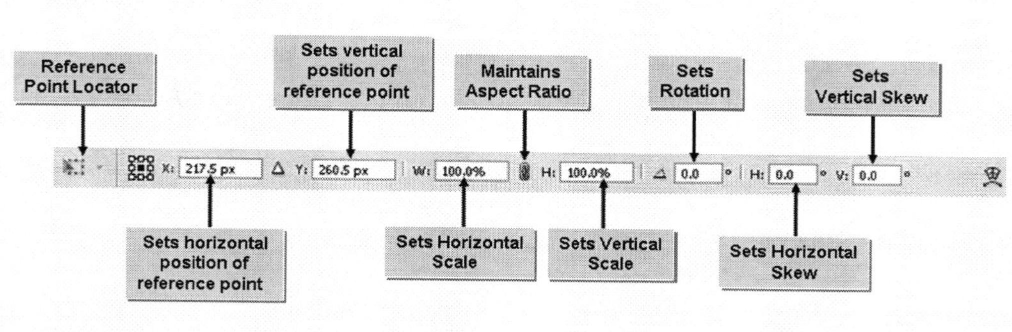

How to Transform Selection

Procedure Reference: Transform a Selection

To transform a selection:

1. Select the desired layer.
2. Make a selection in the selected layer.
   - Create a new selection.
   - Or, load an existing selection.
3. Choose Edit→Free Transform. The transform handles appear around the selection.
4. Transform the selection.
   - Click and drag the transform handle to scale the selection.

Press Shift as you drag the transform handle of the selection to scale proportionately.

- Position the mouse pointer outside the transform handles, and click and drag the double-headed arrow to rotate the selection.
- Hold down Ctrl, and click and drag the corner handles diagonally up or down to warp the selection.
- Hold down Ctrl, and click and drag the top-middle or bottom-middle transform handles to shear the selection.
- Click and drag the transform handle to the opposite side of the bounding box to flip the image.

ACTIVITY 4-8

Transforming Selections

Data Files:

- Kid Stuff.psd

Before You Begin

Open the Kid Stuff.psd file from the C:\084563Data\Image Composites\Activity 8\Starter folder.

Scenario:

You would like to explore the various transform options to resize, rotate and reshape the selected areas of the block.

What You Do	How You Do It
1. **Resize the top of the block with the gray colored letter L.**	a. On the Layers palette, **select the Gray L Block layer.**
	b. **Select the Zoom tool.**
	c. **Click and drag the Zoom tool cursor over the block with the gray colored letter L, at the end of the word SPELL.**
	d. **Select the Polygonal Lasso tool.**

e. **Create a new selection around the top of the block with the gray colored letter L.**

f. **Choose Edit→Free Transform.**

g. **Notice that the transform handles appear around the selection.**

h. **Click and drag the top-center transform handle down by approximately half an inch to decrease the selection's height.**

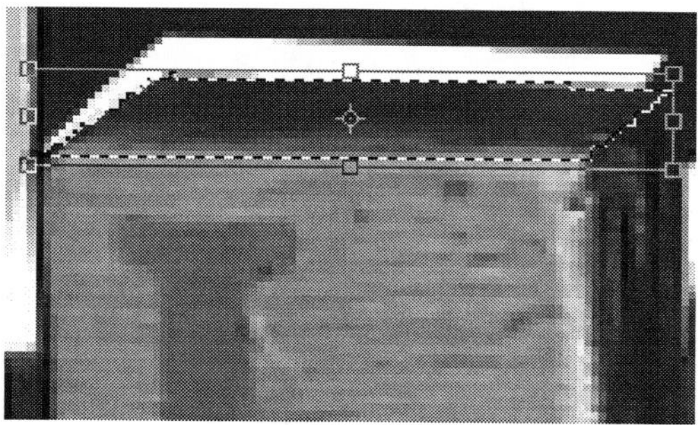

i. **Choose Edit→Undo.**

---

2. **Rotate the selected area.**

a. If necessary, **click the Info palette tab** to display it.

b. **Position the mouse pointer just above the top-left corner handle, and click and drag the curved double-headed arrow until the angle is displayed as -7° on the Info palette.**

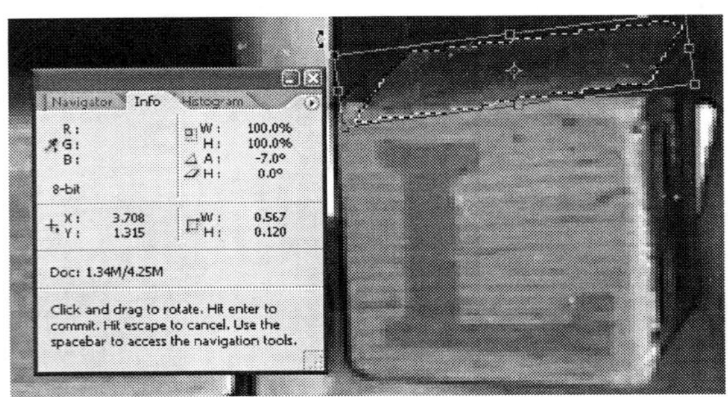

c. **Choose Edit→Undo Free Transform.**

---

3. **Warp the selected area.**

a. **Choose Edit→Free Transform.**

b. **Hold down Ctrl, and click and drag the top-right corner handle diagonally down** to warp the selected area of the image

c. **Choose Edit→Undo.**

---

4. **Shear the selected area.**

a. **Hold down Ctrl and drag the top-middle handle down and then to the left by a few pixels** to shear the selection.

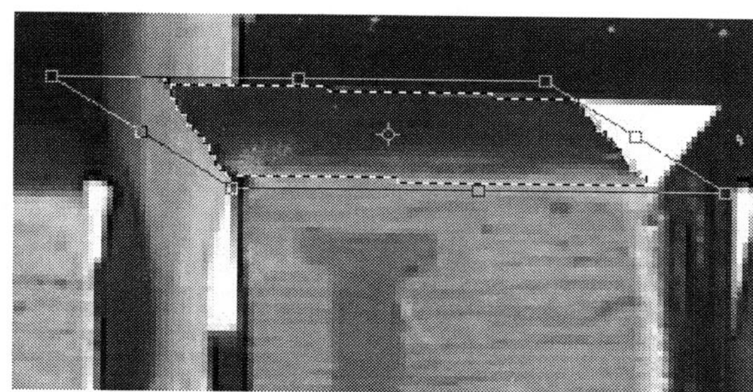

b. **Press Enter** to complete the transformation.

c. **Deselect the selection.**

---

5. **Flip the right side of the gray colored L block horizontally.**

a. If necessary, **select the Polygonal Lasso tool.**

b. **Create a selection around the right side of the block.**

c. **Choose Edit→Free Transform.**

d. **Click the right-middle transform handle and drag the double-headed arrow to the left past the left-middle handle** to flip the selection.

e. **Click inside the selected image area and drag it to the left of the block's front face.**

f. **Hold down Ctrl and drag the top-left and top-right corner handle so that the block's side corners line up to the block more accurately.**

g. **Press Enter** to complete the transformation.

h. **Deselect the selection.**

6. **Reposition the block.**

a. **Select the Move tool.**

b. **Click and drag the block with gray colored letter L diagonally up, approximately by half an inch** to reposition the block with the gray colored letter L within its slot.

c. **Close the file and click No when prompted to save.**

TOPIC G

Copy Layers Between Images

You are now working on images, and editing them using layers. However, while creating images you must be aware that the color mode and resolution can affect its final output. In this topic, you will copy layers between images having the same resolution.

As images created in Photoshop can be used in print or on the web, you need to set up new files so they use the color mode and resolution appropriate to their output. Understanding how to make these choices will ensure you set up a new document appropriately based on its intended use.

The New Dialog Box

Photoshop comes with many presets to automatically set the width, height, and resolution for an image. In addition, you can also set the background color. The New dialog box also features video-sized preset files, with optional settings available for control of non-square pixel document creation. You can set the pixel aspect ratio for video sized files in the Advanced section of the New dialog box.

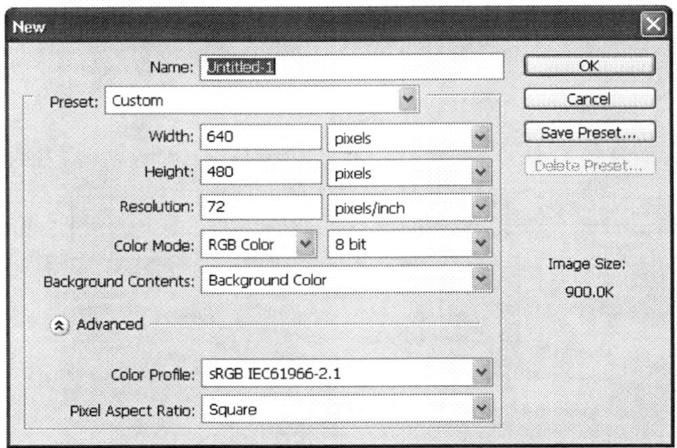

The New Dialog Box

Copy Layers Between Images

You can create layers using the New Layer Via Cut and New Layer Via Copy commands. Another way to create a layer is to drag a selection from one window to another. When you drag a selection into another Photoshop window, the selection is placed as a new, untitled layer. You can also drag an entire layer into a new window, and the correct layer name will appear on the new image's Layers palette. To drag an entire layer between windows, you can either use the Move tool to drag from one window to the other, or you can drag the layer name itself from the first image's Layers palette to the second window. You can hold down Shift as you drag the layer to a new window to center the pixels in the new window.

Image Composite and Resolution

When you create an image composite, it is helpful to make sure that the images use the same resolution. If you drag an image with a lower resolution into the composite, the resolution of the image will change to match that of the composite. Photoshop does not resample the image, so the size of the image changes. You can resize the image once it is part of the composite.

How to Copy Layers Between Images

Procedure Reference: Create a Document

To create a document:

1. Choose File→New.
2. In the New dialog box, specify the desired settings.
   - In the Name text box, specify the desired name.
   - In the Width text box, specify the desired width.
   - In the Height text box, specify the desired height.
   - In the Resolution text box, specify the desired resolution.
   - From the Color Mode drop-down list, select the desired color mode.
   - From the Background Contents drop-down list, select the desired background.

   In Adobe Photoshop, RGB is the default color mode. It is the universally accepted color mode.

3. In the New dialog box, click OK to create a document.

Procedure Reference: Create a New Layer by Dragging Selections Between Windows

To create a new layer by dragging selections between windows:

1. Open the required Photoshop file.
2. Open another document or Photoshop file whose image is to be moved.
3. Select the image area to be moved.
   - Choose Select→All to select the entire image.
   - Or, select a specific portion of the image area using the Marquee or Lasso tools.
4. In the toolbox, select the Move tool.
5. Hold down Shift and drag the selection to the desired window.
6. Position the image in the desired location.
7. On the Layers palette, rename the layer.
   - Double-click the layer name and then type the desired name.
   - Hold down Alt, double-click the layer to be renamed, and then type the desired name.
   - From the Layers palette menu, select Layer Properties and in the Layer Properties dialog box, in the name text box, specify the desired name.

- Or, choose Layer→Layer Properties and in the Layer Properties dialog box, in the name text box, specify the desired name.

Procedure Reference: Create New Layers by Dragging Layer Between Windows.

To create new layers by dragging layers between windows:

1. Open the required Photoshop file.
2. Open another Photoshop file whose layer is to be moved.
3. In the toolbox, select the Move tool.
4. Hold down Shift and drag the layer to the desired Document Window.
5. In the Document Window, position the layer in the desired location.

Procedure Reference: Transform an Image

To transform an image:

1. Open the desired Photoshop file.
2. On the Layers palette, select the desired layer.
3. Choose Edit→Transform.
4. Transform the image using the transform options.

Transform Options

The following table lists the options available for transforming an image.

Option	Description
Scale	Scales the image.
Rotate	Rotates the image.
Skew	Skews the image vertically or horizontally.
Distort	Distorts the image.
Perspective	Changes the angle of the image.
Warp	Distorts text in the type layer.
Rotate 180°	Rotates the image by 180 degree.
Rotate 90° CW	Rotates the image clockwise by 90 degrees.
Rotate 90° CCW	Rotates the image counter-clockwise by 90 degrees.
Flip Horizontal	Flips the image horizontally.
Flip Vertical	Flips the image vertically.

Procedure Reference: Resize the Image

To resize an image:

1. Open the desired Photoshop file.
2. On the Layers palette, select the desired layer.
3. Choose Edit→Free Transform.

4. Resize the image.
   - Resize the image using the mouse pointer.
     a. Position the mouse pointer on the upper-right transform handle hold down Shift and drag down to the left.
     b. Release the mouse button when the Info palette's W and H text boxes indicate the desired size.
   - Resize the image using the Tool Options bar.
     a. On the Tool options bar, click the Maintain Aspect Ratio button.
     b. Specify the desired resize value.
        - Double-click the W text box and type the desired value.
        - Or, double-click the H text box and type the desired value.

ACTIVITY 4-9

Creating a New Document

Data Files:

- backdrop.jpg

Scenario:

You want to create a composite image "This and That collectibles." You intend to use the backdrop.jpg file as the background for the new composite. As the first step, you want to create a new document that is a bit bigger than the backdrop.jpg file.

What You Do	How You Do It
1. **View the file information of backdrop.jpg file.**	a. **Choose File→Open.**
	b. **Navigate to the C:\084563Data\Image Composites\Activity 9\Starter folder.**
	c. In the Open dialog box, **Select Backdrop and click Open.**
	d. In the third section, at the bottom border of the Backdrop.jpg window, **hold down Alt and press the mouse button.**

e. **Notice that a pop-up box containing the file information is displayed.**

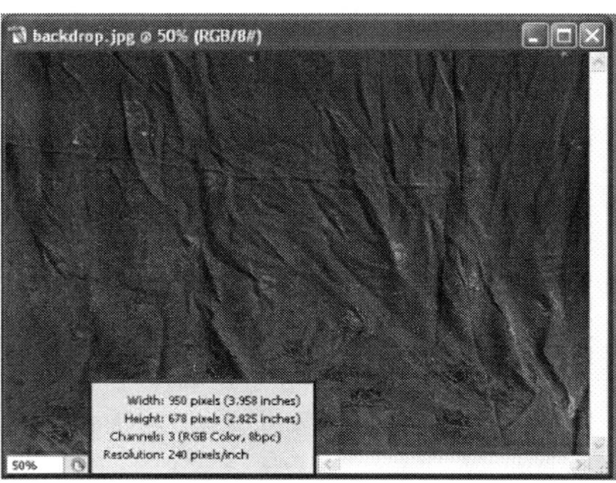

2. **Create a new file.**

a. **Choose File→New.**

b. In the New dialog box, in the Name text box, **type *this and that collectibles***

c. In the Width text box, **double-click and type *4***

d. In the Height text box, **double-click and type *3***

e. In the Resolution text box, **double-click and type *250***

f. **Notice that the color mode is set to RGB Color.**

g. In the New dialog box, from the Background Contents drop-down list, **select Transparent** to make the background transparent.

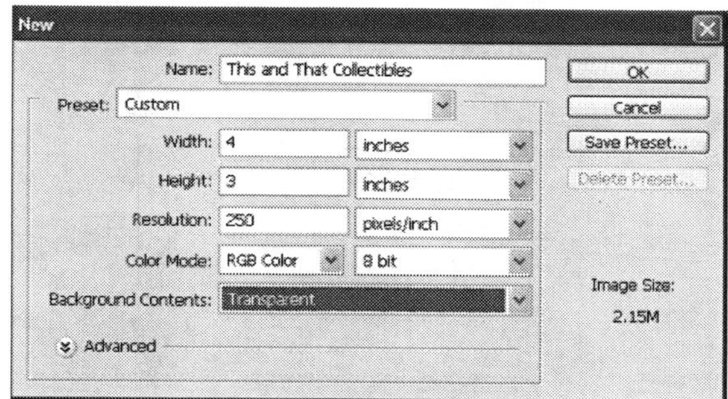

h. In the New dialog box, **click OK** to create a new document.

ACTIVITY 4-10

Copying Layers Between Images

Data Files:

- backdrop.jpg
- this and that collectibles.psd
- dog.psd
- globe.psd
- hand.psd

Before You Begin

1. Open the backdrop.jpg and this and that collectibles.psd files from the C:\084563Data\Image Composites\Activity 10\Starter folder.

Scenario:

You've got a new document ready in Photoshop. You want to proceed with the creation of the composite image by dragging selections and layers from other images.

What You Do	How You Do It

1. **Move the backdrop image into the This And That Collectibles document.**

   a. If necessary, **choose Window→Backdrop.jpg** to make the Background.jpg document active.

   b. **Choose Select→All** to select the entire image.

   c. **Select the Move tool.**

   d. **Hold down Shift and drag the selection to the This And That Collectibles.psd window.**

   e. On the Layers palette, **double click Layer 1 and type *Backdrop***

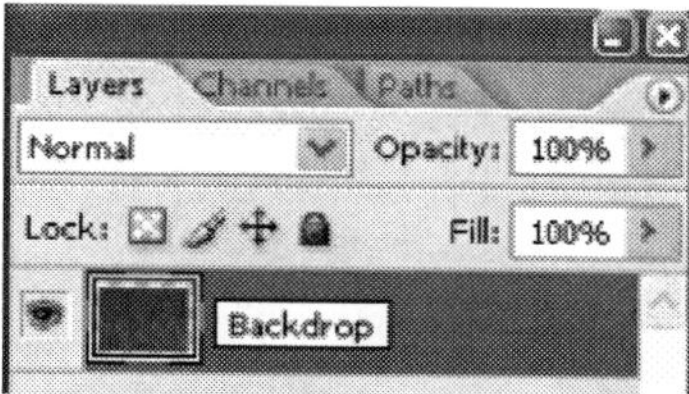

   f. **Choose Window→Backdrop.jpg.**

   g. **Close Backdrop.jpg file.**

If you double-click a layer, but not directly on the layer name, the Layer Styles dialog box will appear. You'll use the Layer Styles dialog box later. If you accidentally double-clicked the layer, click Cancel to close the Layer styles dialog box. Then double-click the layer name to rename the layer.

2. **Move the image of the dog into the This And That Collectibles document.**

a. **Choose File→Open.**

b. **Navigate to the Folder C:\084563Data\Image Composites\Activity 11\Starter.**

c. In the Open dialog box, **select Dog.psd and click Open.**

d. **Choose Select→Load Selection and click OK.**

e. **Hold down Shift and drag the selection to the This And That Collectibles.psd window.**

f. In the This And That Collectibles.psd window, **position the dog image at the bottom-left corner of the Backdrop image.**

g. On the Layers palette, **double click Layer 1 and type *Dog***

---

3. **Reposition the image of the dog.**

a. **Notice that the highlights on the dog's left side indicate that a light source exists to its left. However, the light source in the Backdrop image is from the right.**

b. **Choose Edit→Transform→Flip Horizontal** to flip the image of dog horizontally so that the highlights appear correctly.

4. **Resize the image of the dog.**

a. In the Navigator palette group, **select the Info palette.**

b. **Notice that the Info palette displays the scale percentage of the dog.**

c. **Choose Edit→Free Transform.**

d. **Position the mouse pointer on the upper-right transform handle, hold down Shift, and drag down to the left.**

e. Release the mouse button when the Info palette's W and H fields indicate that the dog is now 60 percent of its original size.

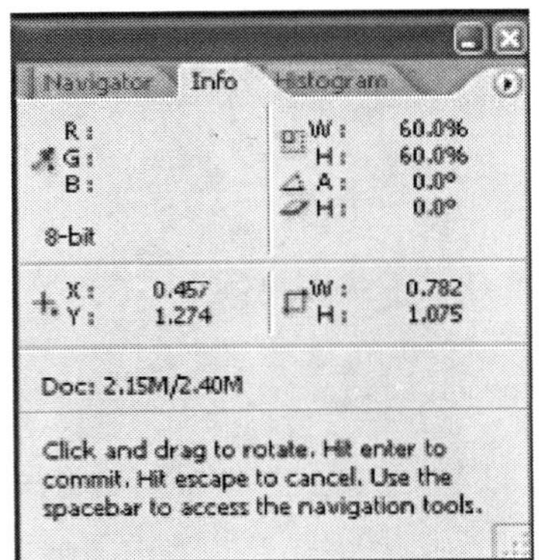

f. Close Dog.psd file.

5. **Move a layer into the This and That Collectibles document.**

a. **Choose File→Open.**

b. **Navigate to the Folder C:\084563Data\Image Composites\Activity 11\Starter.**

c. In the Open dialog box, **select Hand.psd and click Open.**

d. **Notice that the hand image is in a layer named Hand.**

e. **Hold down Shift and drag the hand image to the This And That Collectibles.psd window.**

f. In the This And That Collectibles.psd window, **position the hand image at the bottom-right corner of the Backdrop image.**

g. **Close Hand.psd file.**

h. Similarly, you need open the globe.psd file in the C:\084563Data\Image Composites\Activity 11\Starter, move the Globe layer from the Globe.psd window into the This And That Collectibles window and then position the globe image next to the hand image.

i. Close Globe.psd file.

TOPIC H

Save Images in Photoshop Format

You have created an image using Photoshop. However, you are now required to save the image in its best quality. In this topic, you will save images in the Photoshop format.

You have created the image for a flyer in Photoshop. But to get the right output for web or for print, you have to first save the file in its right format. The format in which the file is saved, reflects the quality of the final product.

Photoshop File Formats

Photoshop can save images in several file formats. Some file formats, such as TIFF and EPS, are most appropriate for printing and for exporting to page layout applications; and others, such as GIF and JPEG, are typically used for putting images on web pages for the Internet. However, when working within Photoshop, you should generally save files in Photoshop's native format, which retains all the original information about the file with the highest quality.

How to Save Images in Photoshop Format

Procedure Reference: Save Images in Photoshop Format

To save images in Photoshop format:

1. Open the required Photoshop file.
2. Choose File→Save As.
3. In the Save As dialog box, in the File Name text box, type the desired name.
4. From the Format drop-down list, select Photoshop (*.PSD;*.PDD).
5. Click Save.

ACTIVITY 4-11

Saving Images in Photoshop Format

Data Files:

- ball.jpg

Before You Begin

1. Open the ball.jpg file from the C:\084563Data\Image Composites\Activity 11\Starter folder.

Scenario:

You have an image in a JPEG format. You now want to save it in a format that allows it to open faster, retain image quality, and contain layers.

What You Do	How You Do It
1. **Save the image.**	a. **Choose File→Save As.**
	b. In the Save As dialog box, in the File Name text box, **type *this and that***
	c. In the Save As dialog box, from the Format drop-down list, **select Photoshop (*.PSD;*.PDD)**
	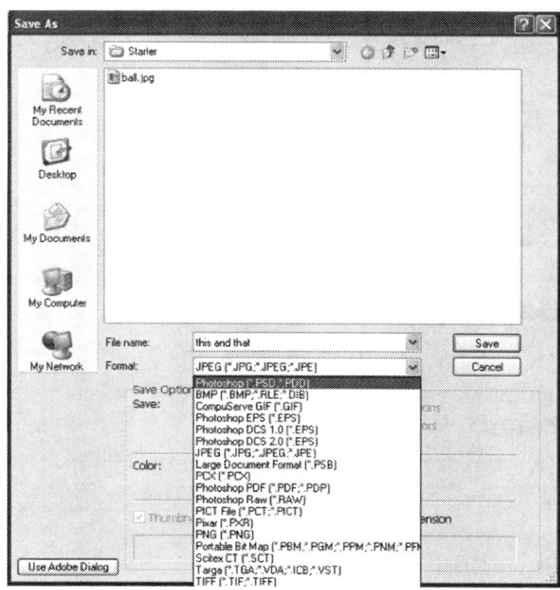
	d. **If necessary, navigate to the C:\084563Data\Image Composites\Activity 11\Starter folder.**
	e. In the Save As dialog box, **Click Save.**

2. **Which is not a valid Photoshop file format?**

   a) .EPS

   b) .PDD

   c) .HTM

   d) .PSD

TOPIC I

Arrange Layers

You have learned to work with layers. This process can however be made easier if these layers are properly organized. In this topic, you will stack layers, link them to each other, and control multiple layers using smart guides.

You want to reposition multiple images within an image. You don't have to spend time trying to align the images individually, as each of them exists on a separate layer. Photoshop enables you to perform the task of controlling multiple layers using layer links and smart guides.

Stacking Order of Layers

When working with multiple layers, you might have parts of an image overlapping with each other. You can change the stacking order of layers, which determines the layers that appear to overlap others. Layers that appear higher on the Layers palette are higher in the stacking order. The pixels in layers that are higher in the stacking order will appear in front of the pixels in layers that are lower in the stacking order. You can change the stacking order by dragging the layer names on the Layers palette.

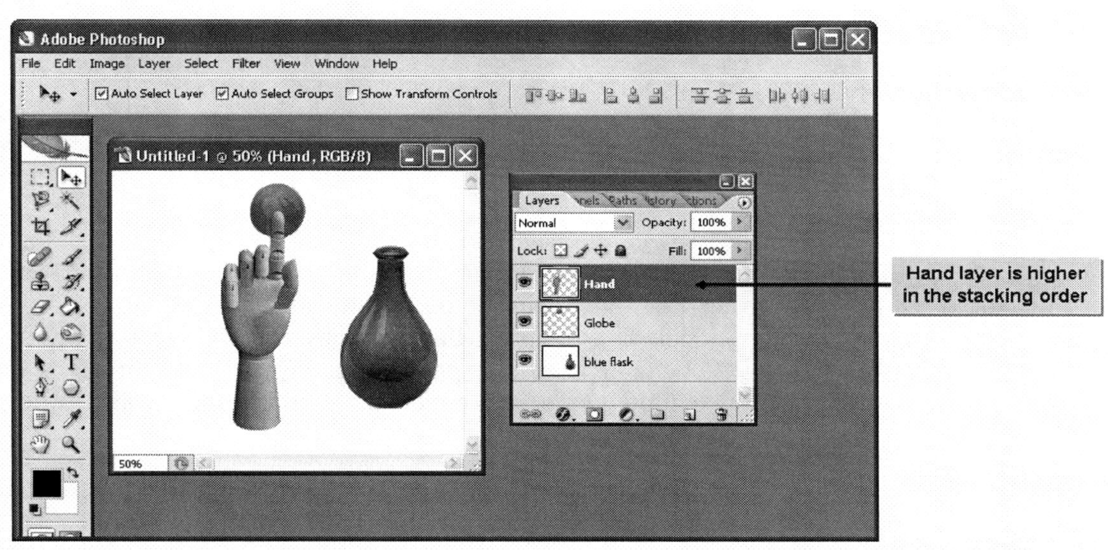

 The Auto Select Layer can be used to move the elements in different layers, without manually clicking on each layer on the Layer palette.

Link Layers

You can link multiple layers to each other. The pixels of the linked layers can be manipulated together, as if they are all on the same layer. The contents of layers that are linked can be moved or transformed together, and be aligned to one another. You can further control and organize layers by making a group that includes multiple layers.

To link layers, you can either click the Link Layers button at the bottom of the Layers palette, or choose Link Layers from the Layer menu.

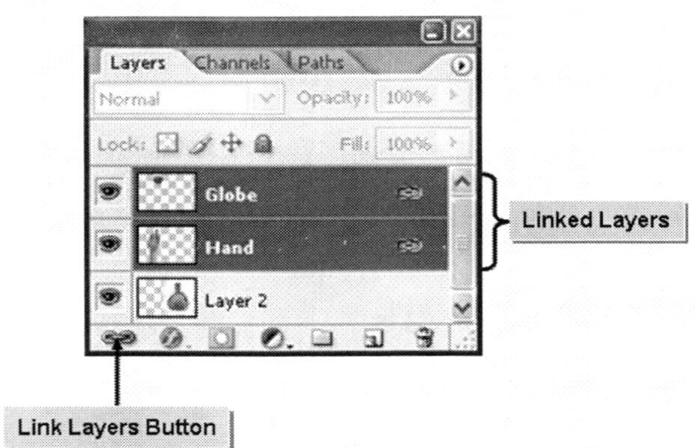

 The commands and buttons on the Layers palette are also available as commands within the Layer menu in the menu bar at the top of the screen. For example, you also could have created a new group by choosing Layer→New→Group. The Layer menu also contains additional commands not found on the Layers palette.

Layer Groups

Layer groups allow you to organize layers into batches that can be collapsed or expanded on the Layers palette. Like linked layers, layers within a group can be moved together. However, unlike linked layers, the layer group will allow you to hide or show all layers at once, and rearrange these layers on the Layers palette as a group. Layer groups also allow you to organize the layers on the Layers palette by collapsing or expanding the layers within the group on the Layers palette. Layer groups also allow you to apply blending options to the layers as a unit.

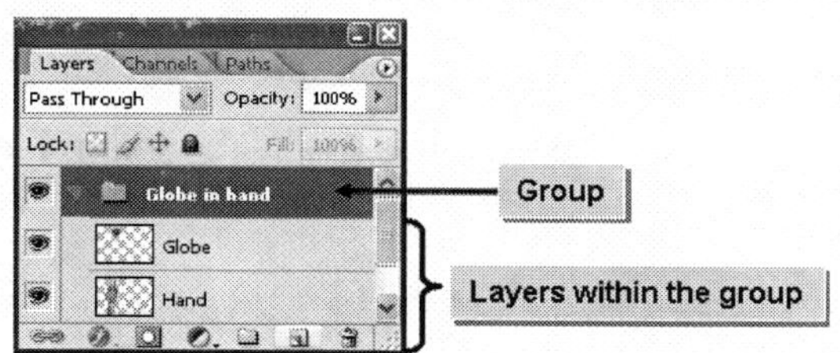

Work with Layer Group

You can create a Layer group by clicking the New Group button on the Layers palette, and then dragging the layers into the group. If the layers you want to add to a layer group are linked, you can choose Layer→New→Group From Layers. A new layer group will be created and the linked layers will automatically be in the group. While you can't create a layer group within an existing layer group, you can nest groups. To nest layers, create the layer group, and drag the new layer group into an existing layer group. To remove a layer from a layer group, drag the layer to the desired location among the other layers that are outside the layer group on the Layers palette. If you want to position the layer directly below the layer group, drag it slightly to the left below the layers in the layer group. You can remove the last layer in a layer group by simply dragging its thumbnail to the left.

Smart Guides

The Smart Guide feature allows you to align objects in different layers. When you turn the Smart Guide option on by selecting it from the View menu, and move objects in your image, guides will appear automatically to help you position the objects in the appropriate place. By default, the guides are displayed as magenta lines. However, you can change the color of the guides using Preferences in the Edit menu. Click on Guides, Grids & Slices, to access the Preferences dialog box, where you can change the color.

How to Arrange Layers

Procedure Reference: Change the Stacking Order of Layers

To change the stacking order of layers:

1. Open the required Photoshop file.
2. On the Layers palette, select the layer you want to move.

3. Drag the selected layer up or down to the desired location and release the mouse button to position the corresponding images accordingly.

Procedure Reference: Align Objects Using Smart Guides

To align objects using smart guides:

1. Open the required Photoshop file.
2. Select the desired layer in which the objects have to be aligned.
3. If necessary, Choose View→Rulers to display the ruler.
4. Choose View→Show→Smart Guides.
5. If necessary, in the toolbox, select the Move tool.
6. In the images window, move the object to be aligned. Magenta guides appear when you move the object.
7. Position the object at the appropriate place.

Procedure Reference: Align objects in Multiple Layers Using Smart Guides

To align objects in multiple layers using smart guides:

1. Open the required Photoshop file.
2. If necessary, in the toolbox, select the Move tool.
3. On the Tool Options bar, select the Auto Select Layer check box.
4. In the document window, draw a marquee around the objects to be selected.
5. Drag the selection to the desired position to reposition the selected objects located in different layers.
6. Magenta guides appear when you move the object.

Procedure Reference: Copy a Selection in the Image to a New Layer

To copy a selection made using the Magnetic Lasso tool to a new layer.

1. Open the required Photoshop file.
2. Select the desired portion of the image to be copied to the new layer.
   a. In the toolbox, select the Magnetic Lasso tool.
   b. Press the Caps Lock key to switch to the cross hair cursor.
   c. Position the Magnetic Lasso tool cursor so that its cross hair appears on the top edge of the object to be selected.
   d. Move the mouse pointer along the object's outline until you return it to the top of the object where you began the selection and click to complete the selection
   e. Press Caps Lock to return to the default Magnetic Lasso tool cursor.
3. Choose Layer→New→Layer Via Copy. A new layer is created on the Layers palette.
4. Rename the layer as desired.
5. On the Layers palette, drag the new layer to the desired position.

Procedure Reference: Set Layer Links

To link layers:

1. Open the required Photoshop file.
2. Select the layers to be linked.
   a. Select a layer.
   b. Hold down Ctrl and select the layers to be linked.
3. Link the selected layers.
   - At the bottom of the Layers palette, click the Link Layers button.
   - Or, choose Layers→Link Layers.

Procedure Reference: Create a New Group with Multiple Layers

To create a new group with multiple layers:

1. Open the required Photoshop file.
2. Create a new group.
   - At the bottom of the Layers palette, click the Create A New Group button.
   - Or, choose Layers→New→Group.
3. On the Layers palette, drag the desired layers into the group, releasing the mouse button when the group tab becomes highlighted.
4. Rename the group.
   - On the Layers palette, double-click the group name and type the desired name.
   - On the Layers palette, double-click the group set and in the Name dialog box, type the desired name.
   - On the Layers palette menu, select Group Properties, and in the Name text box, in the Name dialog box, type the desired name.
   - Or, choose Layer→Group Properties, and in the Name text box, in the Name dialog box, type the desired name.

Procedure Reference: Remove Layer Links

To remove layer links:

1. Open the required Photoshop file.
2. Select any one of the linked layers.
3. Remove the link for the selected layers.
   - At the bottom of the Layers palette, click the Link Layers button.
   - Or, choose Layers→Select Linked Layers and then Layer→ Unlink Layers.

Procedure Reference: Move Images in a Group

To move images in a group:

1. Open the required Photoshop file.
2. On the Layers palette, select the group whose images are to be moved.

3. In the images window, drag any one of the objects. The pixels on all the linked layers within the group now move together.

ACTIVITY 4-12

Changing the Stacking Order

Data Files:

- this and that collectibles.psd

Before You Begin

1. Open the this and that collectibles.psd file from the C:\084563Data\Image Composites\Activity 12\Starter folder.

Scenario:

You have imported images into your document and created layers. You find that some of the images need to be brought to the front and some need to be moved back.

What You Do	How You Do It
1. **Position the Globe layer on the Hand Layer.**	a. **Verify if the Globe layer is selected and the Move tool is active.** b. **Choose View→Show→Smart Guides.** c. **Drag the globe and position it between the thumb and forefinger** so that the hand appears to hold the globe. 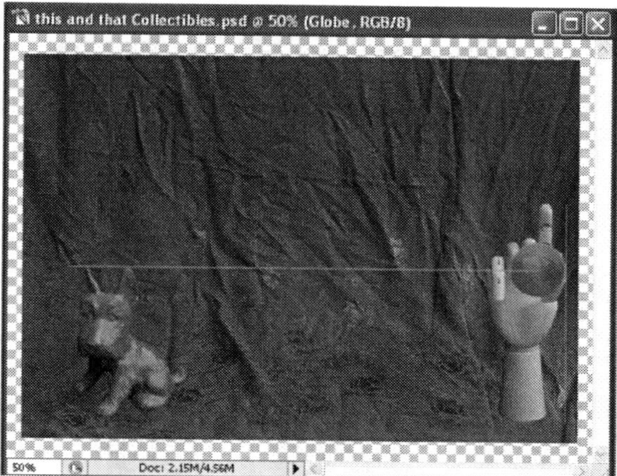 d. **Notice that magenta guides appear to help you position the globe accurately and the globe is in front of the hand, because the Globe layer is placed above the Hand layer on the Layers palette.**

2. **Copy the thumb from the hand image into a new layer named Thumb.**

a. In the Layer Visibility column of the Globe layer, **click the Eye icon** to hide the Globe layer.

b. On the Layers palette, **select the Hand layer.**

c. **Select the Zoom tool and click on the hand image.**

d. **Select the Magnetic Lasso tool.**

e. **Press Caps Lock** to switch to the cross hair cursor.

f. In the This And That Collectibles.psd window, **position the Magnetic Lasso tool so that its cross hair cursor appears on the top edge of the thumb, and click to begin the selection.**

g. **Notice that the mouse pointer appears as a circle, which indicates the area that the Magnetic Lasso tool will look in for contrasting edges.**

h. In the This And That Collectibles.psd window, **move the mouse pointer along the thumb's outline until you return it to the top of the thumb where you began the selection and click to complete the selection.**

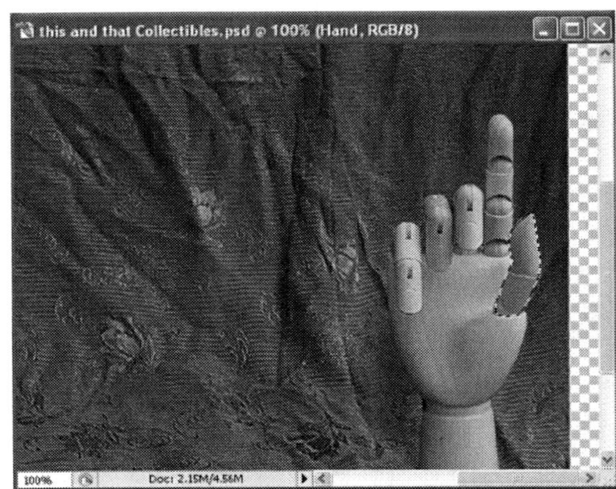

i. **Press Caps Lock** to return to the default Magnetic Lasso pointer.

j. **Choose Layer→New→Layer Via Copy.**

k. **Notice that a copy of the thumb is now moved to a new layer, Layer 1.**

l. On the Layers palette, **double-click Layer 1 and type *Thumb***

3. **Rearrange the layers.**

a. In the Globe layer, **click in the layer visibility column.**

b. On the Layers palette, **drag the Globe layer below the Thumb layer, and release the mouse button when a double black line appears below the Thumb layer.**

c. **Notice that the Thumb layer now appears above the Globe layer, so the thumb now overlaps the globe.**

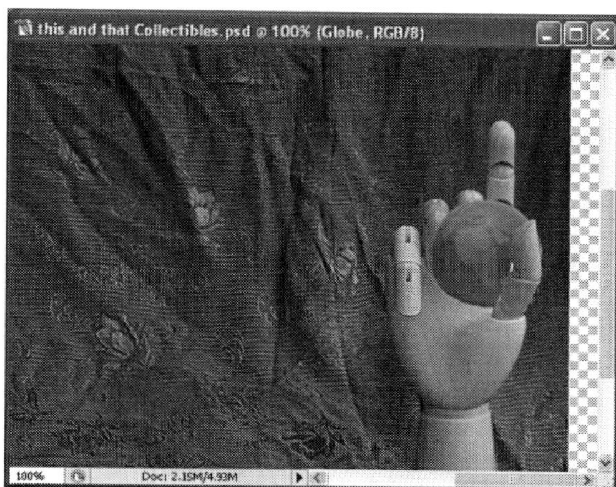

d. **Close the file and click No when prompted to save.**

ACTIVITY 4-13

Linking Layers and Creating A New Group

Data Files:

- this and that collectible.psd

Before You Begin

1. Open the this and that collectibles.psd file from the C:\084563Data\Image Composites\Activity 13\Starter folder.

Scenario:

As you continue to work with the composite image, you have created and added a lot of layers and they look a bit disorganized. You want to organize and link layers that have overlapping objects.

What You Do	How You Do It
1. **Link the Thumb, Globe and Hand Layers.**	a. On the Layers palette, **select the Thumb layer.**
	b. On the Layers palette, **hold down Shift and select the Hand layer.**
	c. **Notice that the Thumb, Globe and Hand layers are selected.**
	d. At the bottom of the Layers palette, **click the Link Layers button.**
	e. **Notice that on the Layers palette, the Link icon appears to the right of the selected layers indicating that all the three layers are linked.** 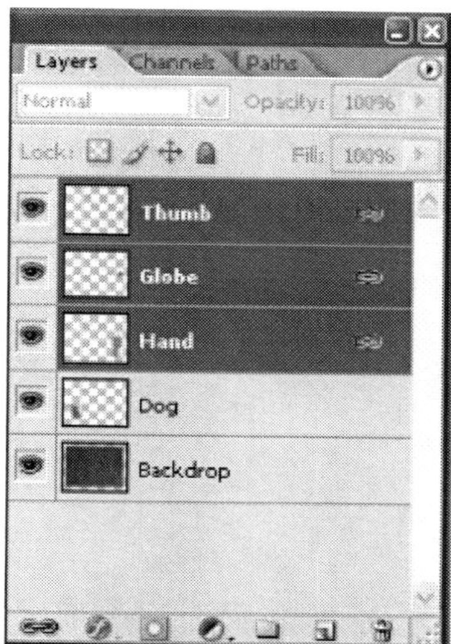
	f. **Select the Move tool.**
	g. In the This And That Collectibles.psd window, **drag the hand** about an inch to the left to move it.
	h. **Notice that the hand, globe, and thumb move together, maintaining their positions relative to one another.**
	i. **Choose Edit→Undo Move.**

2. **Create a new group.**

a. At the bottom of the Layers palette, **click the Create A New Group button.**

b. **Notice that at the top of the Layers palette, a new group named Group 1 appears.**

c. On the Layers palette, **drag the Thumb layer onto the Group 1 set, releasing the mouse button when Group 1 becomes highlighted.**

d. Similarly, **drag the Globe and Hand layers onto the Group 1 set.**

e. **Notice that all the three layers appears below the Group 1 set, indicating that it is now part of the group.**

f. On the Layers palette, **double-click Group 1 and type *Globe in Hand***

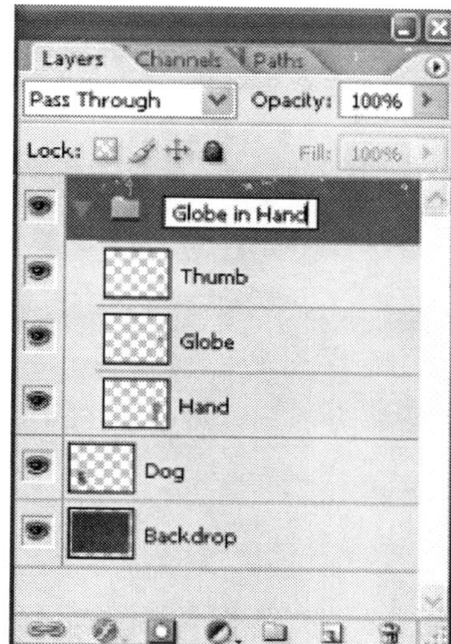

3. **Remove the layer links.**

a. On the Layers palette, **select the Globe layer.**

b. At the bottom of the Layers palette, **click the Link Layers button** to remove the links.

c. **Notice that on the Layers palette, all the link icons in the layers disappear.**

d. On the Layers palette, **select the Hand layer.**

e. At the bottom of the Layers palette, **click the Link Layers button** to remove the link.

f. On the Layers palette, **select the Thumb layer.**

g. In the This And That Collectibles.psd window, **drag the thumb** about an inch to the left.

h. **Notice that only the thumb moves, since the layers are no longer linked.**

i. **Choose Edit→Undo Move.**

4. **Move images in the Globe in Hand group.**
   a. On the Layers palette, **select the Globe in Hand group.**
   b. In the This And That Collectibles.psd window, **drag the globe** about an inch to the left.
   c. **Notice that the images on all the three layers within the set now move together.**
   d. **Choose Edit→Undo Move.**
   e. On the Layers palette, **click the triangle to the left of the Globe in Hand Group** to collapse the group.
   f. **Close the File and click No when prompted to save.**

ACTIVITY 4-14

Selecting Image Areas and Working with Layers

Data Files:

- ball.jpg
- this and that collectibles.psd
- flasks.psd

Before You Begin

1. Open the ball.jpg, flasks.psd, and this and that collectibles.psd files from the C:\084563Data\Image Composites\Activity 14\Starter folder.

Scenario:

You want to add another image to the document you are creating. You find that the image you have is slightly bigger so you decide to scale it down in relation to the other objects in the document.

What You Do	How You Do It
1. **Move the image of the ball to the this and that collectibles document.**	a. If necessary, **choose Window→Ball.jpg.**
	b. From the Marquee tool flyout, **select the Elliptical Marquee Tool.**
	c. In the Ball.jpg window, **click to position the mouse pointer at the top of the ball and drag around it** to select it.
	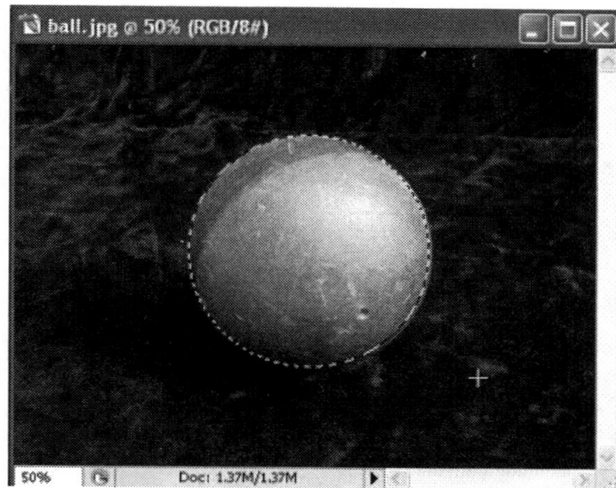
	d. **Select the Move tool.**
	e. **Drag the selected ball image to the This And That Collectibles window and place it between the hand and the dog images.**

	f. On the Layers palette, **double-click Layer 1 and type *Ball***

2. **Resize the image of the ball.**

a. If necessary, on the Layers palette, **select the Ball layer.**

b. **Choose Edit→Free Transform.**

c. **Position the mouse pointer on the upper-right transform handle, hold down Shift, and drag down to the left.**

d. **Release the mouse button when the Tool Options bar W and H text boxes indicate that the ball is now 30 percent of its original size.**

e. In the This And That Collectibles.psd window, **position the ball so that it is slightly behind the hand image.**

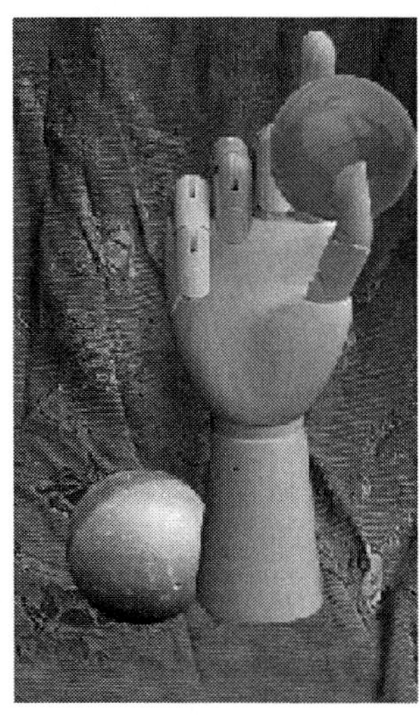

f. **Choose Window→Ball.jpg.**

g. **Choose File→Close.**

3. **Save the blue flask selection.**

a. If necessary, **choose Window→Flasks.psd.**

b. From the Marquee tool flyout, **select the Lasso Tool.**

c. In the Flasks.psd window, **click to position the mouse pointer at the top of the blue flask and drag around it** to select it.

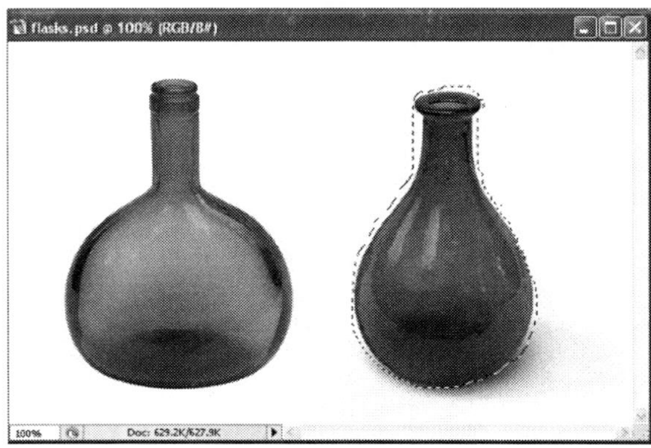

d. **Choose Select→Save Selection.**

e. In the Save Selection dialog box, in the Name text box, **type *blue flask* and click OK.**

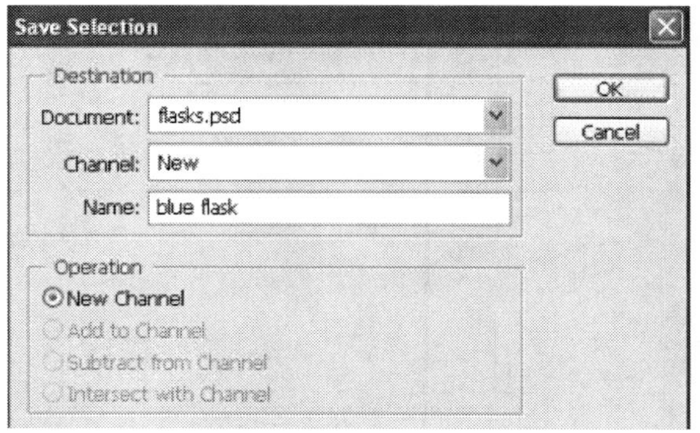

f. **Choose File→Save As.**

g. If necessary, **navigate to the C:\084563Data\Image Composites\Activity 14\Starter folder.**

h. In the Save As dialog box, in the File Name text box, **type *my collectibles* and click Save.**

i. Choose File→Close.

Lesson 4 Follow-up

In this lesson, you used layers to isolate specific parts of an image. You also used several techniques to create and manipulate layers, and undo steps.

1. **Which tool is more useful in undoing the previous steps?**

2. **Give examples of instances when you copied layers between images for a project.**

Notes

LESSON 5

Blending Composite Images

Lesson Time
25 minutes

Lesson Objectives:

In this lesson, you will apply blending effects to composite images so that they appear more realistic.

You will:

- Remove a halo effect using the Defringe command.
- Apply transparency to a layer.
- Apply feathering to a selection edge.

Introduction

You have started working with multiple layers and images in Photoshop. Blending composite images is important so that any image area you add appears as a natural part of the image to which it was added. In this lesson, you will use several techniques for applying blending effects to composite images.

When moving an image from one background to another, the edges of the added image area may contrast with the background. In addition, if the added image area contains transparent material, you may have to apply transparency to ensure the new background's visibility through the added image area. Blending composite images is important so that added image areas seem like they belong naturally to the new background.

TOPIC A

Defringe Images

You have learned to combine images in Photoshop. When you select an area from one image, and add it to another, the added area may look unnatural against the new background. In this topic, you will defringe a selection by removing the unwanted pixels around images that have been included to other backgrounds, to make sure they blend with their new backgrounds.

When you move an image to a new background, a halo effect appears along the edges of the selection. Photoshop enables to you seamlessly blend images with new backgrounds, by removing unwanted pixels that surround it.

The Defringe Command

By default, each of Photoshop's selection tools is set to apply antialiasing to every selection. Antialiasing softens the color transitions at the edge of a selection, thereby making jagged edges of a selection softer. However, these softened pixels along the selection edge may create a halo around the selected image area. This becomes apparent when the selection is moved to a new image background.

You can use the *Defringe command* to remove unwanted pixels around the edge of a selection. The Defringe command changes the color of pixels along the current layer's edge to a color from within the layer.

Defringe Images

Procedure Reference: Remove a Halo Effect

To remove a halo effect:

1. Open the required Photoshop file.
2. Select the layer containing the object whose halo effect is to be removed.
3. Choose Layer→Matting→Defringe.
4. In the Defringe dialog box, specify the desired width and click OK to specify the area in which the pixels are to be replaced.
5. Save the file.

ACTIVITY 5-1

Removing a Halo Effect

Data Files:

- this and that collectibles.psd
- flasks.psd

Before You Begin

1. Open the this and that collectibles.psd and flasks.psd files from the C:\084564Data\Blending Composite Images\Activity 1\Starter folder.
2. The flasks.psd file is active.

Scenario:

You have moved certain image selections to a new document. You now notice some stray pixels around the object that appear unrealistic against the background.

What You Do	How You Do It
1. **Load the blue flask selection to the this and that collectibles document.**	a. **Choose Select→Load Selection.**
	b. In the Source section of the Load Selection dialog box, from the Document drop-down list, verify that Flasks.psd is selected and from the channel drop-down list blue flask is selected. **Click OK.**
	c. **Notice that the saved selection is loaded, and appears around the blue flask.**
	d. **Select the Move tool.**
	e. **Drag the selected blue flask to the This And That Collectibles.psd and position it next to the dog image.**

	f. **Notice that the blue flask is added as a new layer, and appears within the image.**
	g. On the Layers palette, **double-click Layer 1 and type *Blue Flask***
2. **Remove the fringe of white pixels around the blue flask.**	a. **Choose Layer→Matting→Defringe.**

b. In the Defringe dialog box, in the Width text box, verify that the width is set to 1.**Click OK.**

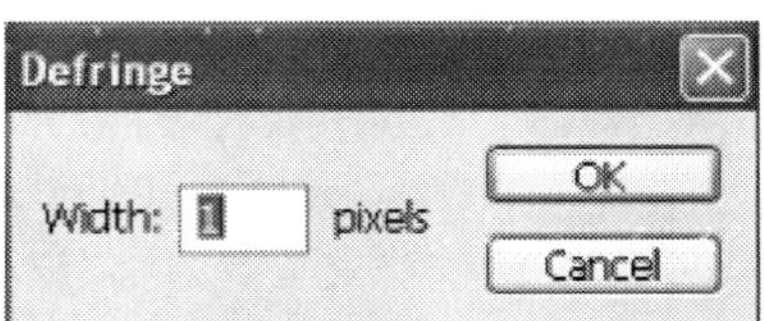

c. **Notice that the fringe of white pixels around the blue flask is removed.**

d. **Choose Edit→Transform→Flip Horizontal** to flip the blue flask so that the highlights appear correctly.

3. **Load the green flask image and move the Blue Flask layer above the Green Flask layer.**

   a. **Choose Window→Flasks.psd**

   b. **Choose Select→Load Selection.**

   c. In the Source section of the Load Selection dialog box, from the Document drop-down list, **select Green Flask and click OK.**

   d. **Drag the selected green flask to the This And That.psd and position it before the ball image.**

   e. **Notice that the green flask is added as a new layer, and appears within the image.**

   f. On the Layers palette, **double-click Layer 1 and type *Green Flask***

   g. On the Layers palette, **drag the blue flask layer above the green flask layer.**

h. **Notice that defringing is not required as both the layers blend seamlessly.**

i. **Choose File→Save As.**

j. If necessary, **navigate to the C:\084564Data\Blending Composite Images\Activity 1\Starter** folder.

k. In the Save As dialog box, in the File Name text box, **type *my this and that collectibles* and click Save.**

l. **Choose Window→Flask.psd.**

m. **Choose File→Close.**

TOPIC B

Simulate Transparency with Opacity and Blending Modes

You are familiar with blending images in Photoshop. In some instances you may be required to apply blending modes to simulate transparency for a layer that has moved over a new background. In this topic, you will adjust a layer's opacity and apply blending modes to simulate transparency.

While adding an image area that contains smoke, glass, water, or similar transparent material, you may need to apply transparency so that the new background is visible through the added image area. You can easily apply transparency to a Photoshop layer by adjusting the layer's opacity. Also, in some cases, a more realistic transparency effect can be achieved by using layer blending modes.

Opacity

Opacity is the amount of transparency in a layer. The lower you set the layer opacity, the more transparent the layer appears. However, adjusting opacity is not always sufficient for creating realistic transparency effects. If you lower a layer's opacity, it will apply transparency equally to the entire layer. However, some areas within the layer may need a higher opacity in comparison to other areas so that the effect appears realistic.

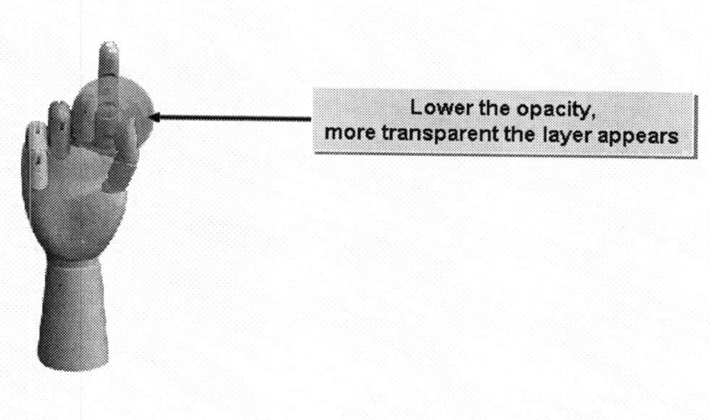

Adjust the Layer Opacity

You can adjust the transparency by adjusting the Opacity slider on the Layers palette to the required opacity value. You can also adjust the currently selected layer's opacity by typing the opacity value you want to use. You can type the opacity value at any time, without having to first select the Opacity field on the Layers palette. You must type the two numbers in fairly rapid succession so that Photoshop correctly interprets the number as a single, two-digit number. If you type the numbers too slowly, Photoshop interprets each number as a separate opacity value. Whenever you type a single digit for the layer opacity, Photoshop makes the number a multiple of 10. For example, if you type the number 8, the opacity will be set to 80 percent. To type a single digit opacity value, you must type 0 before the single digit number.

Blending Modes

Blending modes can be used to create a variety of effects by blending pixels in a layer or between layers. To maintain transparency while strengthening the solidity of the dark areas in an image, you can duplicate the layer and apply the Multiply blending mode to the original layer that is lower in the stacking order. The Multiply blending mode multiplies the colors in the selected layer and the layers below it in the stacking order. This results in a darker image in the selected layer, making the image appear more solid, while maintaining its transparency.

 Layer blending mode is the method that Photoshop uses to combine pixel colors in a layer with those in underlying layers. For example, Normal mode does not blend the colors at all, and Multiply mode combines the layers similarly to colored transparencies on an overhead projector.

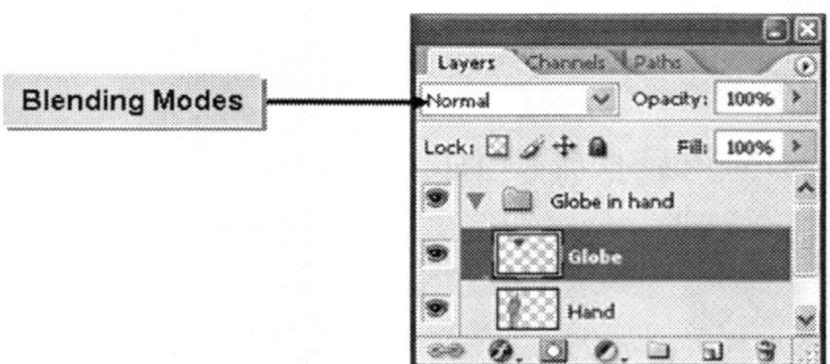

Several other blending modes can create semitransparency effects, including Overlay, Hard Light, and Soft Light. The Overlay blending mode multiplies colors based on the colors below; and the Soft Light blending mode darkens or lightens the image based on the color being blended. The Hard Light blending mode is similar to Soft Light, but it produces a more pronounced effect.

Layer Blending Mode

Layer blending mode is the method Photoshop uses to combine pixel colors in a layer with those in underlying layers. For example, Normal mode does not blend the colors at all, and Multiple mode combines the layers similarly to colored transparencies on an overhead projector.

Apply Blending Mode To A Group

You can apply a blending mode to a group. By default, the blending mode of a group is Pass Through, which means that the group has no blending properties. When you choose a blending mode for a group, the group is treated as a single unit, and it is blended with the rest of the image using the selected blending mode. The blending mode for a group will override any blending modes applied to a layer inside the group.

Simulate Transparency with Opacity and Blending Modes

Procedure Reference: Set the Opacity for a Layer

To set the opacity for a layer:

1. Open the required Photoshop file.
2. Select the layer whose opacity is to be set.
3. On the Layers palette, specify the opacity level for the layer.

- Click the triangle to the right of the Opacity text box, and drag the opacity slider to the desired opacity level.
- Or, in the Opacity text box, specify the desired opacity value.

Procedure Reference: Apply Blending Mode

To apply blending mode:

1. Open the required Photoshop file.
2. On the Layers palette, select the layer to which the effect is to be applied.
3. On the Layers palette, from the Blending Mode drop-down list, select the blending mode to be applied.
4. If necessary, on the Layers palette, set the opacity to 100 percent.

Blending Modes

There are certain blending modes that you can apply to enhance the effects of the images in your document. The following table lists the different types of blending modes.

Blending Mode	Description
Dissolve	This mode randomly replaces the pixels in the base color with those in the blend color.
Behind	This mode edits or paints the transparent part of the layer alone.
Clear	This mode makes each pixel transparent.
Darker	This mode selects the darker color in each channel as the blend color.
Multiply	This mode multiplies the base color with the blend color.
Color Burn	This mode darkens the base color and displays the blend color by increasing the contrast.
Linear Burn	This mode darkens the base color and displays the blend color by reducing the brightness.
Lighten	This mode chooses the lightest between the base and blend color as the blend color.
Screen	This mode multiplies the inverse of the blend and base colors.
Color Dodge	This mode brightens the base color and displays the blend color by reducing the contrast.

Activity 5-2

Simulating Transparency with Opacity and Blending Modes

Data Files:

- this and that collectibles.psd

Before You Begin

1. Open the this and that collectibles.psd file from the C:\084563Data\Blending Composite Images\Activity 2\Starter folder.

Scenario:

You have moved certain images into your document. However you find that they have solid color pixels. They look out of place in your document. You want them to blend with the background and other objects in your documents, and appear realistic.

What You Do	How You Do It
1. **Set the opacity of the Blue Flask layer.**	a. If necessary, on the Layers palette, **select the Blue Flask layer.**
	b. If necessary, **select the Move tool.**
	c. **Drag the blue flask so that it partially overlaps the dog figurine.**

	d. On the Layers palette, **click the triangle to the right of the Opacity text box, and drag the opacity slider to 80 percent.**

2. **Set the opacity of the Green Flask layer.**

a. On the Layers palette, **select the Green Flask layer.**

b. **Drag the green flask so that it partially overlaps the ball.**

c. On the Layers palette, in the Opacity text box, **double-click and type *75***

3. **Duplicate the Green Flask layer.**

a. On the Layers palette, **drag the Green Flask layer to the New Layer button at the bottom of the palette.**

b. **Notice that the layer is copied to a new layer named Green Flask Copy.**

c. On the Layers palette, in the Layer Visibility column of the Green Flask copy layer, **click the Eye icon** to hide the Green Flask Copy layer.

4. **Apply a blending mode to the Green Flask layer.**

a. On the Layers palette, **select the Green Flask layer.**

b. On the Layers palette, from the Blending Mode drop-down list, **select Multiply.**

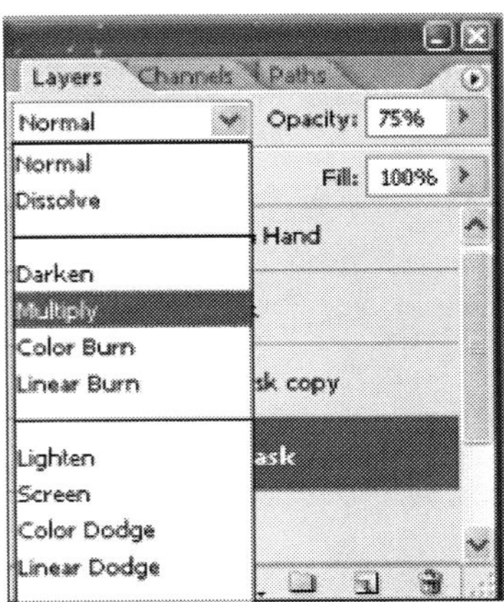

c. **Notice that the flask now darkens as it merges with the background.**

d. On the Layers palette, in the Opacity text box, **double-click and type *100***

e. **Notice that the flask is darkened, and appears more like a shadow than a solid flask.**

f. On the Layers palette, **click in the Layer Visibility column of the Green Flask copy layer** to make the layer visible.

5. **Link the Green Flask and Green Flask Copy layers.**

   a. On the Layers palette, **select the Green Flask Copy layer.**

   b. **Hold down Ctrl and select the Green Flask layer.**

   c. At the bottom of the Layers palette, **click the Link icon.**

   d. **Choose File→Save As.**

   e. If necessary, **navigate to the C:\084564Data\Blending Composite Images\Activity 2\Starter** folder.

   f. In the Save As dialog box, in the File Name text box, **type *my this n that collectibles* and click Save.**

   g. **Close the file.**

TOPIC C

Feather Edges

Using the Defringe command, you have learned to blend the image with its new background. However, certain situations will require more command over the softening of the image that is being transferred to a new background. In this topic, you will use the Feather command to manipulate the softening or blurring of images.

You are now working on a project, where the edges of a certain image are to be softened. For example, you want to place the image of a moon in an image displaying the clear dark sky. You want edges of the moon to have a blurred or softened effect. Antialiasing and defringing might not give you satisfactory results. You can make use of the feathered effect to attain satisfactory results.

Feathered Effect

Antialiasing can soften a selection's edges by blending the colors along the edge of the selection with the colors just outside it. However, when you want to control the softening or blurring of a selection border, you apply feathering. *Feathering* creates a blurred transition between the selection edge and the surrounding pixels, and it allows you to specify the width of the feathered edge. Feathering doesn't actually change the colors of any pixels. Instead, it reduces the opacity of pixels gradually over the specified feather distance. A feathered selection doesn't actually display feathering until you move, cut, copy, or fill the feathered selection. Feathering can be used to create a variety of effects, such as silhouetting.

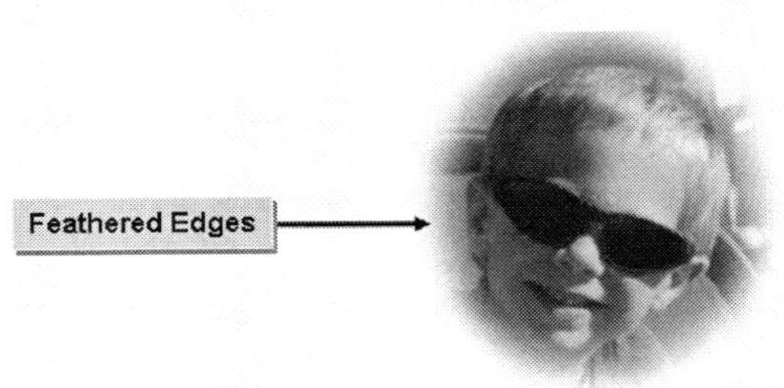

You can specify the feather amount to be used by selections created with the Marquee and Lasso tools by specifying a value in the Feather text box on the Tool Options bar. The value must be entered before making the selection, or it will have no effect. If you want to add a feather to an existing selection, you must use the Feather command in the Select menu. The feathered selection edge will not become apparent until you move, cut, copy, or fill the selection.

How to Feather Edges

Procedure Reference: Feather an Image

To apply the feather effect to an image:

1. Open the required Photoshop file.
2. Select the layer to be feathered.
3. Apply the feather settings.
    - On the Tool Options bar, in the Feather text box, specify the desired feather settings.
    - Or, select the image to which feather settings are to be applied, choose Select→Feather and in the Feather Selection dialog box, specify the desired feather settings.

Procedure Reference: Create a Spotlight Effect

To create a spotlight effect:

1. Open the required Photoshop file.

2. Specify the feather settings.
3. Using the Elliptical Marquee tool, create a large oval selection that includes most of the image to which the effect is to be applied.
4. Choose Select→Inverse to select the image area outside the oval selection.
5. If necessary, in the toolbox, click the Default Foreground And Background Colors button and set it to the desired color.
6. Choose Edit→Fill and in the Fill dialog box, click OK.
7. In the image window, click outside the selection to deselect the image.

ACTIVITY 5-3

Feathering to Create a Spotlight Effect

Data Files:

- this and that collectibles.psd

Before You Begin

1. Open the this and that collectibles.psd file located from the C:\084563Data\Blending Composite Images\Activity 3\Starter folder.

Scenario:

You have imported all the objects to be used in the this and that collectibles document. You now want to emphasize the presence of the objects by applying a special effect.

What You Do	How You Do It
1. **Create a new layer.**	a. On the Layers palette, **select the Globe in Hand layer set.** b. **Hold down Alt and click the New Layer button at the bottom of the Layers Palette.** c. In the New Layer dialog box, in the Name text box, **type *feather* and click OK.** 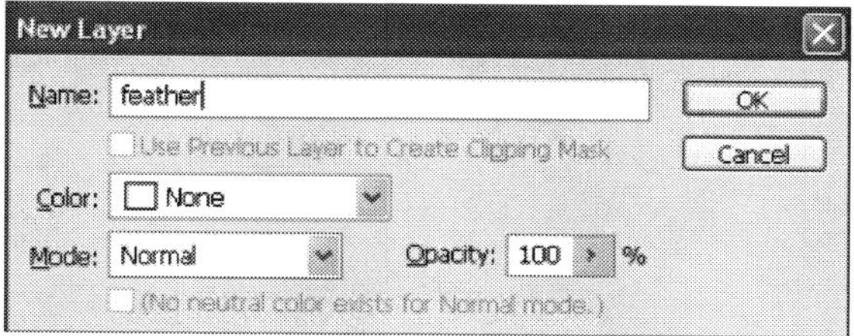

2. **Create a spotlight effect in the image.**

a. **Select the Elliptical Marquee tool.**

b. On the Tool Options bar, in the Feather text box, **double-click and type *20***

c. In the This And That Collectibles.psd window, **drag the mouse pointer to create an oval selection that includes all the images in the document.**

d. **Choose Select→Inverse** to select the image area outside the oval selection.

e. If necessary, on the Color palette, **click the Default Foreground And Background Colors button.**

f. **Choose Edit→Fill.**

g. In the Fill dialog box, **click OK.**

h. In the This And That Collectibles.psd window, **click outside the selection** to deselect the image.

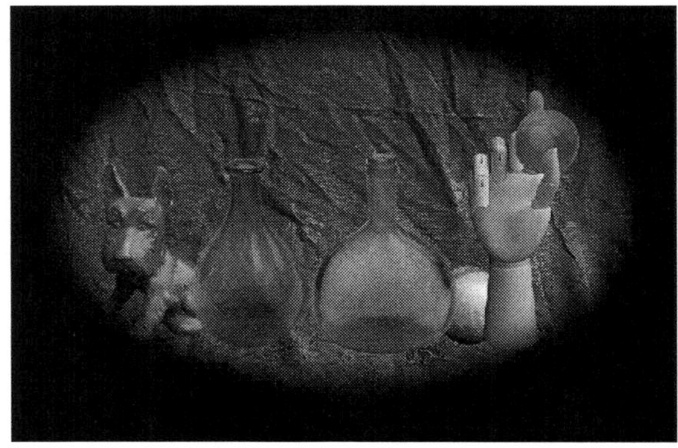

i. On the Layers palette, in the Visibility Column of the Feather layer, **click the**

Eye icon.

j. **Choose File→Save As.**

k. If necessary, **navigate to the C:\084564Data\Blending Composite Images\Activity 3\Starter** folder.

l. In the Save As dialog box, in the File Name text box, **type *my this n that* and click Save.**

m. **Choose File→Close.**

Lesson 5 Follow-up

In this lesson, you used several techniques for applying blending effects to composite images.

1. **Give an example of a situation where you had to use realistic transparency effects.**

2. **Which common effects do you use to soften images?**

Notes

LESSON 6
Exploring Image Modes

Lesson Time
25 minutes

Lesson Objectives:

In this lesson, you will identity the various image modes characteristics and select the appropriate image mode for specific purposes.

You will:

-
- Change the image modes.
- Explore the Photoshop color modes.

Introduction

You are now skilled at creating and blending composite images. It is important to understand the similarities and differences in image types or modes to best utilize Photoshop for specific purposes. The modes vary in complexity from black and white to color. In this lesson, you will explore the different image modes.

Photoshop enables you to select one of several image types or modes to work with. The modes vary in complexity from black and white to color. Using the correct image mode can minimize the file size and processing time, and is essential for obtaining quality output.

TOPIC A

Examine Mode Characteristics

You've been working on different kinds of images. While working with Photoshop, it is necessary to understand the characteristics that differentiate different image modes. In this topic, you will examine the image mode characteristics.

Photoshop enables you to work with color and black and white images. In doing so, it therefore becomes imperative to recognize the different color channels that an image gets broken down to, or to determine the different shades or colors that can be used in an image.

Channels

Photoshop uses channels to divide some color images into components, much like a prism divides white light. For example, the RGB images you have been working with, are divided into red, green, and blue channels. Non-color images such as grayscale, and black and white, need only one channel, since there is no need to divide the colors into components.

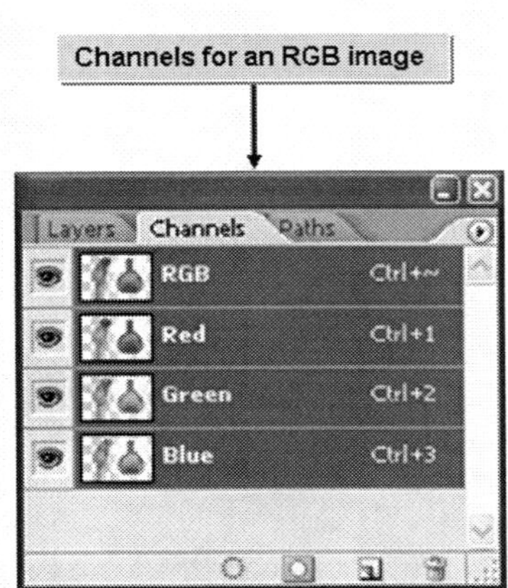

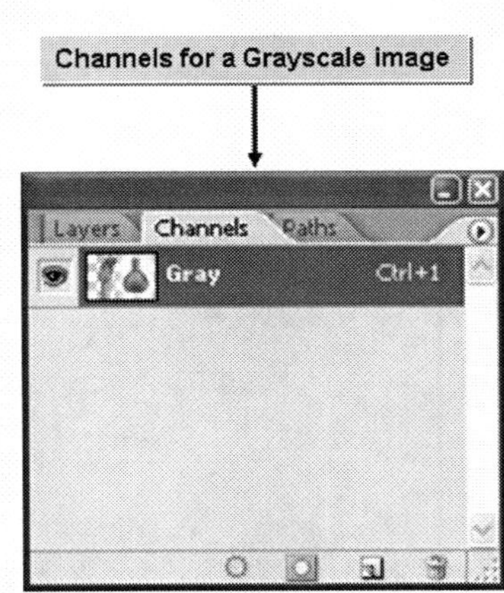

Pixel Depth

The *pixel depth*, measured in bits, determines the total number of colors or shades of brightness an image can utilize. The greater the pixel depth, the more accurately the image is represented. A simple formula, determines the number of colors or shades based on the pixel depth.

$$\text{Colors or shades} = 2^{\text{(pixel depth)}}$$

A simple formula determines the number of colors or shades based on the pixel depth.

Determine the Number of Colors

The formula for determining the number of colors or shades based on the pixel depth is $2^{\text{pixel depth}}$. For example, a 1-bit image has a total of 2 shades, since 2^1 is 2. An 8-bit image has a total of 256 shades, since 2^8 is 256.

Photoshop Modes

All Photoshop modes, from the simplest to the most complex, differ only in the number of channels and the pixel depth per channel. The complexity and file size of an image increases depending on the number of channels and pixel depth.

ACTIVITY 6-1

Examining Mode Characteristics

Scenario:

The following questions will test your knowledge of mode characteristics.

1. **What does pixel depth determine?**
   a) The total number of shades of brightness an image can utilize.
   b) The accuracy of the image.
   c) The way the image is printed.
   d) The file size.

2. **True or False? Photoshop uses channels to divide color images into components.**
   ___ True
   ___ False

3. **How many channels does a grayscale image require?**
   a) One
   b) Two
   c) Three
   d) Four

TOPIC B

Explore Grayscale and Bitmap Modes

You've examined image mode characteristics. While working on Photoshop, you will encounter several situations that will warrant the use of black and white images. But before you begin, you must recognize the technical differences in separating different kinds of black and white images. In this topic, you will explore Bitmap and Grayscale modes in Photoshop.

Grayscale and Bitmap images are similar, as neither carry color information. However, while working with images in Photoshop, it becomes important to distinguish between the two image modes.

Bitmap

Bitmap images have single 1-bit channels that result in two available shades of brightness: black and white. They contain no gray levels in between. Bitmap images are typically used for simple logos and line art, and for creating special effects such as mezzotinting.

Bitmap Image

 A random pattern of black and white areas to create illusion of raised areas of an image.

Grayscale

Grayscale images are also one channel images. However, the channel is 8 bits rather than one. This results in 256 brightness levels, ranging from 0 or pure black to 255 or pure white.

Grayscale is a more accurate term for black and white photos. Although they are printed using only black ink, the pixels in the version you edit on the screen are levels of gray, with the conversion to a black and white halftone occurring during the printing process.

Grayscale Image

Duotone

A *Duotone* is a one-channel, 8-bit image that is similar to a Grayscale image. However, it differs in the way in which the image is printed. The Duotone mode allows you to assign two, three, or four inks namely duotone, tritone, or quadtone, to print certain tones of the image in different colors. For example, you could create a duotone that prints black ink in areas that were dark green to black in the original image, and brown ink in areas that were middle green to white in the original.

Duotones are typically used to print tinted images, such as sepia tones, and images with special ink requirements, such as shiny objects like coins. They can also be used to add subtle shading to Grayscale images. Since fewer printing plates are used, duotones are more cost effective than four-color printing.

Print Duotone Images

While you can print a Duotone image on an inkjet printer, it will be a simulation of how it would appear when printed with the specific inks you designated. This is because inkjet printers mix colors from a specific set of inks typically the process colors Cyan, Magenta, Yellow, and Black, and they don't use other ink colors.

Traditionally, a duotone is an image printed with two inks, typically for tinting it or creating effects at lower cost than four-color printing. In Photoshop, a duotone is an image saved in Duotone mode, which specifies one (monotone), two (duotone), three (tritone) or four (quadtone) inks to be applied to a base Grayscale image.

How to Explore Grayscale and Bitmap Modes

Procedure Reference: Change Image Mode

To change an image mode.

1. Open the required Photoshop file.

2. Choose Image→Mode.
3. From the Mode submenu of the Image menu, choose the desired mode.

ACTIVITY 6-2

Changing Image Modes

Data Files:

- dog.psd

Scenario:

You have an image in your document. You would like to see how it is displayed in the Grayscale mode before deciding on the mode that suits your needs best.

What You Do	How You Do It
1. **Open the image and change the color mode to grayscale.**	a. **Choose File→Open.**
	b. **Navigate to C:\084563Data\Exploring Image Modes\Activity 2\Starter** folder.
	c. In the Open dialog box, **select dog.psd and click Open.**
	d. **Choose Image→Mode.**
	e. **Notice that a list of image modes is displayed.**
	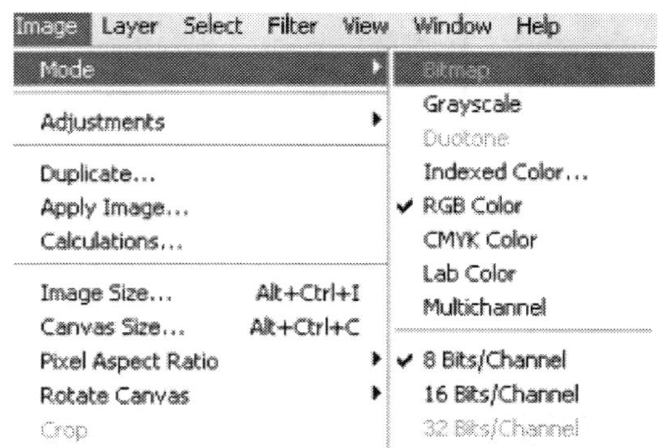
	f. From the Mode submenu of the Image menu, **choose Grayscale.**
	g. In the Adobe Photoshop dialog box, **click OK.**
	h. **Choose File→Close.**
	i. **Click No when prompted to save.**

2. **Which image does not contain any gray level?**
   a) BMP
   b) JPEG
   c) PNG
   d) GIF

3. **True or False? Duotone is a one-channel 8-bit image.**
   ___ True
   ___ False

TOPIC C

Explore Color Modes

You are familiar with Grayscale and Bitmap modes in Photoshop and are now going to work on color images. However, before you begin you must recognize that images in Photoshop fall under one of the four color modes that contain its color information. In this topic, you will identify the attributes that distinguish each of Photoshop's color modes.

You are creating an image for a print advertisement, in Photoshop. However, the result on screen is visibly different from the printed output. To get the best results, you need to understand the different color modes.

Indexed Color

Indexed color is a single-channel mode, much like Grayscale and Duotone modes. The bit depth can be set from 1 to 8 bits. However, each pixel will be a color instead of a shade of gray. A color table is used to establish which colors are available.

Features of Indexed Colors

Indexed color images are often saved in the CompuServe GIF format for use on web pages. Its small file sizes result in fast transfer rates. However, the limit of 256 colors makes smooth color transitions and realistic display of color photos difficult. Therefore indexed color is best suited for color illustrations.

RGB Color

RGB color has three 8-bit channels. Each color component which is red, green, or blue, can use 256 shades. The three channels combine to make a 24-bit image, resulting in 2^{24} or 16.7 million colors. Since each color channel has the same amount of information as a Grayscale or Indexed Color image, the file size is three times bigger. The RGB color mode is most commonly used for images that are distributed electronically and viewed on a monitor. In addition, you will most likely work in RGB mode during editing and painting.

Primary Colors

Red, green, and blue are often referred to as the three additive primary colors, because they add together to create white, when projected from a light source such as light bulbs or the phosphors of your computer monitor. However, you cannot use RGB color for printing, as red, green, and blue inks darken when they overlap, instead of becoming brighter.

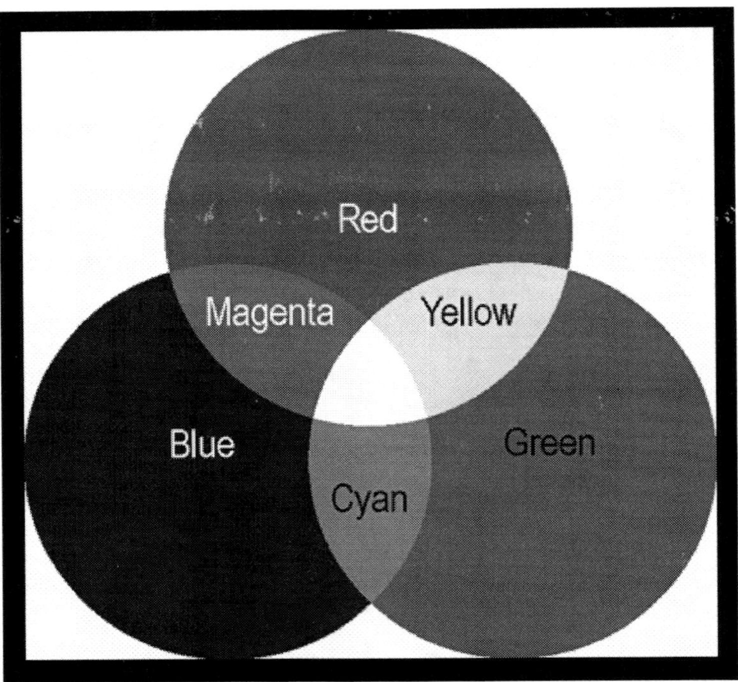

CMYK Color

For printing purposes, it is necessary to convert RGB images into the subtractive primary colors that are cyan, magenta, and yellow. In theory C, M, and Y added together form black. However, since semitransparent inks are used in printing, overprinting C, M, and Y inks will result in a dark, muddy color. Therefore, black ink or K is introduced to produce the dark tones in an image, to create solid blacks. The resulting image is 32 bits or 4 channels x 8 bits, which result in over 4 billion available colors.

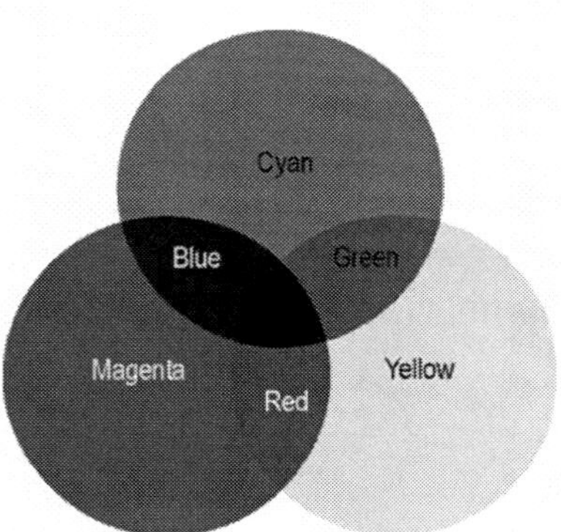

CMYK colors overlap to create other colors

 Although mathematically, *CMYK color* can hold more colors, its color gamut or the total range of colors is more limited than RGB in many areas, such as bright blues, greens, pastels, and flesh tones.

Color Separation

Although color inkjet printers use cyan, magenta, yellow, black inks, and occasionally other additional inks, most color inkjet printer drivers are optimized for printing RGB images. Therefore, you shouldn't convert from RGB to CMYK in Photoshop. However, during commercial printing or while using more expensive printers that use the PostScript® printing language, you should convert the image to CMYK. This process is called color separation, because for commercial printing, the four ink colors are printed separately on a press. To perform the conversion, you can choose the CMYK color mode in the Mode submenu.

Lab Color

The *Lab color mode* defines colors mathematically, and is an independent device, unlike RGB, which is used for monitors and scanners, and CMYK, which is used for printing. Lab color, like RGB color, uses three 8-bit channels to represent color. L is the luminance component, ranging from black to white; A is a chromatic component ranging from green to red; and B is a chromatic component ranging from blue to yellow.

Application of Lab Color

The Lab color mode is used internally by Photoshop when converting colors between image modes such as from RGB to CMYK. It is also used by a color management software that modifies images automatically to appear the same on different printers and monitors. Also, as it separates luminance from color, Lab color is useful for editing image lightness without modifying the color.

ACTIVITY 6-3

Identifying the Attributes of Color Modes

Scenario:

The following questions will test your knowledge of identifying the attributes of color modes.

---

1. **Which color mode has three 8-bit channels?**

    a) Indexed

    b) RGB

    c) CMYK

    d) Lab

---

2. **Which color mode defines colors mathematically?**
   a) Indexed
   b) RGB
   c) CMYK
   d) Lab

3. **True or False? Color separation is the process of converting an image to CMYK by printers that use the PostScript printing language.**
   __ True
   __ False

Lesson 6 Follow-up

In this lesson, you identified attributes that distinguish each of Photoshop's image modes. Using the correct image mode is essential for obtaining quality output.

1. **When do you prefer using Grayscale image and when do you prefer using a Bitmap image?**

2. **In previous projects, what errors did you encounter as a result of picking the wrong image mode? How do you hope to correct them now?**

LESSON 7
Applying Colors

Lesson Time
40 minutes

Lesson Objectives:

In this lesson, you will select colors and paint image using the various color and painting tools in Photoshop and duplicate parts of an image using the Clone Stamp tool.

You will:

- Work with colors in Photoshop.
- Apply colors using the painting tools.
- Use the Clone Stamp tool to duplicate parts of an image.

Introduction

You have customized the Photoshop environment, selected image areas, and worked with image composites. You now want to begin using the color and painting tools of Photoshop CS2 to make your images look even better. In this lesson, you will select colors and apply them using the painting tools.

Selecting colors accurately is among the most important skills in professional image editing. You can use color for painting images, filling areas, and for gradient fill effects. Photoshop offers several tools for working with color. Once you have selected the color you want, you can use the Photoshop tools to apply it.

TOPIC A

Select Colors

You've been working with different kinds of images, both color, and black and white. While working with color images, you must understand that selecting colors accurately is the key to professional image editing. In this topic, you will select colors for painting images using the Color palette, the Color Picker, and the Eyedropper tool.

While working with images that require different shades of color, you aren't merely faced with the mundane task of picking colors from a pre-existing list. You can define different shades of colors by choosing them from a color spectrum or by typing numerical values for percentages of color components.

Foreground and Background Colors

Photoshop offers a variety of methods for selecting colors to use as the foreground and background colors. The foreground color, which appears within an icon as well as on the Color palette, is the color used by Photoshop's painting tools. The background color, which appears within an icon, to the right of the foreground color icon, is used to replace pixels in the background layer that are removed.

 A gradient is a blend of multiple colors. The color in the Set background color icon can be used within gradients.

The Color Palette

The Color palette provides straightforward and comprehensive features for selecting colors. The *Color palette* is used to select an available color from the color ramp. You can select a foreground color from the Color palette by either clicking within the color ramp at the bottom of the palette, or by specifying color values within the palette's fields. You can select a background color by holding down Alt and clicking within the Color palette's color ramp.

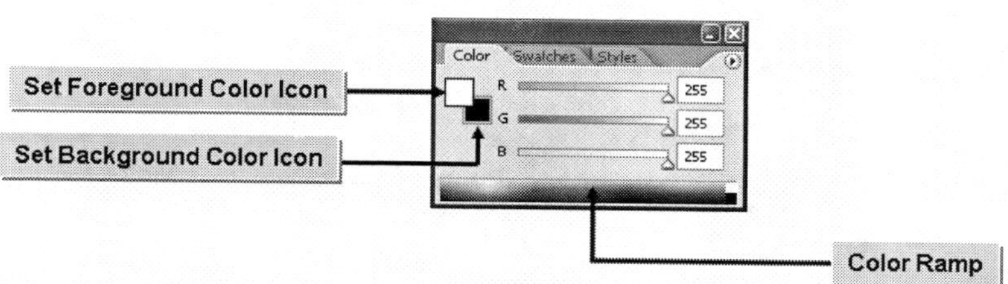

Color Gamuts

When choosing colors, it is important to consider the device that you will use for final output, as each device has a different gamut, or range of usable colors. For example, monitors display colors using red, green, and blue phosphors, and can generate much more vivid colors than printers using cyan, magenta, yellow, and black inks. The Color palette displays a warning when you choose a color that is not reproducible by CMYK colors for printing. Then the color is labeled an out-of-gamut color. This means that although the color may be suitable for computer or video work, it will appear different when printed. This warning prevents you from getting an unpredictable output of your colors.

When you select an out-of-gamut color, a triangle with an exclamation point appears at the bottom-left corner of the Color palette. This symbol lets you know that the color you have chosen is too bright to be adequately printed. The nearest printable color appears next to the exclamation point. Click the triangle, or the color next to it to choose a substitute that is within the gamut. If you choose a color from the Color palette's color ramp, you will automatically select a color within the CMYK gamut. By default, the color ramp only displays colors that are in the CMYK gamut.

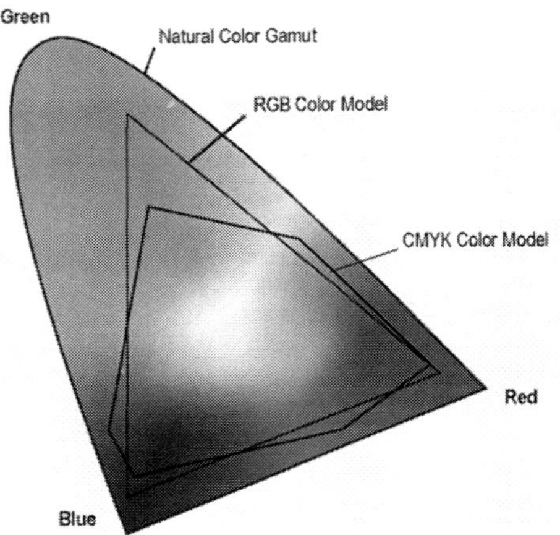

 If you are using the web color sliders, the gamut warning icon is a cube. This icon indicates that the selected color is not a web-safe color. Clicking the icon or the swatch next to it will select the closest web-safe color.

The Color Picker

Photoshop's Color Picker, which is accessible through the toolbox, gives you greater flexibility in selecting foreground and background colors. Photoshop's Color Picker, provides options for selecting foreground and background colors by choosing from a color field or by entering color values numerically. Its color spectrum is larger, and it provides additional controls for displaying colors within the color field.

Selecting colors from the Color Picker is easier than selecting them from the Color palette because on the Color palette, the ramp is very small, and it offers limited methods for choosing colors.

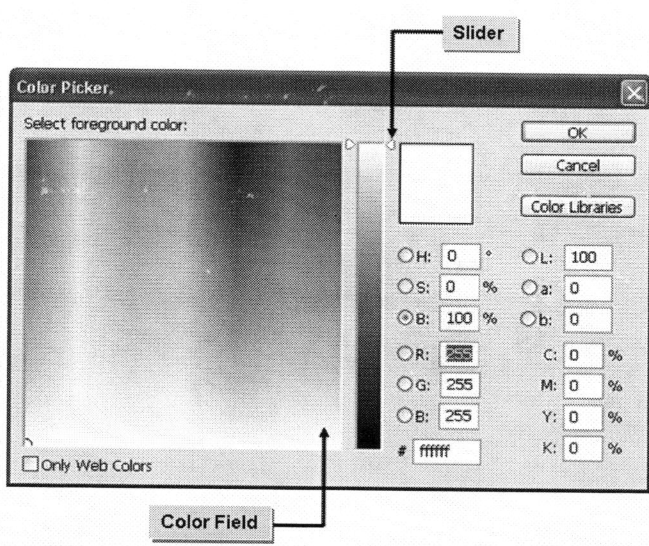

The Color Picker Dialog Box

You can use the Color Picker to select a foreground color by clicking the Set foreground color icon. Likewise, you can use the Color Picker to select a background color by clicking the Set background color icon. Shades of the hue color appear in the color field. The shades vary in saturation, or intensity, from left to right, and in brightness from top to bottom. To change the colors displayed in the color field, drag the slider upwards or downwards.

Change Colors Displayed in the Color Field

You can also change which parameter is affected by the slider in the Color Picker. For example, if the "S" or saturation option is selected, the complete range of saturation of the selected color is displayed on the slider bar. The color field then shows varying hues and brightness according to the saturation you select with the slider.

The Eyedropper Tool

The Eyedropper tool is used to pick up an existing color as if it were wet paint being drawn off a canvas. You can select a foreground or background color from within an image by sampling colors from the image using the Eyedropper tool. You can choose a foreground color by clicking with the Eyedropper tool within an image. You can choose a background color by holding down Alt as you click with the Eyedropper tool within an image.

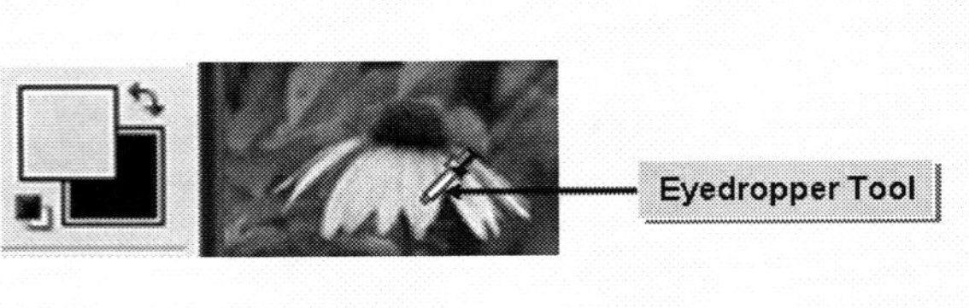

Select Colors

Procedure Reference: Select a Foreground Color

To select a foreground color:

1. Open the required Photoshop file.
2. Select a foreground color.
    - In the toolbox, click the Foreground Color icon and in the Color Picker dialog box, drag the slider in the color ramp to select the desired color.
    - On the Color palette, click the Foreground Color icon and from the color ramp at the bottom of the palette select the desired color.
    - On the Color palette, click the Foreground Color icon and drag the Red, Green and Blue color sliders to set the desired color.
    - On the Color palette, click the Foreground Color icon and specify values in the Red, Green and Blue color sliders text boxes to set the desired color.
    - Select the Eyedropper tool and click the image whose color is to be set as the foreground color.
    - Or, on the Swatches palette, click the desired color.
3. If necessary, specify the HSB values to adjust the Hue, Saturation and Brightness of the foreground color.

Procedure Reference: Select a Background Color

To select background color:

1. Open the required Photoshop file.
2. Select a background color:

- In the toolbox, click the Background Color icon and in the Color Picker dialog box, drag the slider in the color ramp to select the desired color.
- On the Color palette, click the Background Color icon and from the color ramp at the bottom of the palette select the desired color.
- On the Color palette, click the Background Color icon and drag the Red, Green and Blue color sliders to set the desired color.
- On the Color palette, click the Background Color icon and specify values in the Red, Green and Blue color sliders text boxes to set the desired color.
- Select the Eyedropper tool, hold down Alt and click the image whose color is to be set as the background color.
- Or, on the Swatches palette, Hold down Ctrl and click the desired color.

3. If necessary, specify the HSB values to adjust the Hue, Saturation and Brightness of the background color.

ACTIVITY 7-1

Selecting Foreground and Background Color

Data Files:

- this and that collectibles.psd

Before You Begin

1. Open the this and that collectibles.psd file from the C:\084563Data\Applying Colors\Activity 1\Starter folder.

Scenario:

You have prepared the images required and want to select a foreground color that will enhance their visual appeal.

What You Do	How You Do It
1. **Select a foreground and a background color using the color ramp on the Color palette.**	a. If necessary, **Choose Window→Color** to display the Color palette. b. On the Color palette, **position the mouse pointer on the color ramp at the bottom of the Color palette.** 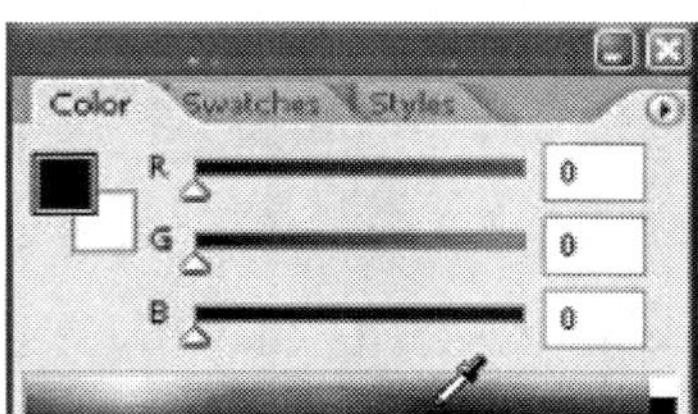 c. **Notice that the mouse pointer becomes an eyedropper, indicating that you can pick up color from the bar.** d. On the color palette, from the color ramp, **select dark blue.** e. **Notice that the foreground color in the Foreground Color icon at the top-left corner of the Color palette changes to blue.** f. **Hold down Alt and select a red color from the color ramp.** g. **Notice that the background color in the Background Color icon at the top-left corner of the palette changes to red.**
2. **Select an in-gamut foreground color using the color slider on the Color palette.**	a. On the Color palette, **drag the red slider to the left till it reaches zero.** 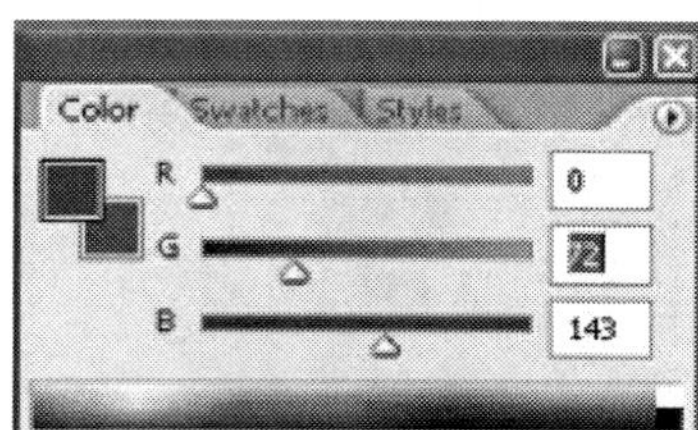

b. **Drag the green slider to the left till it reaches zero.**

c. **Notice that the red and green color components have been eliminated from the color that was selected, so now a pure blue hue is displayed.**

d. **Position the mouse pointer on the Gamut Warning icon before the Color Selection Box.**

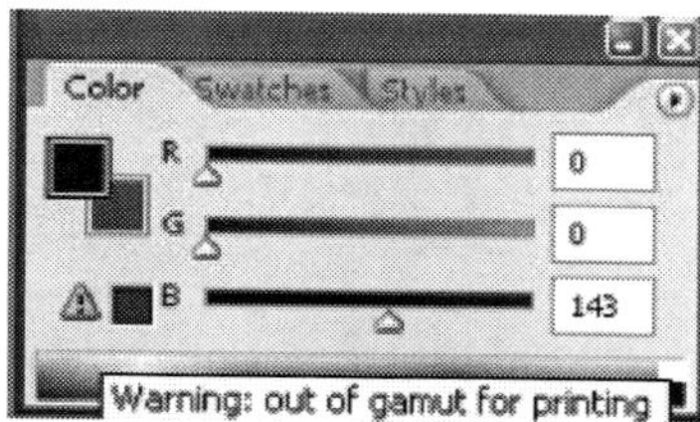

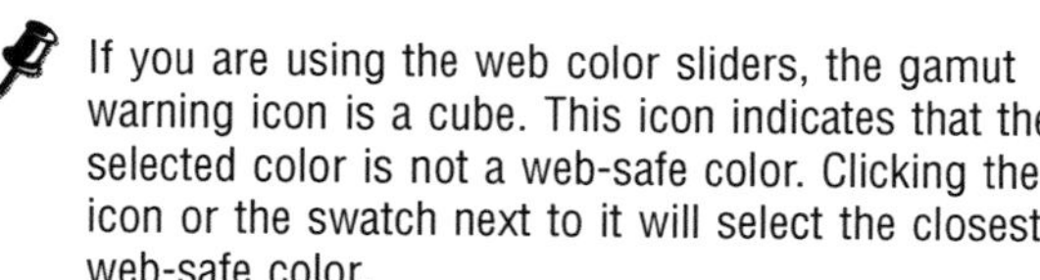
If you are using the web color sliders, the gamut warning icon is a cube. This icon indicates that the selected color is not a web-safe color. Clicking the icon or the swatch next to it will select the closest web-safe color.

e. **Notice that it displays the warning Out Of Gamut For Printing.**

f. **Click the color selection box next to the warning box** to select an in-gamut foreground color.

g. **Notice that on the Color palette, the color in the Foreground Color icon at the top-left corner of the Color palette is replaced by the in-gamut color selected.**

h. **Choose File→Close.**

ACTIVITY 7-2

Selecting Colors with the Color Picker

Data Files:

- this and that collectibles.psd

Before You Begin

1. Open the this and that collectibles.psd from the C:\084563Data\Applying Colors\Activity 2\Starter folder.

Scenario:

You are not satisfied with the color that was selected using the color ramp. You are still unable to find the exact shade you are looking for. You decide to explore other possibilities.

What You Do	How You Do It
1. **Select a color.**	a. In the toolbox, **click the Foreground Color icon.**
	b. In the Color Picker dialog box, **click at the top-right corner of the color field.**
	c. **Notice that the Gamut Warning icon appears to the right of the current color selection box.**

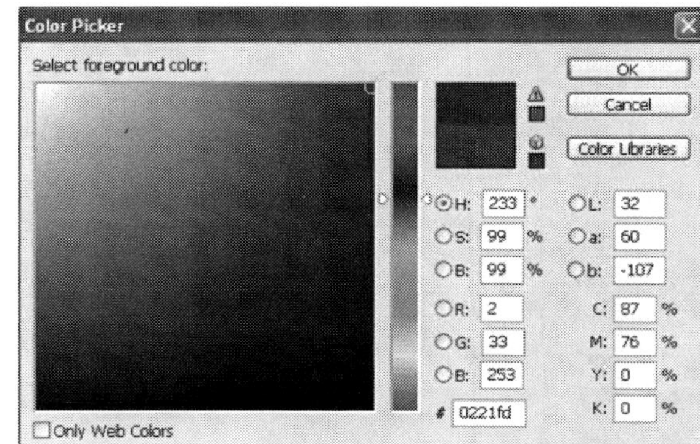

d. In the Color Picker dialog box, in the color ramp, **click in the middle of the area that displays shades of green.**

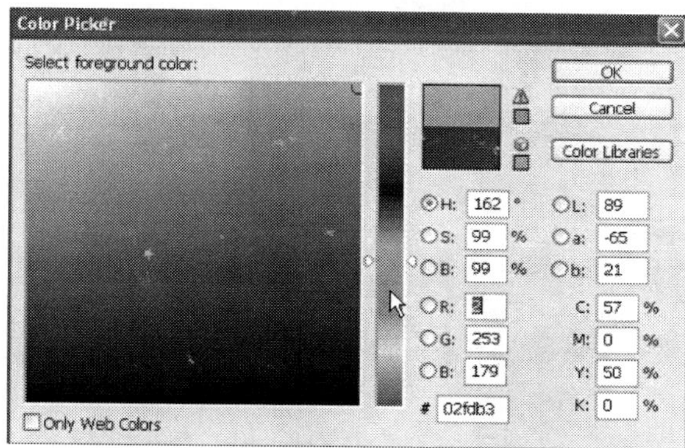

e. In the Color Picker dialog box, **click in the middle of the color field** to select a light green shade.

---

2. **Select the level of saturation.**

a. In the Color Picker dialog box, **select the S radio button.**

b. In the Color Picker dialog box, in the S text box, **double-click and type *0***

c. **Notice that the colors within the field are all gray, since there is no saturation.**

d. In the Color Picker dialog box, in the S text box, **double-click and type *100***

e. **Notice that the colors are very vivid.**

---

3. **Select a color by specifying RGB values.**

   a. In the Color Picker dialog box, **select the G radio button.**

   b. In the Color Picker dialog box, in the G text box, **double-click and type *0***

   c. **Notice that all the shades of green color have been eliminated from the color field.**

   d. In the Color Picker dialog box, in the G text box, **double-click and type *100***

   e. **Notice that all the available colors include full-intensity green.**

   f. In the Color Picker dialog box, in the color ramp, **click in middle of the area that displays shades of green.**

   g. **Notice that to the right of the current color selection, near the upper-right corner of the Color Picker, a Gamut Warning icon and a Web Safe Color Warning icon appear.**

   h. In the Color Picker dialog box, **click the Gamut Warning icon** to select the nearest in-gamut color.

ACTIVITY 7-3

Sampling Color with the Eyedropper Tool

Data Files:

- this and that collectibles.psd

Before You Begin

1. Open the this and that collectibles.psd from the C:\084563Data\Applying Colors\Activity 3\Starter folder.

Scenario:

You are still unsatisfied with the foreground and background colors in the image. You now decide to try and use the colors of the objects as the foreground and background colors.

What You Do	How You Do It
1. **Select the foreground color.**	a. **Select the Eyedropper tool.**
	b. In the This And That Collectibles.psd window, **click the blue flask.**
	c. **Notice that the foreground color in the Set Foreground Color icon changes to that of the blue flask.**
2. **Select the background color.**	a. **Hold down Alt and click anywhere on the green flask.**
	b. **Notice that the background color in the Set Background Color icon changes to that of the green flask.**
	c. **Choose File→Close.**

Topic B

Work with Painting Tools

You have selected the correct shade of color for an image you are working on. As you will be drawing new elements in the image with a chosen color, you must recognize appropriate painting tools used in Photoshop. Selecting the right tool will give you the right effect you want for your drawing. In this topic, you will use the Brush and Pencil tools, and use the Brush tool with the airbrush enabled to create shading effects within an image.

Photoshop enables you to draw images and bring them to life with color. As a graphic designer, Photoshop makes sure that you aren't limited only to selecting and editing existing images. The right painting tools will enable you to bring forth your own creations.

The Brush Tool

The *Brush tool* applies foreground color as you drag within an image, in the form of freehand lines that can have soft or hard edges. The Tool Options bar includes options for choosing a brush type and size. It also has an option to enable an airbrush effect, which applies more paint the longer you drag over an area. This allows you to easily create soft shadows and transitions from the paint to the background.

 You can also select preset brushes from the Brushes palette, located in the palette well. The Brushes palette can also be used to create custom brushes. When creating a custom brush, you can use the dynamic options to vary the size, color, and opacity of the brush over the course of the stroke.

The Brush Tool Options Bar

The Brush Tool Options bar, located below the menu bar, is context-sensitive. When you select the Brush tool, the Brush Tool Options bar displays settings for brush selection, mode, opacity, and flow. The flow setting controls how quickly paint is applied. A low flow value lightens the color of the paint applied, so it may look similar to painting at low opacity. However, low flow values also thin the brush stroke, and overlapping strokes with low flow will appear darker at the intersection.

Using the Brush Tool with the Airbrush

When using the Brush tool with the airbrush enabled to add shadows for items in an image, it is best to create the shadows on separate layers. The paint you apply to create the shadows will exist only in the active layer. Therefore, no pixels in the rest of the image are replaced by the shadows you draw in the active layer. This allows you to be much more creative and experimental with your painting and change the image later if you need to.

The Pencil Tool

The *Pencil tool* also applies foreground color as you drag within an image. It creates freehand lines that are always hard edged. The Tool Options bar includes options for choosing a brush type and size.

Work with Painting Tools

Procedure Reference: Paint Shadows in a New Layer

To paint shadows in a new layer:

1. Open the required Photoshop file.
2. Create a new layer.
    a. Hold down Alt and click the Create A New Layer button at the bottom of the Layers palette.
    b. In the Layer Properties dialog box, specify the desired layer name and click OK.
3. If necessary, select the Eyedropper tool.
4. Select the desired color for the shadow.
5. Select the Brush tool.
6. On the Tool Options bar, specify the desired settings.
    - From the Brush drop-down list, select the desired brush size.
        - Drag the Master Diameter slider to set the desired brush size.
        - Or, double-click the Master Diameter text box and type the desired value to set the brush size.
    - Click the Enable Airbrush button.
    - In the Flow drop-down list, specify the desired flow value.
7. In the document window, drag along the image you want to apply the shadow effect to.
8. On the Layers palette, from the Blending Mode drop-down list, select the desired blending mode.
9. If necessary, link the new layer to its image layer.
    a. Select the new layer.
    b. Hold down Ctrl and select the image layer.
    c. Click the Link Layers icon at the bottom of the Layers palette to link the new layer to its image layer.

ACTIVITY 7-4

Painting Shadows in a New Layer

Data Files:

- this and that collectibles.psd

Before You Begin

1. Open the this and that collectibles.psd file from the C:\084563Data\Applying Colors\Activity 4\Starter folder.

Scenario:

You have got the perfect color that you wanted. You now decide to add shadows to some images in your document to make them appear realistic.

What You Do	How You Do It
1. **Create a new layer.**	a. **Hold down Alt and click the New Layer button.** b. In the New Layer dialog box, **type *blue flask shadow* and click OK.** c. On the Layers palette, **drag the blue flask shadow layer you just created and place it just below the blue flask layer.**

2. **Apply shadow effects.**

   a. If necessary, **select the Eyedropper tool.**

   b. In the This And That Collectibles.psd window, **click in the middle of the blue flask.**

   c. **Select the Brush tool.**

   d. On the Tool Options bar, **click the Brush drop-down list and drag the Master Diameter slider till it reaches 21.**

   e. On the Tool Options bar, **click the Enable Airbrush button.**

   f. On the Tool Options bar, **double-click in the Flow text box and type *10***

   g. In the This And That Collectibles.psd window, **drag along the bottom of the blue flask, and extend the shadow to the left of the flask's base.**

3. **Apply a blending mode and link the layers.**

   a. On the Layers palette, from the Blending Mode drop-down list, **select Multiply** to apply a lending mode.

   b. **Hold down Ctrl and select the Blue Flask layer.**

   c. At the bottom of the Layers palette, **click the Link Layers button.**

   d. **Notice that the Blue Flask and the Blue Flask Copy Layer are linked.**

   e. **Choose File→Save As.**

   f. If necessary, **navigate to the C:\084563Data\Applying Colors\Activity 4\Starter** folder.

   g. In the Save As dialog box, in the File Name text box, **type *my thisnthat collectibles* and click Save.**

   h. **Choose File→Close.**

ACTIVITY 7-5

Painting Shadows

Data Files:

- this and that collectibles.psd

Before You Begin

1. Open the this and that collectibles.psd file from the C:\084563Data\Applying Colors\Activity 5\Starter folder.

Scenario:

You are pleased with the shadow effect that you created. You want to add shadows to all the images in the document. You also decide to create each object's shadow in a separate layer and use black as the foreground color for the remaining shadows.

What You Do	How You Do It
1. **Add a shadow effect to the dog image.**	a. In the toolbox, **click the Default Foreground and Background Color button.**
	b. **Hold down Alt and click the New Layer button.**
	c. In the New Layer dialog box, **type *dog shadow* and click OK.**
	d. On the Layers palette, **drag the dog shadow layer you just created and place it just below the Dog layer.**
	e. In the This And That Collectibles.psd window, **drag along the bottom of the dog image and extend the shadow between the dog's front legs.**
	f. On the Layers palette, from the Blending Mode drop-down list, **select Multiply.**
	g. **Hold down Ctrl and select the dog layer.**
	h. At the bottom of the Layers palette, **click the Link Layers button** to link the layers.

2. **Add a shadow effect to the green flask image.**	a.	**Hold down Alt and click the New Layer button.**
	b.	In the New Layer dialog box, **type *green flask shadow* and click OK.**
	c.	On the Layers palette, **drag the green flask shadow layer and place it just below the green flask layer.**
	d.	**Add a shadow effect to the green flask image, and link the green flask shadow and green flask layers.**
3. **Add a shadow effect to the ball image.**	a.	**Hold down Alt and click the New Layer button.**
	b.	In the New Layer dialog box, **type *ball shadow* and click OK.**
	c.	On the Layers palette, **Drag the ball shadow layer you just created and place it just below the ball layer.**
	d.	**Add a shadow effect to the ball image, and link the ball shadow and ball layers.**

4. **Add a shadow effect to the base of the hand image.**

a. **Hold down Alt and click the New Layer button.**

b. In the New Layer dialog box, **type *hand shadow* and click OK.**

c. On the Layers palette, **click the triangle to the left of the Globe in Hand group.**

d. **Verify that it is a part of the Globe in Hand group.**

e. **Add a shadow effect to the hand image, and link the hand shadow and hand layers.**

f. **Choose File→Save As.**

g. In the Save As dialog box, in the File Name text box, **type *my collectibles* and click Save.**

h. **Choose File→Close.**

TOPIC C

Clone Image Areas with the Clone Stamp Tool

You have learned how to paint an image. You may need to edit the image to make it look more professional, and one of the most common image editing options is retouching an image. In addition, you can even recreate effects within an image, by creating clones. In this topic, you will use the Clone Stamp tool to sample parts of an image and paint it elsewhere.

Retouching images, and re-creating similar elements with an image can be time consuming. The tools and features of Photoshop CS2 take care of these painting needs in very little time.

The Clone Stamp Tool

The *Clone Stamp tool* is useful for duplicating parts of an image. This is used to correct blemishes or mistakes, in addition to copying one part of an image to another. Instead of making a selection and copying it, you can use the Clone Stamp tool to clone part of the image and paint it elsewhere.

Clone Image Areas

You can sample a part of an image and clone it to produce a duplicate of it using the Clone Stamp tool. To do so, you need to hold down the Alt key and click to sample the pixels that need to be cloned. After taking a sample of the image, you need to click and drag the mouse pointer in the area, where you want the cloned image to appear. As you drag to paint the cloned image area, a cross hair appears, which is the original reference point created by holding down Alt. The cross hair moves in order to clone different areas of the original image.

How to Clone Image Areas with the Clone Stamp Tool

Procedure Reference: Clone a Part of an Image with the Clone Stamp Tool

To clone a part of an image with the Clone Stamp tool:

1. Hold down Alt and click the part of the image that needs to be sampled for cloning.
2. Position the Clone Stamp tool cursor at the place where you want to duplicate the sample pixels.
3. Click and drag the mouse pointer back and forth to clone different areas with the sampled pixels.
4. If necessary, resample the reference point for the Clone Stamp tool to create a realistic effect.

ACTIVITY 7-6

Cloning Image Areas

Data Files:

- Kid Stuff.psd

Before You Begin

Open the Kid Stuff.psd file from the C:\084563Data\Applying Colors\Activity 6\Starter folder.

Scenario:

You have selected and moved the yellow E block in the Kid Stuff image. This edit has created a white space at the top row of the crate. You would like to clone parts of an empty slot to the right of the white space, and paint the sampled pixels into the white space to enhance the appearance of the crate.

What You Do	How You Do It
1. **Select a soft type brush tip.**	a. **Select the Zoom tool.** b. At the top of the crate, **click and drag the Zoom tool cursor over the white space and the empty slot to its right.** c. **Select the Brush tool.** d. On the Tool Options bar, **click the Brush Preset Picker drop-down arrow.** e. **Scroll down the Brush Preset Picker list box and double-click the Soft Round 27 Pixels brush tip.**
2. **Sample an area of the empty slot.**	a. On the Layers palette, **select the Background Layer.** b. **Select the Clone Stamp tool.** c. At the top row, **position the mouse pointer in the empty slot to the right of the white space, in a location that roughly corresponds to the top-right corner of the white space. Hold down Alt and click** to sample the image.

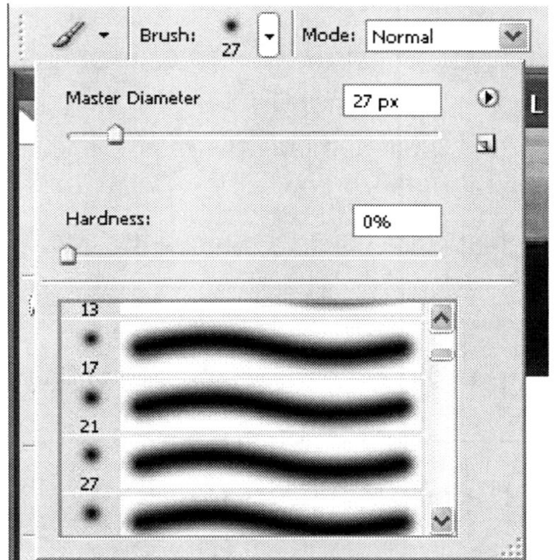

d. **Position the Clone Stamp tool mouse cursor at the top-right corner of the white area, and click and drag it to the left.** The pixels from the right slot are duplicated in the left slot as you drag.

e. **Drag back and forth across the white area to finish painting over it.**

3. **Resample the bottom area of the empty slot to create a realistic cloning effect.**

a. At the bottom of the empty slot at the right, **hold down Alt and click** to create a more realistic effect by resampling again.

b. **Click at the bottom-right corner of the white area in the empty slot at the right, and drag back and forth** to paint over it.

c. **Choose View→Fit On Screen.**

d. **Save the file as *Kid Stuff_cloned* and close the file.**

Lesson 7 Follow-up

In this lesson, you selected colors and painted images using the various color and painting tools in Photoshop. You also duplicated parts of an image using the Clone Stamp tool.

1. **Which painting tools will be the most useful to you in your work environment?**

2. **In you current project, give examples of instances when you used the Clone Stamp tool.**

Notes

LESSON 8

Enhancing Images with Text and Special Effects

Lesson Time
40 minutes

Lesson Objectives:

In this lesson, you will add type to an image, format it, and create special effects by applying filters.

You will:

- Create a type layer in which you will add and format type.
- Apply multiple effects to a type layer.
- Apply filter effects.
- Merge layers into a single layer, and merge all layers within an image.

Introduction

You have created and edited images in Photoshop. To make those images more professional, you need to enhance them. In this lesson, you will enhance images with text and special effects.

Photoshop provides numerous options for applying special effects to an image or to a layer within an image. Combining these options can result in a limitless variety of interesting effects that range from realistic to abstract. Photoshop also enables you to quickly enhance the quality of images with the addition of text effects.

TOPIC A

Create Type Layers

By now, you are reasonably comfortable with Photoshop and its different tools. However, in addition to creating and editing images, you can add text to your images. In this topic, you will create type layers.

While looking through advertisements and brochures, how many times have you been impressed with an illustration that has a catchy slogan laid out in attractive type? An image complimented with text is not only visually appealing but conveys the message more clearly.

Type Layers

Type layers are not composed of pixels, and they hold editable text to which you can apply formatting. Since Photoshop draws the type to the screen dynamically, you can resize the type to any size without it appearing jagged. This is different from when you resize pixel-based selections or layers.

Photoshop text must be contained within a type layer. Clicking or dragging in an image with the Type tool creates a new type layer. When you click with the Type tool to begin adding text, you can type to add text, and press Enter to add text in a new line.

Point and Paragraph Text

When you drag with the Type tool to add text, the area you drag becomes a type bounding box. Within this box, text will wrap itself automatically. Text that wraps within a bounding box is called *paragraph text*, and text that does not wrap within a bounding box is called *point text*. Point text is useful when you want each line of text to flow independent of other lines. Paragraph text is useful when you want the text to flow within a specified bounding box. You can resize the bounding box for paragraph text at any time.

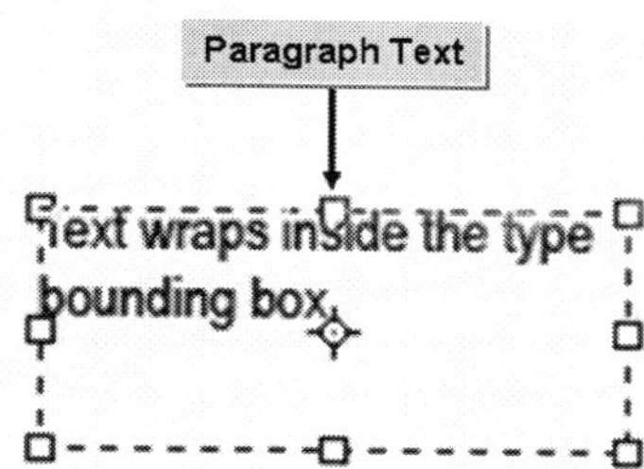

Convert Paragraph to Point Text

You can convert Paragraph text to Point text by choosing Layer→Type→Convert To Point Text. Similarly, you can convert Point text to Paragraph text by choosing Layer→Type→Convert to Paragraph Text.

The Edit Mode

When you click or drag to add text to a new type layer, the Type tool is in edit mode. When the Type tool is in edit mode, you can add, edit, and format text. However, you will be unable to perform other Photoshop operations. In order to exit edit mode and keep the changes you've just made to the Type layer, click the Commit Any Current Edits button on the Tool Options bar. If you decide that you do not want to keep the changes you have made in edit mode, you click the Cancel Any Current Edits button on the Tool Options bar. To select the Type tool and enter edit mode, you can double-click the layer thumbnail for the type layer.

Format Type

The text you added uses the current foreground color displayed in the Set foreground color icon. When the Type tool is selected, the Tool Options bar contains type formatting options, including a color selection box for choosing a new type color.

Photoshop CS2 includes What You See Is What You Get (WYSIWYG) font menus. In Photoshop CS2, that means typeface samples right in the Font menu, so you can choose your typeface visually instead of having to remember them by name. You can access the font menu on the Character palette or the Tool Options bar. If other types of fonts are installed in your system, the font on the font menu will then be followed by T1 for T1 fonts, TT for True Type fonts, or OT for Open Type fonts. T1 and TT fonts appear only in Adobe applications, while Open Type fonts were developed jointly by Adobe and Microsoft.

 Choose Edit→Check Spelling to spell check text. If Photoshop questions the spelling of a word, you can ignore the possible misspelling, choose the correct spelling from a list of suggestions, or add the word to Photoshop's dictionary. If you want to spell check text for a different language, choose the language from the Character palette.

Type layers can be created to add text to your images, using the Type tools. In addition to setting font type, type layers possess other properties, which include size, antialiasing, alignment, and color. The following table shows the different properties of type.

Option	Description
Rasterizing	Converts a type layer into a normal layer, so that text can be edited.
Changing orientation	Determines orientation by the direction of the type lines in relation to the window or bounding box they are contained in. For example, if a type is horizontal, the type flows from left to right.
Anti-aliasing	Allows the creation of smooth edges by partly filling in the pixels around the edge. Consequently, the edges are blended in with the background.
Converting between point type and paragraph type	Helps you control the character flow in a bounding box.

Type Formatting in Edit Mode

If you apply any type formatting while in edit mode, including changing type color, the formatting you choose will only apply to any type that is currently selected. If you are not in edit mode, the formatting you choose will apply to all the text in the selected type layer.

How to Create Type Layers

Procedure Reference: Add Text to a Document

To add text to a document:

1. Open the desired Photoshop File.
2. On the Layers palette, select the topmost layer.
3. Select the desired Type tool.
4. In the document window, position the mouse pointer and drag it to create a bounding box.
5. In the bounding box, type the desired text.
6. On the Tool Options bar, click the Commit button to commit changes made to the type layer.

Procedure Reference: Format Text in a Document

To format text in a document:

1. Open the desired Photoshop File.

2. On the Layers palette, select the text layer.
3. On the Tool Options bar, specify the format settings.
    - From the Font Family drop-down list, select the desired font.
    - From the Font Style drop-down list, select the desired style.
    - In the Font Size text box, specify the desired size.
        - — Double-click and type the desired value.
        - — Or, from the font size drop-down list, select the desired value.
    - From the Anti-aliasing Method drop-down list, select the desired antialias method to be used.
    - From the Align section, select the desired alignment style.
    - From the Text color text box, select the desired color.

ACTIVITY 8-1

Working with Text

Data Files:

- this and that collectibles.psd

Before You Begin

1. Open the this and that collectibles.psd file from the C:\084563Data\Enhancing Images with Text and Special Effects\Activity 1\Starter folder.

Scenario:

You have finished working with the images. You now want to add the name of your company to the document.

What You Do	How You Do It
1. **Add text to the image.**	a. On the Layers palette, **select the feather layer.**
	b. **Select the Horizontal Type tool.**

c. In the This And That Collectibles.psd window, **position the Type tool cursor about 1/2 inch below and to the right of the top-left corner of the image and drag down to the right, to just above the second closed finger in the hand.**

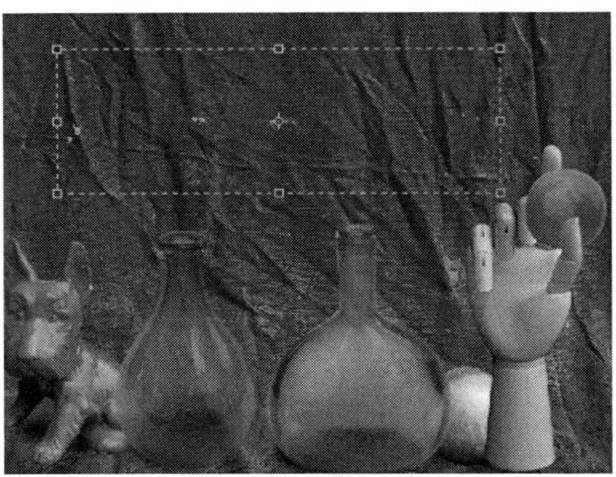

d. In the This And That Collectibles.psd window, in the bounding box, **type *This and That Collectibles***

e. On the Tool Options bar, **click the Commit button.**

f. **Notice that on the Layers palette, the type layer is now named This and That Collectibles and the bounding box and insertion points disappear.**

2. **Format the text.**

a. On the Tool Options bar, **click the Text Color box.**

b. In the Color Picker dialog box, **drag the mouse pointer in the color field and select the color whose RGB values are 146, 134, and 205 respectively.**

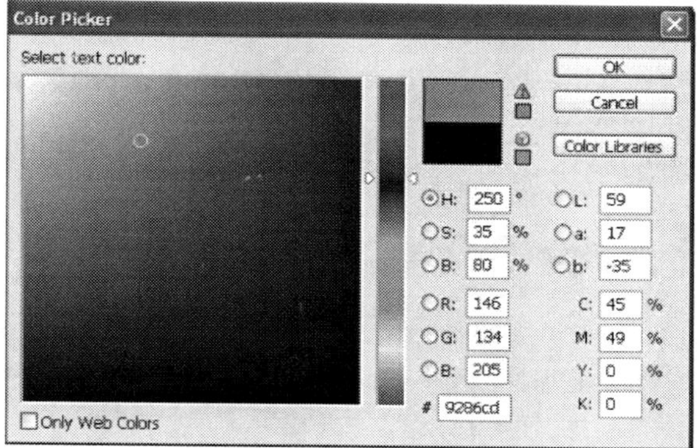

c. **Notice that light blue is applied to the text, and also appears in the Text Color box on the Tool Options bar.**

d. On the Tool Options bar, from the Font Family drop-down list, **select Comic Sans MS.**

e. On the Tool Options bar, from the Font Style drop-down list, **select Bold.**

f. On the Tool Options bar, in the Font Size field, **double-click, type *16* and press Enter.**

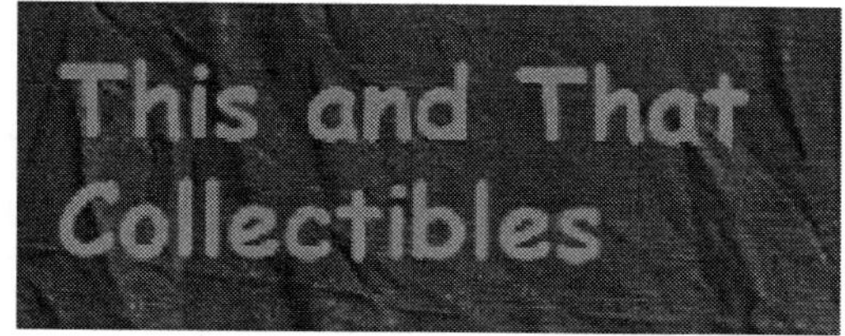

g. **Close the file and click No when prompted to save.**

TOPIC B

Apply Layer Effects

You are familiar with adding text to an image. But in addition to just typing text, you can apply a wide range of effects on them. In this topic, you will use layer effects to quickly apply highlight and shadow effects to a layer.

Text with special style effects compliments the graphics and makes it more appealing than a graphic with just plain text. Photoshop offers many built-in effects for layers, such as drop shadows, embossing, and beveling that can be applied to a type layer.

Layer Effects

Photoshop allows you to apply effects to layers such as shadows, embossing, beveling, cutouts, glows, and color fills. In Photoshop CS2, these processes are simplified dramatically. You can either apply layer effects either by double-clicking a layer to bring up the Layer Style dialog box, or you can use a layer style from the Layer Style button on the Layers palette.

On the Layer Style dialog box, you can check the check box of an effect to apply the style effect without viewing its options. If you click the effect name, you will view the effect's options as well as apply the effect to the image.

Edit Layer Effects

Each of the layer effects you apply is dynamic. For example, changes to the layer, such as editing type, automatically change the effect as well. Additionally, they are all editable, so you can modify the effects or combine multiple effects. Also, you can break any of the effects into component layers for greater flexibility while editing. After applying layer effects, you can continue to modify the layer. The layer effect will automatically get updated as necessary, making it possible for you to edit or modify text.

The Bevel and Emboss Effect

The Bevel and Emboss effect adds highlights and shadows to the image to create a 3-D look. The bevel and emboss effect has many options you can change to control the amount and type of bevel. These options can be accessed by clicking Layer→Layer Style→Bevel and Emboss. This will open up the Layer Style dialog box.

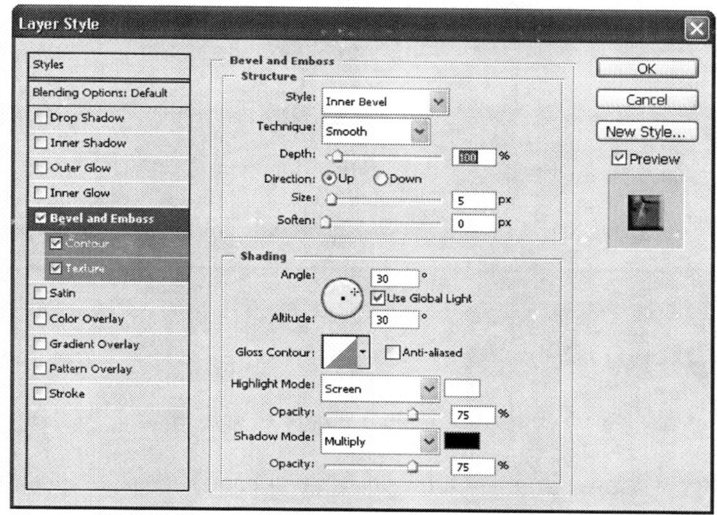

Bevel and Emboss Options

The Structure section of the Layer Style dialog box provides you with different options that affect the bevel settings.

Structure Option	Description
Style and Technique	This drop-down list contains choices for the style of the bevel.
Depth	This field controls the strength of a shading effect. A higher depth percentage increases the shading applied to the layer.
Direction	These options, Up and Down, allow you to specify whether the bevel appears raised from a surface or carved into a surface.
Size text box	This field controls the size of the bevel.
Soften text box	This field blurs the shading.

The Shading section within the Layer Style dialog box provides options for controlling the light source, and how it interacts with the layer to create shadows and highlights.

Shading Option	Description
Global Light check box	This option causes the light source angle you set to apply to other layer effects in the image. This is done so that it appears as if the same light source is shining throughout the image.

Shading Option	Description
Altitude	This field controls the altitude of the light source.
Gloss Contour drop-down	This drop-down list allows you to apply a variety of contour effects to the bevel/emboss effect.
Anti-aliased check box	This check box allows you to smoothen the contour effect.
Other options	The remaining options in the Shading section allow you to choose blending modes and opacity values for the highlights and shadows.

The Outer Glow Effect

The Outer Glow effect adds a glow to the outside edges of the image. The Outer Glow effect has many options you can change to control the amount and type of glow. To control the Outer Glow effect, click Layer→Layer Style→Outer Glow. You can then make changes in the Layer Style dialog box.

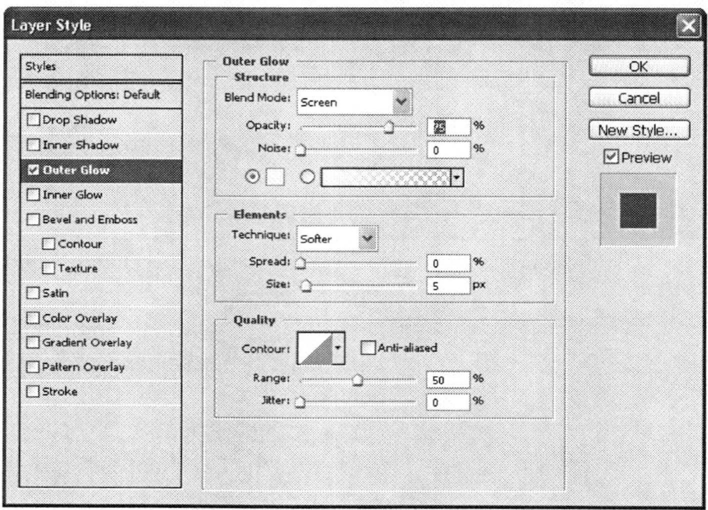

On selecting the Outer Glow option, the Layer Style dialog box displays three sections that provide various options to manipulate the Outer Glow effect.

Option	Description
Structure section	In the Structure section, by default, the Blend Mode for the glow is set to Screen, which is appropriate since the Screen mode multiplies the inverse of the colors being blended, creating a lighter color than either of the original colors. This creates the appearance of a glow. Increasing the value in the Noise field adds noise to the opacity, creating a more pixelated appearance instead of a smooth glow.
Elements section	In the Elements section, the Technique drop-down list allows you to choose how the glow effect is created. The default Softer option creates the glow as a blur, which loses detailed features at larger sizes. The Precise option creates the glow using a distance measurement technique, which preserves detailed features better than the Softer option. Increasing the Spread percentage enlarges the size of the shapes the blur is created from.
Quality section	In the Quality section, the Contour drop-down list can apply transparent rings within and around the glow. The Range field allows you to control the part of the glow the contour is applied to. The Jitter field affects how a gradient's color and opacity are applied.

How to Apply Layer Effects

Procedure Reference: Apply Layer Effects using Blending Options

To apply layer effects using blending options:

1. Open the required Photoshop file.
2. On the Layers palette, right-click the layer to which the effect has to be applied and choose Blending Options.
3. From the Blending Options (Default) section of the Layer Style dialog box, select the desired effect.
4. In the Layer Style dialog box, change the desired structural and shading settings and click OK.

Procedure Reference: Add ™ Symbol to the Layer

To add ™ symbol to a layer:

1. Open the required Photoshop file.
2. On the Layers palette, select the Text layer.
3. On the Layers palette, double-click the layer thumbnail of the text layer.
4. In the image window, position the insertion point where the symbol is to be inserted.

5. Hold down Alt and simultaneously on the numeric keyboard, hold the numbers 0,1,5, and 3 and press enter.

ACTIVITY 8-2

Applying Layer Effects

Data Files:

- this and that collectibles.psd

Before You Begin

1. Open the this and that collectibles.psd file from the C:\084563Data\Enhancing Images with Text and Special Effects\Activity 2\Starter folder.

Scenario:

The text that you added to the document looks simple and flat. You want to make it stand out and appear noticeable.

What You Do	How You Do It
1. **Apply the Bevel And Emboss effect to the text.**	a. On the Layers palette, **(right) click the This and That Collectibles layer and select Blending Option.**
	b. In the Blending Options (Default) section of the Layer Style dialog box, **click the words Bevel And Emboss.**
	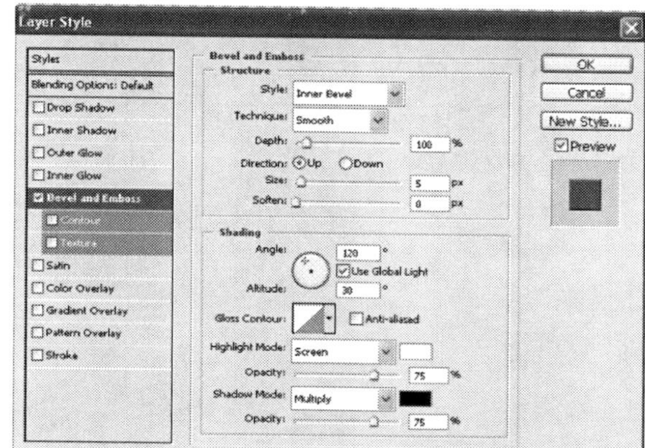
	c. Verify the Preview check box is checked, and **move the Layer Style dialog box down so that the This and That Collectibles text is visible in the background.**
	d. In the Layer Style dialog box, in the Structure section, from the Technique drop-down list, **select Chisel Soft.**
	e. In the Structure section, **drag the Size slider till it reaches 3.**
	f. In the Structure section, **drag the Soften slider till it reaches 3.**
	g. In the Shading section, **double-click in the Angle text box and type** - ***8***

2. **Apply the Outer Glow effect to the text.**

a. In the Blending Options (Default) section of the Layer Style dialog box, **click the words Outer Glow.**

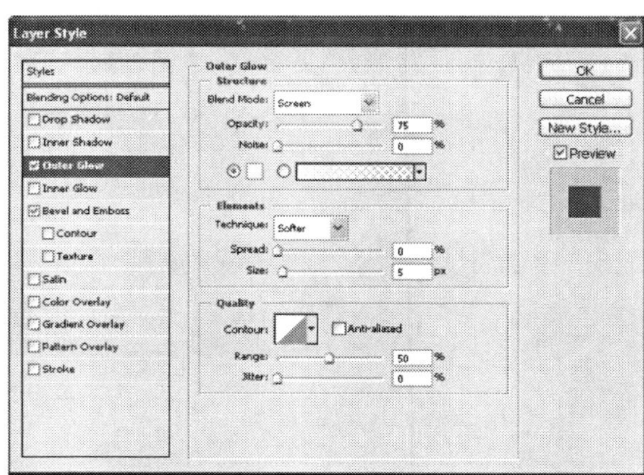

b. In the Layer Style dialog box, in the Structure section, **drag the Opacity slider to a value of 35%.**

c. If necessary, in the Elements section, **drag the Spread slider to a value of 0.**

d. In the Elements section, **drag the Size slider to a value of 33% and click OK.**

3. **Add the ™ symbol to the text.**

a. On the Layers palette, in the This and That Collectibles layer, **click the triangle to the right of the *f* symbol** to expand it.

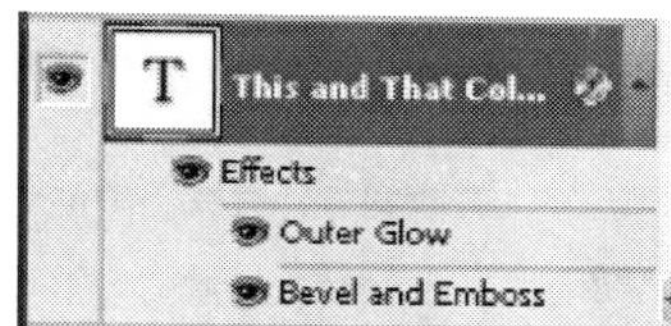

b. On the Layers palette, in the This and That Collectibles layer, **double-click the layer thumbnail of the type layer.**

c. **Notice that a bounding box appears around the text, indicating that you are in edit mode.**

d. In the This And That Collectibles window, **click at the end of the text** to position the insertion point.

e. **Hold down Alt and simultaneously on the numeric keyboard, hold down the numbers 0,1,5, and 3 and press enter.**

f. **Notice that the ™ symbol is now added to the text.**

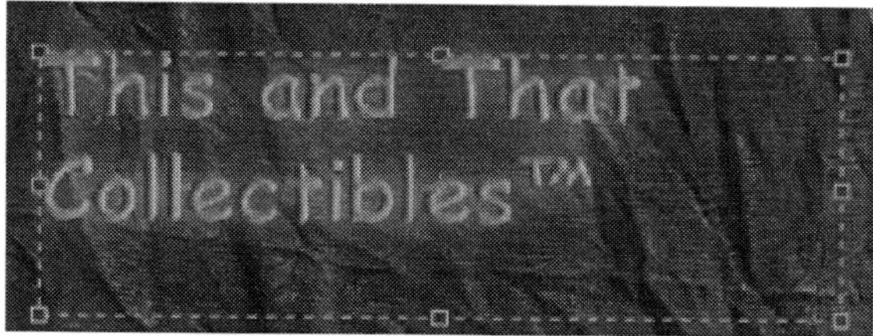

g. **Choose File→Save As.**

h. If necessary, **navigate to the C:\084563Data\Enhancing Images with Text and Special Effects\Activity 2\Starter** folder.

i. In the Save As dialog box, in the File Name text box, **type *my collectibles text* and click Save.**

j. **Choose File→Close.**

TOPIC C

Work with Filters

You have used a few of Photoshop's features to enhance text and images. Photoshop also has a variety of filters to help enhance an image. In this topic, you will apply filters to enhance an image.

The filters available in Photoshop expand your ability to enhance images without spending a lot of time doing it. The four new filters available in Photoshop CS2 will expand your image editing skills and spark your creativity.

Filters

Filters are features in Photoshop that allow you to change the appearance of images. With filters, images can be altered, retouched, polished, or given different lighting.

Photoshop provides dozens of filters, divided into 14 submenus in the Filter menu. You can apply filters to the active layer, or to selected areas of an image. Filters can be used to create original textures and effects, or to alter existing images or artwork. By combining Photoshop's filters, you can create a nearly limitless variety of effects. The Filter Gallery is divided into three panes. The left pane displays a preview; the middle pane displays the selected filter, and the right pane displays the settings for the filter. You can view the original image without the effect by clicking the Eye icon in the lower-right section of the dialog box.

New Filters in Photoshop CS2

Photoshop CS2 offers four new filters that will expand your image editing skills.

Filter	Description
Reduce Noise filter	Reduces noise in an image while maintaining image detail and edge sharpness.
Smart Sharpen filter	Enables greater control over sharpening rules, with increased edge detection. Focuses on sharpening the shadows and highlights of an image.
Vanishing Point filter	Defines perspective planes, allowing you to correct and edit perspective within an image.
Lens Correction filter	Fixes common wide angle and telephoto lens flaws, such as barrel and pincushion distortion.

The Filter Gallery

The Filter Gallery lets you apply many filters to a single image. It also allows you to use a filter on an image, more than once. In the Filter Gallery dialog box, you can see a preview of how the filter will be applied on the image. In addition, you can view thumbnails on the function of each filter, and rearrange and change filter settings.

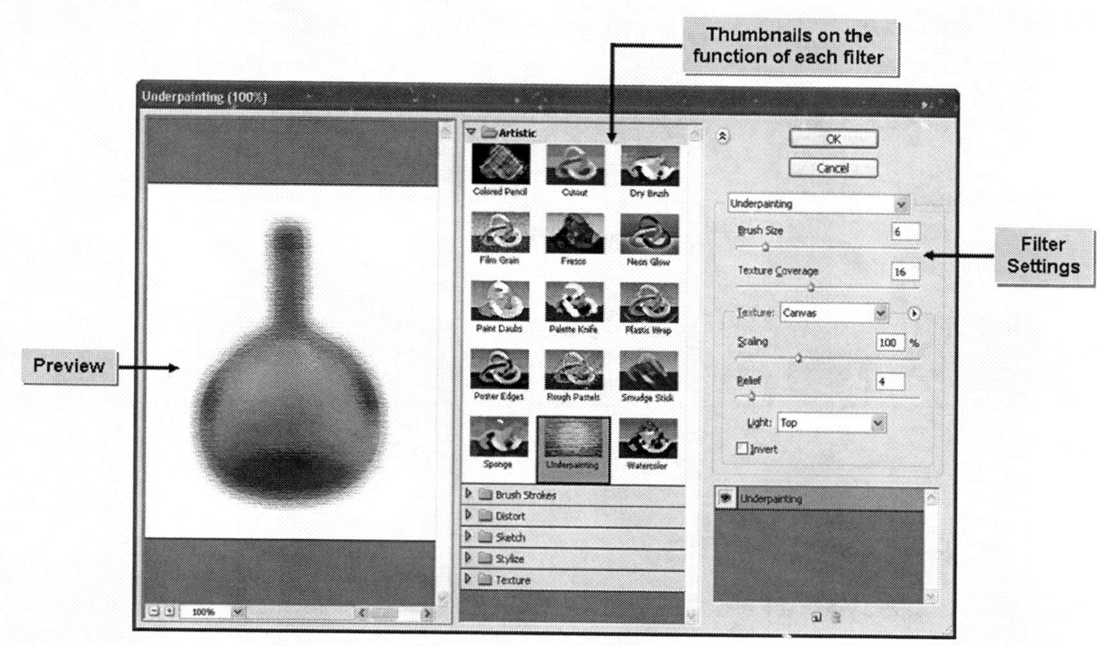

The Glass Filter

The Glass filter creates an effect that looks like glass. The Distortion text box controls how significantly the original layer pixels are distorted, and the Smoothness text box controls how smooth the final image appears. A lower, smooth setting results in a more jagged, broken up distortion. You can choose from a variety of preset glass textures, or you can load a custom texture created by you or someone else.

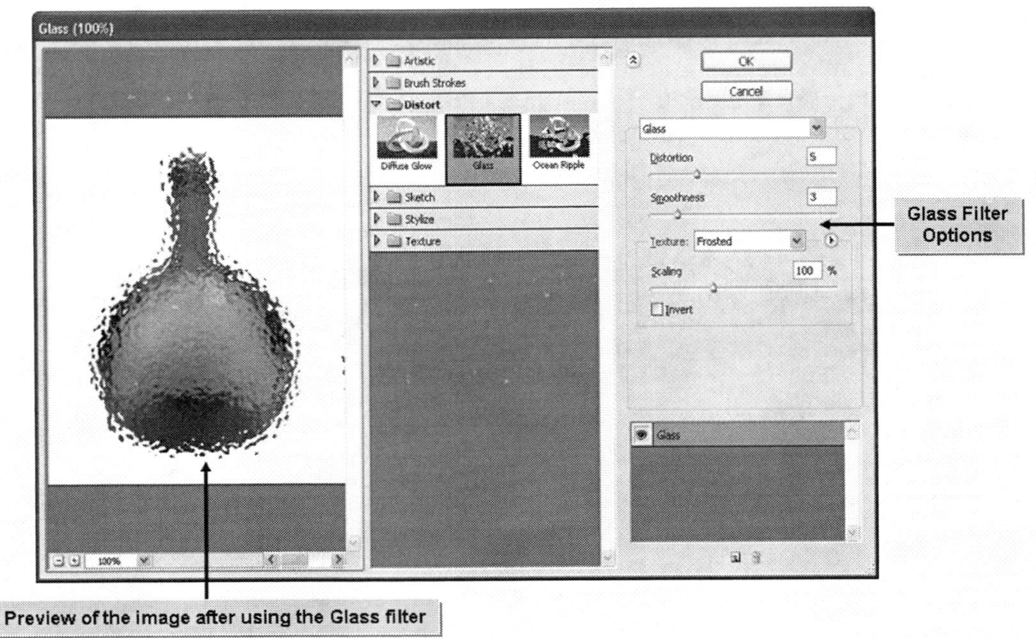

The Fade Command

After applying a filter, you can use the *Fade command* on the Edit menu to change the opacity and blending mode of the filter, changing how the filter impacts the image. The Fade command can also be used to change the opacity and blending mode of a painting tool, erasing tool, or color adjustment. The Fade command allows you to apply blending modes and opacity to these types of effects as though they existed on their own layer. .

How to Work with Filters

Procedure Reference: Apply the Glass Filter

To apply the Glass filter:

1. Open the required Photoshop file.
2. Select the layer to which the filter effect is to be applied.
3. Choose Filter→Distort→Glass.
4. In the Glass dialog box, in the third section, adjust the desired settings.
    - Specify the distortion settings.
    - Specify the desired smoothness setting.
    - From the Texture drop-down list, select the desired texture.
    - Specify the scaling setting.
5. Choose Edit→Fade Glass.
6. If necessary, in the Fade dialog box, specify the opacity settings.
    - Drag the Opacity slider, to select the desired distortion setting.
    - Double-click the Opacity text box and type the desired distortion setting value.

7. In the Fade dialog box, from the Mode drop-down list select the desired blending mode and click OK.

Procedure Reference: Apply the Vanishing Point Filter

To apply the Vanishing Point filter:

1. Open the required Photoshop file.
2. Copy the image to be placed in the editing plane.
3. Choose Filter→Vanishing Point.
4. Click the four corners of a perspective plane or object in the image to create the editing plane.
5. Paste and move the image to be applied to the editing plane.
6. Click OK to apply the Vanishing Point filter.

Procedure Reference: Apply the Add Noise Filter

To add noise to an image:

1. Open the required Photoshop file.
2. Choose Filter→Noise→Add Noise.
3. Adjust the percentage of noise and select the Distribution option.
   - Select the Uniform option distribute color values of noise using random numbers.
   - Select the Gaussian option to distribute color values of noise along a bell-shaped curve.
4. Click OK to apply the Noise filter.

Procedure Reference: Apply the Reduce Noise Filter

To apply the Reduce Noise filter:

1. Open the required Photoshop file.
2. Choose Filter→Noise→Reduce Noise.
3. Adjust filter settings.
   - Adjust the Strength setting to control the amount of luminance.
   - Adjust the Preserve Details setting to preserve the texture of images or objects.
   - Adjust the Reduce Color Noise setting to remove random color pixels.
   - Adjust the Sharpen Details setting to sharpen the image.
4. Click OK to apply the Reduce Noise filter.

Procedure Reference: Apply the Smart Sharpen Filter

To apply the Smart Sharpen filter:

1. Open the required Photoshop file.
2. Choose Filter→Sharpen→Smart Sharpen.
3. Adjust filter settings.

- Adjust the Amount setting to set the amount of sharpening.
- Adjust the Radius setting to determine the number of pixels affected due to sharpening.
- Adjust the Remove setting to set the sharpening algorithm.
- Adjust the Angle setting to set the direction of movement.
- Select the More Accurate setting for finer removal of blurring.

4. Click OK to apply the Smart Sharpen filter.

Procedure Reference: Apply the Lens Correction Filter

To apply the Lens Correction filter:

1. Open the required Photoshop file.
2. Choose Filter→Distort→Lens Correction.
3. Adjust filter settings.
    - Adjust the Remove Distortion setting to remove distortion.
    - Adjust the Chromatic Aberration setting to remove color fringes along the edges of the objects.
    - Adjust the Vignette setting to brighten the corners of the image.
    - Select the Transform option to scale the image.
4. Click OK to apply the Lens Correction Filter.

Procedure Reference: Apply a Filter from the Filter Gallery

To apply a filter from the Filter Gallery:

1. Open the required Photoshop file.
2. Choose Filter→Filter Gallery.
3. Select a filter name and expand the category to display the thumbnail list.
4. Click the desired thumbnail and apply any desired settings.
5. Click OK.

ACTIVITY 8-3

Applying Glass Filter

Data Files:

- this and that collectibles.psd

Before You Begin

1. Open the this and that collectibles.psd file from the C:\084563Data\Enhancing Images with Text and Special Effects\Activity 3\Starter folder.

Scenario:

You are still not happy with the effects in some of the images in the document. You decide to apply a filter effect to make the images appear realistic.

What You Do	How You Do It
1. **Apply the Glass filter to the green flask image.**	a. On the Layers palette, **select the green flask copy layer.**
	b. **Choose Filter→Distort→Glass.**
	c. **Verify that in the third section, the distortion section shows a value of 5.**
	d. In the Glass 100% dialog box, in the third section, at the bottom-right corner of the Glass dialog box, **click the Eye icon next to the Glass filter preview.** 
	e. **Notice that the green flask in the preview appears with no distortion.**

2. **Specify filter settings.**

a. In the Glass 100% dialog box, in the third section, at the bottom-right corner of the Glass dialog box, **click the box next to the Glass filter preview.**

b. In the third section, **drag the Smoothness slider to a value of 2.**

c. If necessary, in the third section, from the Texture drop-down list, **select Frosted.**

d. In the third section, **drag the Scaling slider to a value of 60% and click OK.**

e. **Choose Edit→Fade Glass.**

f. In the Fade dialog box, **drag the Opacity slider to a value of 75%.**

g. From the Mode drop-down list, **select Darken and click OK.**

h. **Close the file and click No when prompted to Save.**

ACTIVITY 8-4

Applying Vanishing Point Filter

Data Files:

- art_cube.psd
- art_cube_text.psd

Before You Begin

1. Open the art_cube.psd and art_cube_text.psd files from the C:\084563Data\Enhancing Images with Text and Special Effects\Activity 4\Starter folder.

Scenario:

You are working on a presentation that requires you to place a text layer on an image with an angled perspective. You realized that adjusting it manually could take a long time. You will use the Vanishing Point filter to define the area and place the text layer so it appears correctly.

What You Do	How You Do It
1. **Copy the image.**	a. **Choose Window→Art_Cube_Text.psd** to make it active. b. **Choose Select→All.** c. **Choose Edit→Copy.** You are copying the text here to paste it in the next step. Once you have entered Filter mode, you can go back to Photoshop without cancelling the filter.
2. **Apply the Vanishing Point filter.**	a. **Choose Window→Art_Cube.psd.** b. **Choose Filter→ Vanishing Point.** c. In the cube image, **click the upper-left corner.** d. **Click the upper-right corner.** e. **Click the lower-right corner.**

f. **Click the lower-left corner.**

g. **Press Ctrl+V to paste the copied image.**

h. In the top of the image box, **drag the text into the centre of the cube image and double-click it.**

i. In the Vanishing Point dialog box, **click OK.**

j. **Choose File→Save As.**

k. In the Save As dialog box, in the Name text box, **type *my_art_cube* and click Save.**

l. **Choose File→Close All.**

TOPIC D

Merge Layers and Flatten Images

You are familiar with applying filters to images. Photoshop provides you with the option of applying filter effects to images with multiple layers easily. In this topic, you will merge layers and flatten images.

When working on images with multiple layers, it can be tedious to apply the desired filter effect to one layer at a time. Just as creating layers simplifies your work process, merging layers helps you to apply a filter effect to the entire file.

Flatten Images

Photoshop filters can apply to only one layer at a time. Therefore, if you want to apply a filter to multiple layers, you must first merge the layers into a single layer. This is known as flattening the image. Merging layers or flattening an image is also useful for reducing the file size of an image. File size is based on the number of pixels in the image, and combining layers or flattening the image reduces the number of pixels in the image, as pixels on lower layers are replaced by pixels that overlap them on higher layers.

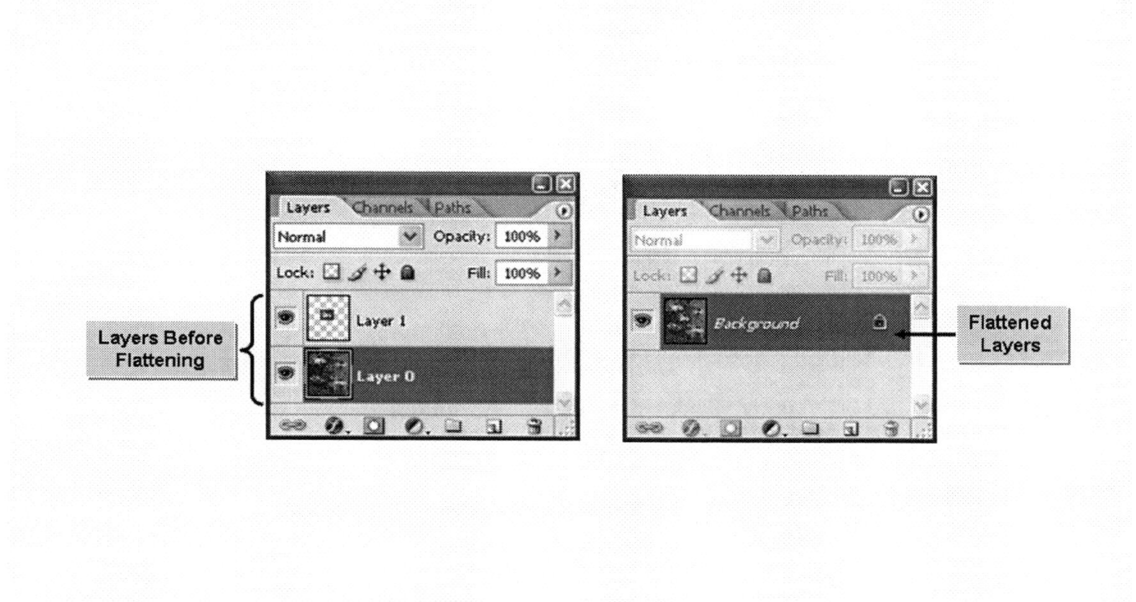

 To reduce all layers in a Photoshop image down to one Background layer.

Save a Copy

When merging layers or flattening an image, it is a good idea to first save a copy of the image that includes all the layers. That way, if you ever need to return to the image with all layers intact, you will have a copy.

Merge Layers

You can use the Merge Down and Merge Visible commands from the Layers palette menu to merge layers in an image. You can also use the Flatten Image command to merge all the layers into a single layer. Before merging layers, select the appropriate layer. If you want to merge layers in a group, you must then select the group on the Layers palette, and choose Merge Group. If you want to merge linked layers, then you must select one of the linked layers, and choose Merge Down. To merge a layer with the layer below it, select the top layer and choose Merge Down. Then, the selected layer's name will be used for the merged layers. To merge visible layers, hide any layers you do not want to merge, and then choose Merge Visible.

How to Merge and Flatten Images

Procedure Reference: Merge Layers

To merge layers:

1. Open the desired Photoshop file.
2. On the Layers palette, select the layers to be merged.
   a. Select a layer.
   b. Hold down Ctrl and select the layers to be merged.
3. From the Layers palette menu, choose the desired merging method.
   - Choose Merge Group, to merge layers in a group.
   - Choose Linked Layers and Merge Layers, to merge linked layers.
   - Choose Merge Down, to merge all layers into a single layer.

Procedure Reference: Flatten Images

To flatten images:

1. Open the desired Photoshop file.
2. On the Layers palette, select the layer to be flattened.
3. From the Layers palette menu, choose Flatten Image.
4. If necessary, choose Filter→Blur→Blur to soften the image.

ACTIVITY 8-5

Merging and Flattening Images

Data Files:

- this and that collectibles.psd

Before You Begin

1. Open the this and that collectibles.psd file from the C:\084563Data\Enhancing Images with Text and Special Effects\Activity 5\Starter folder.

Scenario:

You have created multiple layers. Now you have two problems, one you are finding it difficult to work with multiple layers and two the file size is becoming bigger. You decide to merge and flatten the layers in the document before continuing to work with it.

What You Do	How You Do It
1. **Replicate the file.**	a. **Choose File→Save As.**
	b. In the Save As dialog box, in the File Name text box, **type *this and that merged.psd* and click Save.**

2. **Merge Groups.**

a. On the Layers palette, **scroll down and select the Globe in Hand group.**

b. On the Layers palette menu, **choose Merge Group.**

3. **Merge the linked layers.**

a. On the Layers palette, **scroll up and select the Blue Flask layer.**

b. **Notice that the link icon appears in the Link column for the blue flask shadow layer, indicating that the two layers are linked.**

c. From the Layers palette menu, **choose Select Linked Layers.**

d. From the Layers palette menu, **choose Merge Layer.**

4. **Unlink and merge the layers using the Merge Down option.**

   a. On the Layers palette, **select the Green Flask Copy layer.**

   b. At the bottom of the Layers palette, **click the Link Layers button.**

   c. On the Layers palette menu, **choose Merge Down.**

   d. **Notice that the selected Green Flask copy layer is now merged with the Green Flask layer.**

   e. **Choose Edit→Undo Merge Down.**

5. **Flatten the image.**

a. **Notice that the image file size displayed on the right side of the File Information box at the bottom of the window.**

b. From the Layers palette menu, **choose Flatten Image.**

c. In the Adobe Photoshop warning box, **click OK.**

d. **Notice that all layers are now merged to the Background layer and the File Information box indicates a much smaller file size.**

e. **Choose Filter→Blur→Blur** to soften the image.

f. **Close the file and click No when prompted to save.**

Lesson 8 Follow-up

In this lesson, you enhanced images with text and special effects.

1. **When selecting filter types, which effects have been most beneficial to you? Why?**

2. **Do you feel that adding text to graphics enhances the image?**

Notes

LESSON 9
Adjusting Images

Lesson Time
25 minutes

Lesson Objectives:

In this lesson, you will adjust an image's brightness, contrast, hue, and saturation.

You will:

- Adjust the brightness and contrast of the images using adjustment layers.
- Lighten or darken image areas using the toning tools.
- Change specific colors in an image using the Hue/Saturation command.

Introduction

You have created image composites, and applied colors and filter effects to layers. In addition to focusing on the color and mode alone, you must also adjust the contrast and brightness levels in an image to perfect it. In this lesson, you will adjust the brightness of an image, its contrast; hue, and saturation.

Factors such as an image's brightness, contrast, hue, and saturation play an important role in enhancing the quality of an image. Photoshop lets you lighten an image, and increase its contrast, darken specific areas, and change the hue and saturation of certain colors.

TOPIC A

Create Levels Adjustment Layers

You have now worked with layers, and the effects you can use on them. But while working on an image, you may first want to test the effect of brightness, contrast, or color modifications, before making permanent changes to the image. In this topic, you will create adjustment layers.

Photoshop allows you to create adjustment layers that let you adjust an image's brightness, contrast, and color without permanently modifying any existing pixel values in the image.

The Levels Command

The Levels command allows you to adjust the shadows, highlights, and midtones of an image independently and with precision. The Levels dialog box is used for precise adjustments, because it offers much more control in adjusting brightness and contrast than the Brightness/ Contrast dialog box.

It allows you to adjust the highlights and shadows of the image while leaving the midtones as is. The Shadow/ Highlight command is useful for correcting overexposed or underexposed areas of an image.

Brightness is the relative lightness or darkness of the color. Images can be classified based on brightness, as shadows, highlights, and midtones. The shadow refers to the darkest area in an image. The highlight is the brightest area in an image, and the midtone is the area of an image that falls between the lightest and darkest points, usually around 50 percent brightness in an image. Contrast refers to the difference between light and dark pixels.

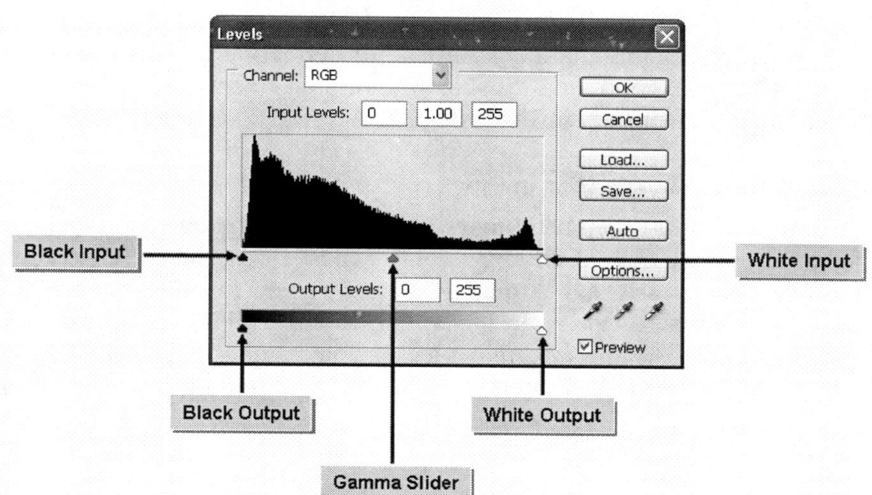

The output levels slider at the bottom of the Levels dialog box is used to reduce the contrast in the image. Sliding the left slider to the right reduces shadows, making the deepest blacks appear lighter. Similarly, moving the right slider to the left reduces highlights, making the brightest whites darker. Input levels enable you to increase contrasts in the highlights and shadows. Unlike the output levels sliders, the input levels sliders allow you to adjust the midtones of an image.

 The brightness of an image through the midtones.

Histogram

A histogram Illustrates the number of pixels at each brightness level. Dark parts of the image are represented on the left, and light parts on the right. You can also use the Histogram palette to view a histogram for the image. The histogram updates as you make changes in the image.

Above the input levels sliders is a histogram representing the image. The dark parts of the image are represented on the left, and the light parts on the right. The height of each bar indicates the number of pixels at that brightness level.

The triangles below the histogram tell you where the black point or shadows, white point or highlights, and gamma or midtones, are located. Any pixel to the left of the black point is pure black, and any pixel to the right of the white point is pure white. The black point and white point are originally at either end of the spectrum. Moving the black point and white point sliders inward spreads the range of brightness of the pixels in the image, thereby increasing the contrast.

Adjusting Gamma Values

If an image is too dark, you can adjust the gamma, the brightness of an image through the midtones, to lighten the image without lightening the shadow areas or making the highlights too bright. If you have to make gamma adjustments of over 1.20, you should consider rescanning the image instead of correcting it. This is suggested as it is always better to get a good scan to which minor adjustments can be made, as opposed to making larger adjustments in Photoshop.

Brightness/Contrast vs. Levels Command

The Brightness/Contrast command may seem to be the obvious choice in controlling the brightness and contrast of an image, but in most cases, the Levels command is far superior. The Brightness/Contrast dialog box allows you to adjust the brightness and contrast for a selection or the entire layer, but does not allow you to isolate pixels and adjust the highlights, shadows, or midtones. If you use the Brightness/Contrast dialog box to brighten the image highlights, the shadows and midtones will be brightened as well.

Levels Dialog Box

The Levels dialog box allows you to adjust the individual Red, Green, and Blue channels separately to adjust the color balance. You can select Red, Green, or Blue from the Channels drop-down list on the Levels dialog box to adjust any one of those channels individually. To adjust all image colors together, select RGB from the Channels drop-down list.

Adjustment Layers

The *adjustment layer* is a special type of layer used for making adjustments to the tonality of an image without changing the pixels on any existing layers. For example, you could use a levels adjustment layer to brighten or darken an image. Adjustment layers let you experiment with brightness, contrast, and color modifications without permanently modifying pixel values in the image. This is important, because if you apply brightness, contrast, and color modifications directly to the image pixels, those pixels are permanently changed. If you then need to further adjust the brightness, contrast, and the color of the image, work with modified pixels, rather than the original pixels in the image.

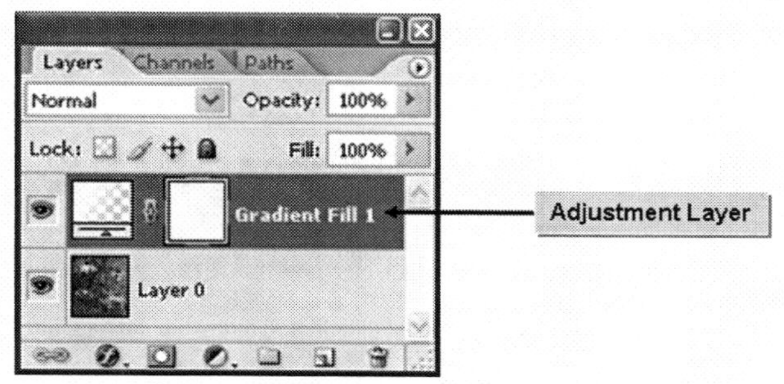

Adjustment layers appear on the Layers palette, and are manipulated in similar ways to image layers. You can create adjustment layers for applying a variety of image adjustment commands, including the Brightness/Contrast and Levels commands. Choose Layer→New Adjustment Layer to select the new adjustment layer from a list.

Adjustment Layer Actions

The following table lists the actions that can be performed to simplify the process of working with adjustment layers.

Option	Description
Group	You can choose to group the adjustment layer with the layer directly below it, by checking the Use Previous Layer to Create Clipping Mask check box on the New Layer dialog box.
Adjust	You can further adjust an adjustment layer at any time by double-clicking the layer thumbnail to the far left of the layer's name on the Layers palette.
Create	You can create a new adjustment layer by clicking the New Adjustment Layer button at the bottom of the Layers palette. The New Layer dialog box does not appear when you use the New Adjustment Layer button, unless you hold down Alt as you select it.

Application of Adjustment Layers

If you brighten an image too much, bright pixels of various shades may all be converted to pure white. Later, you will be unable to apply adjustments that bring back the original color variations that are now uniform in color, as pure white pixels. When using an adjustment layer, the color and contrast changes reside within the adjustment layer. This is like a photographer's filter over a camera lens that is used to affect the underlying image. One image can have several different adjustment layers to perform different color correction functions.

How to Create Levels Adjustment Layers

Procedure Reference: Create a New Adjustment Layer

To create a new adjustment layer:

1. Open the desired Photoshop file.
2. Select the layer for which an adjustment layer is to be created.
3. Choose Layer→New Adjustment Layer.
4. Select the desired Adjustment Layer option.
5. In the New Layer dialog box, in the Name text box, specify the name for the layer.
6. If necessary, choose Layer→Create Clipping Mask to link the adjustment layer to the layer below it.
7. On the Layers palette, double-click the Layer Thumbnail to the far left of the layer's name and specify the desired settings.

New Adjustment Layer Options

The following table lists the adjustment layer options that you can choose while creating a new adjustment layer.

Options	Description
Levels	Allows you to specify highlight, shadow and midtones values.
Curves	Allows to specify the intensity values of a pixel on a scale of 0–255.
Color Balance	Allows you to increase or decrease a specific color in the image.
Brightness/Contrast	Allows you to specify the brightness and contrast settings in an image.
Hue/Saturation	Allows you to specify the Hue, Saturation and Lightness (HSL) values.
Selective Color	Allows you to adjust the components within a specific color.
Channel Mixer	Allows you to edit color values by mixing them with other channels.
Gradient Map	Allows you to specify gradient settings.

Options	Description
Photo Filter	Allows you to simulate the effect of a filter in front of a camera lens.
Invert	Allows you to create inverted adjustment layers that do not have any options.
Threshold	Allows you to specify a threshold level.
Posterize	Allows you to specify the tonal level for a color channel.

ACTIVITY 9-1

Creating a Levels Adjustment Layer

Data Files:

- this and that collectibles.psd

Before You Begin

1. Open the this and that collectibles.psd file from the C:\084563Data\Adjusting Images\Activity 1\Starter folder.

Scenario:

You want to make some changes to the ball image. However, you only want to experiment with brightness, contrast, and color modifications without permanently modifying pixel values in the image.

What You Do	How You Do It
1. **Create a new adjustment layer.**	a. On the Layers palette, **select the Ball layer.** b. **Choose Layer→New Adjustment Layer→Levels.** c. In the New Layer dialog box, in the Name field, **type *levels* and click OK.**

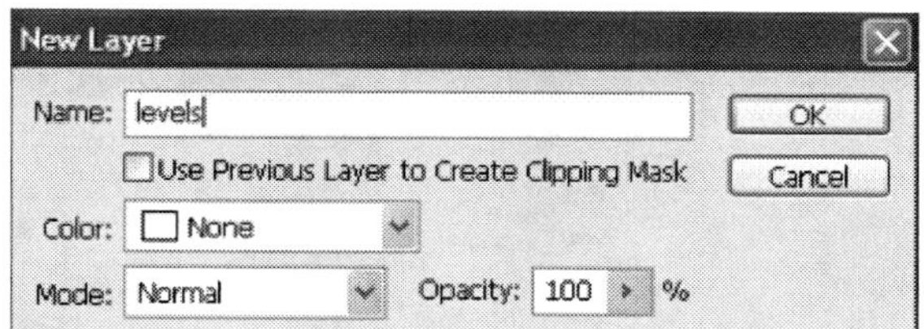

d. At the bottom of the Levels dialog box, **click and drag the white output slider to the left till it reaches 200.**

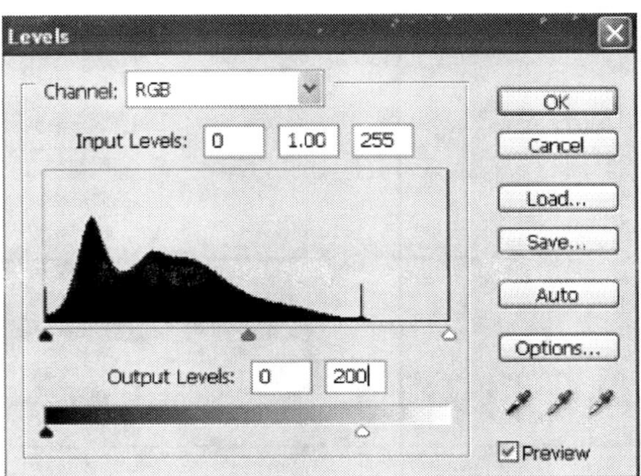

e. **Notice that the adjustment affects several layers in the image, and not just the Ball layer.**

f. **Click and drag the white output slider to the left till it reaches 0.**

g. **Click and drag the black output slider to the right till it reaches 255.**

h. **Notice that the affected layers display as negatives.**

i. **Return the black output slider to it's original positions and click OK.**

---

2. **Group the adjustment layer with the ball layer.**

a. **Choose Layer→Create Clipping Mask.**

b. **Notice that the levels adjustment layer is now grouped with the Ball layer below it. The adjustment layer's effects are now applied only to the Ball layer, and a downward-pointing arrow indicates that it is grouped with the layer below.**

---

3. **Adjust the input levels.**

a. On the Layers palette, **double-click the Layer Thumbnail to the far left of the levels layer's name.**

b. In the Levels dialog box, **drag the black input slider to the right till it reaches 30.**

c. **Click and drag the gamma slider to the right till it reaches 0.10.**

d. **Notice that more pixels fall below middle gray, resulting in a darker image.**

e. **Click and drag the gamma slider to the right till it reaches 0.90.**

f. **Notice that ball image is slightly darker.**

g. In the Layer Visibility column of the Levels layer, **click the Eye icon.**

h. **Notice that the ball becomes brighter.**

i. In the Levels layer, **click in the Layer Visibility column** to restore the adjustment.

j. **Choose File→Save As.**

k. If necessary, navigate to the C:\084563Data\Adjusting Images\Activity 1\Starterfolder.

l. In the Save As dialog box, in the File Name text box, **type *my collectibles adjustment* and click Save.**

m. **Choose File→Close.**

TOPIC B

Enhance Images Using Toning Tools

You have used different effects on layers, while working with Photoshop. However, at times you may need to selectively lighten or darken image areas. In this topic, you will enhance images using the toning tools.

While compositing images, you may move an object from a light setting to a dark setting. The moved image may still contain highlights or light pixels near its edges that look unattractive against the new darker background. Photoshop helps you correct this flaw in the image.

The Toning Tools

Photoshop enables you to enhance images using the toning tools.

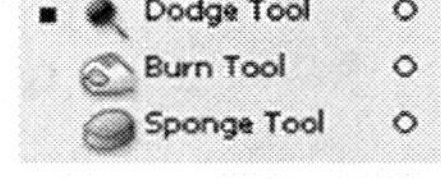

Toning Tools

Tool	Description
Burn	Used to darken part of the image by painting over it.
Dodge	Used to lighten part of an image by painting over it.
Sponge	Used to increase or decrease the intensity of the color in part of an image.

 The Dodge and Burn tools simulate the actions of professional photographers in a darkroom. To lighten a small part of an image or dodge, a photographer holds a disk on a wand over the paper to block a bit of the light as it is being exposed. Similarly, a photographer can block most of the image with his or her hand, leaving only a small hole for light to pass through to areas the photographer wishes to darken or burn.

The toning tools create results similar to those generated by the Levels command. However, since you paint directly in the image with the toning tools, they can be used to selectively darken or lighten specific areas of an image. You can use the toning tools to change the midtones, shadows, or highlights that you drag over. You will also choose an exposure, which determines the strength of the dodge or burn. A smaller exposure will result in a weaker dodge or burn, and a larger exposure will result in a stronger dodge or burn.

How to Enhance Images Using Toning Tools

Procedure Reference: Darken Image Areas

To darken image areas:

1. Open the desired Photoshop file.
2. Select the layer corresponding to the image that needs to be darkened.
3. Select the Burn tool.
4. On the Tool Options bar, specify the settings.
   - From the Brush drop-down list, select the desired brush size.
   - From the Range drop-down list, select the desired shading option.
   - From the Exposure drop-down list, select the desired exposure setting.
5. Click and drag around the area to be darkened.

Range Options

The Range options helps you set the desired shading tone. The following table lists the Range options available in Photoshop.

Range	Description
Midtones	Changes the middle range of grays.
Shadows	Changes the dark areas.
Highlights	Changes the light areas.

ACTIVITY 9-2

Darkening Image Areas with the Burn Tool

Data Files:

- this and that collectibles.psd

Before You Begin

1. Open the this and that collectibles.psd file from the C:\084563Data\Adjusting Images\Activity 2\Starter folder.

Scenario:

You find that certain images in your document do not blend with the dark background. You decide to darken the edges of those images to make the objects in the document blend together.

What You Do	How You Do It
1. **Darken the edges of the green flask.**	a. On the Layers palette, **Select the Green Flask Copy layer.**
	b. From the Dodge tool flyout, **select the Burn tool.**
	c. On the Tool Options bar, from the Range drop-down list, **select Shadows.**
	d. In the Exposure text box, **double-click and type *50***
	e. In the Brush drop-down list, **drag the Master Diameter slider to a value of 50.**
	f. In the This And That Collectibles.psd window, **click on the top edge of green flask and drag around it.**
	g. **Choose Edit→Undo Burn Tool** to remove the burn effect.
	h. **Choose Edit→Redo Burn Tool** to apply the burn effect.
2. **Darken the edges of the blue flask.**	a. On the Layers palette, **Select the Blue Flask layer.**

b. In the This And That Collectibles.psd window, **click on the top edge of blue flask and drag around it.**

c. **Choose File→Save As.**

d. If necessary, **navigate to the C:\084563Data\Adjusting Images\Activity 2\Starter** folder.

e. In the Save As dialog box, in the File Name text box, **type *collectibles darkened* and click Save.**

f. **Choose File→Close.**

TOPIC C

Adjust the Hue/Saturation of Images

You have learned to adjust the tonal differences using toning tools. To achieve the best possible result, you need to correct unwanted color casts in images. In this topic, you will use the Hue/Saturation command to change specific colors in an image.

In general, when printing or scanning images, you can find problems with the color output. You need to ensure that the unwanted color casts are corrected and the output looks as you intended. Correcting the hue and saturation of colors in images will help you achieve the desired output.

The Hue/Saturation Command

You can use the Hue/Saturation command to change the hue, saturation, and lightness of a layer. In addition, you can apply the effect only to specific hues within the layer. This is useful for changing the hue, saturation, or lightness of a specific color within a layer. To limit the adjustments to a certain color, select a color from the Edit drop-down list. The sliders along the color spectrum at the bottom indicate the range of colors that will be affected. You can adjust the sliders to narrow or broaden the range of colors.

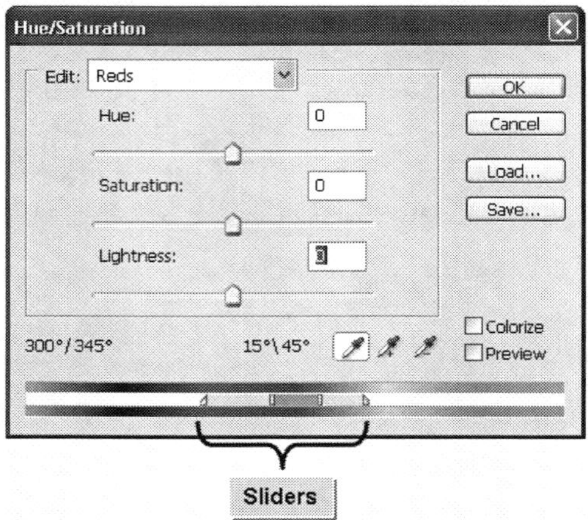

Change the Hue/Saturation of Images

Procedure Reference: Change Image Colors with the Hue/Saturation Command

To change image colors with the Hue/Saturation command:

1. Open the desired Photoshop file.
2. Select the desired layer corresponding to the image whose color needs to be adjusted.

3. Choose Image→Adjustments→Hue/Saturation.
4. In the Hue/Saturation dialog box, specify the desired settings.
   - From the Edit drop-down list, select the color to be edited.
   - Specify the desired Hue value.
   - Specify the desired Saturation value.
   - Specify the desired Lightness value.
5. Click OK.

ACTIVITY 9-3

Changing Image Colors with the Hue/Saturation Command

Data Files:

- this and that collectibles.psd

Before You Begin

1. Open the this and that collectibles.psd file from the C:\084563Data\Adjusting Images\Activity 3\Starter folder.

Scenario:

You are not satisfied with the color of the dog image. You want to change the color. You decide to explore other possibilities.

What You Do	How You Do It

1. **True or False? The Hue/Saturation command allows you to change specific hues within a layer.**

   __ True

   __ False

2. **Change the color of the dog image.**

a. On the Layers palette, **select the dog layer.**

b. **Choose Image→Adjustments→Hue/ Saturation.**

c. In the Hue/Saturation dialog box, from the Edit drop-down list, **select Reds.**

d. In the Hue text box, **double-click and type *42***

e. In the Saturation text box, **double-click and type *-74***

f. In the Lightness text box, **double-click, type *-29* and click OK.**

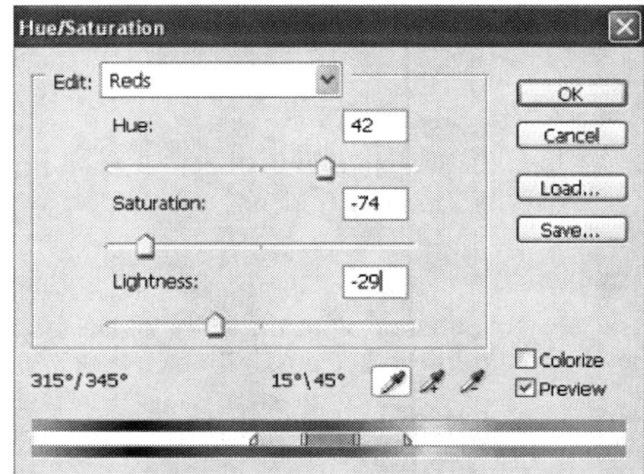

g. **Close the file and click No when prompted to save.**

Lesson 9 Follow-up

In this lesson, you adjusted the brightness of an image, and its contrast, hue, and saturation.

1. **In your environment, which toning tools are more widely used? Why?**

2. **How often do you work with adjustment layers in your projects? Explain.**

LESSON 10
Saving Completed Images

Lesson Time
30 minutes

Lesson Objectives:

In this lesson, you will save completed images for printed applications and for the web and also save the images as PDF documents.

You will:

- Prepare images for print.
- Prepare images for the web.
- Work with PDF documents in Photoshop.

Introduction

You know how to create and edit images in Photoshop. This process is incomplete if you haven't kept in mind the intended use of the image, while saving it. In this lesson, you will save completed images for printed applications and for the web. In addition, you will also save the images as PDF documents.

Images need to be saved in different formats to get the best possible output for different applications. A file format that suits print requirement may not necessarily satisfy the web requirements. Understanding the different file formats and their usage ensures that you get the best output for a specific media.

TOPIC A

Save Images for Use in Print Applications

You know how to create images and the final step is to save the images. But while saving the images, it becomes imperative for you to recognize the different file formats. These formats differ for print applications. In this topic, you will save images for use in print applications.

Photoshop enables you to save a copy of an image in formats best suited for printing, thereby ensuring high quality output.

File Formats for Print Applications

Files to be used in print applications are typically saved in TIFF, which refers to the Tagged Image File Format, or the EPS format that refers to the Encapsulated PostScript File Format. Photoshop images that are imported into documents designed for print are also saved in these formats. TIFF can support layers, but some applications can't properly import layered TIFF files. Therefore, it is a good idea to uncheck the Layers check box in the Save Options section, while saving.

Save As A Copy Option

Photoshop automatically saves a copy of your file when you save the file in the TIFF or EPS. This ensures that the original file with the layers intact will not be replaced when you save the file in a different format. This is important, because you may need to return to the original file that includes layers to make changes later. Saving a copy of an image is also convenient. This allows you to continue to work with the original file, since the original file remains open when you use the Save As A Copy option.

TIFF Options

When you save a Photoshop image in TIFF, you can use the TIFF Options dialog box to set options for compression, compatibility, resolution, and transparency.

Option	Description
Image Compression	Compresses the image to decrease the file size.
Byte Order	Specifies the platform (PC or Macintosh) on which the file will be read. Most programs can read either byte order.
Multi-resolutions	Checks the Save Image Pyramid check box to preserve multi-resolutions in an image.
Transparency	Preserves the transparency as an alpha channel, when the Save Transparency check box is checked.
Layer Compression	Compresses the data in each layer, as opposed to the entire image, if layers are saved as TIFF files.

The Print Commands

Photoshop provides a variety of Print commands.

Print Command	Description
Page Setup And Print	These options display the print options for your printer, printer drivers, and operating system.
Print With Preview	This option displays the printing, output, and color management options in Photoshop.
Print Online	This option sends your print file to an online service so you don't have to print it yourself. This option only works with JPEG files.
Print One Copy	This option prints only one copy of the file and doesn't display the Print dialog box.

Photoshop images can be output to a variety of sources. When preparing to print images to a non-commercial local or network printer, Photoshop provides options to help control how your image will print. By default, Photoshop prints a composite of visible layers. To print an individual layer, hide the other layers and then choose the Print command.

Your monitor displays images using light, while a printer reproduces images using inks and pigments. As a result, the hard copy image can appear quite different. Options, such as a color management system, can increase the predictability of the printed image.

How to Save Images for Use in Print Applications

Procedure Reference: Save in TIFF Format

To save in TIFF format:

1. Open the required Photoshop file.
2. Choose File→Save As.
3. In the Save As dialog box, from the Format drop-down list, select TIFF(*.TIF,*.TIFF) format.

4. Specify the desired Save Options and click Save.
5. In the TIFF Options dialog box, specify the desired options and click OK.

ACTIVITY 10-1

Saving in TIFF Format

Data Files:

- this and that.psd

Before You Begin

1. Open the this and that.psd file from the C:\084563Data\Saving Completed Images\Activity 1\Starter folder.

Scenario:

You have completed working on an image, which you intend to use for a print advertisement. You want to print a hard copy to see how it looks.

What You Do	How You Do It
1. **Save the file.**	a. **Choose File→Save As.**

b. In the Save As dialog box, from the Format drop-down list, **select TIFF(*.TIF,*.TIFF) format.**

c. **Uncheck the Alpha Channels check box.**

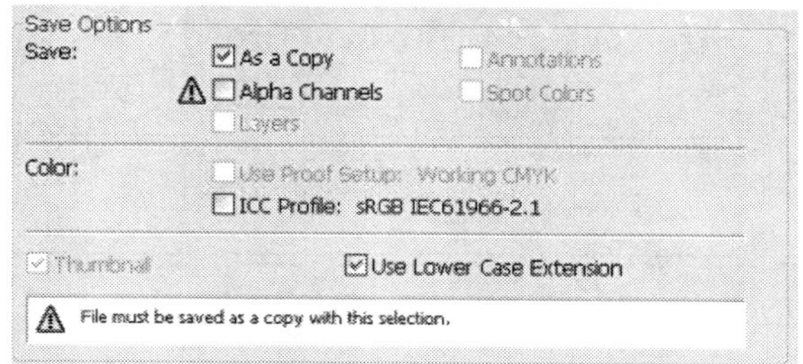

d. **Notice that the As A Copy check box is now checked, indicating that the version you are saving now will be saved as a separate file.**

e. If necessary, **navigate to theC:\084563Data\Saving Completed Images\Activity 1\Starter folder.**

f. **Click Save.**

g. **Notice that the TIFF Options dialog box opens and the IBM PC option is selected for compatibility with the IBM PC desktop publishing applications.**

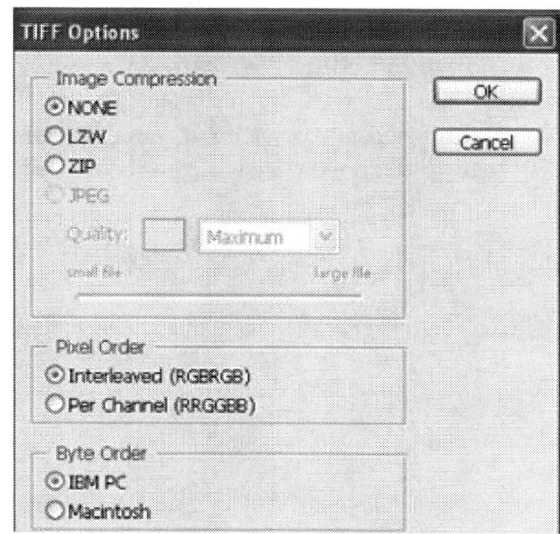

h. In the TIFF Options dialog box, **click OK** to save a copy of the image in TIFF format.

---

2. **In which formats do you save Photoshop images designed for print?**
   a) TIFF
   b) EPS
   c) PSB
   d) PICT

---

3. **True or False? The Byte Order allows you to specify the platform on which the file will be read.**
   ___ True
   ___ False

TOPIC B

Save Images for the Web

You now know how to save images for print applications. It is essential that the right balance is struck between image quality and file size when saving images for the web. In this topic, you will save images for the web.

A lot of files that are created in Photoshop, are often created for the web. Saving them in the right format becomes important to ensure the best quality online.

File Formats for the Web

Web graphics are traditionally saved in either JPEG or GIF, despite the existence of other formats for web graphics. JPEG images can contain millions of colors and shades, while GIF images can contain only 256 colors or shades. Since fewer colors are used in GIF images, some banding and color shifts can occur within the image. Therefore, JPEG is preferable for continuous tone images, such as photographs. JPEG also allows you to specify a quality setting. A higher quality setting creates an image with high quality and high file size. A lower quality setting decreases image quality and file size.

Joint Photographic Experts Group file format, typically used for saving files to be used on web pages.

The Save For Web Command

The Save For Web command allows you to preview several versions of an image to see how the image will appear when exported using a variety of web formats such as JPEG, GIF, PNG, and Bitmap. In addition, you can also set options specific to these formats in the Save For Web dialog box. This allows you to choose the format and the format options that provide the best balance between small file size and image quality. You can use the Zoom tool in the Save For Web dialog box to view the image previews at larger or smaller magnifications. Changing the magnification for one image preview automatically changes it for all of them.

 Click within any image preview using the Zoom tool to zoom in, and hold down Alt and click an image preview to zoom out.

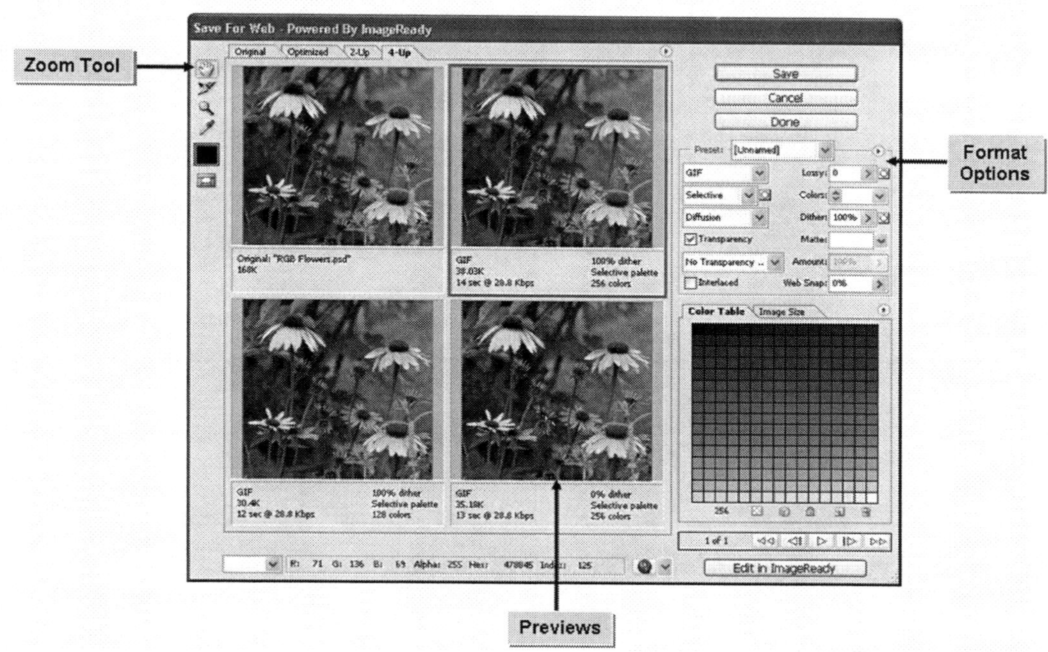

The 2-Up and 4-Up tabs in the Save For Web dialog box show the original image as well as one or three web-optimized versions. The bottom-left corner of each preview of the image displays the image file size, and the time it would take to download the image using a 28.8 Kbps modem. When saving an image using the Save For Web dialog box, the selected image preview is the one that will be saved. It is recommended that images placed on web servers use names that are in all lowercase characters, have no spaces, and use a file extension.

How to Save Images for the Web

Procedure Reference: Save Images in JPEG Format

To save images for the web using the Save For Web command:

1. Open the required Photoshop file.
2. Choose File→Save For Web.
3. In the Save For Web-Powered By ImageReady dialog box, select the 4-Up tab.
4. Select the desired preview and verify that the JPEG file format is selected.
5. Specify the desired optimization options for JPEG format.

6. In the Image Size panel, specify the desired size setting and click Apply.
7. Click Save.
8. In the Save Optimized As dialog box, in the File Name text box, specify the desired file name.
9. Click Save to save a copy of the file in JPEG format.

Optimization Options for JPEG

There following table lists the options for optimizing JPEG images.

Option	Description
Quality	Determines the level of compression.
Optimized	Creates an enhanced JPEG image with a smaller file size.
Progressive	Displays the image progressively in a web browser.
Blur	Specifies the amount of blur.
ICC Profile	Preserves the ICC profile of the images in the file.
Matte	Specifies a fill color for transparent pixels.

ACTIVITY 10-2

Using the Save for Web Command

Data Files:

- this and that collectibles.psd

Before You Begin

1. Open the this and that collectibles.psd file from the C:\084563Data\Saving Completed Images\Activity 2\Starter folder.

Scenario:

You have designed an advertisement that is to be posted on the web. You want to save it in a format that would allow the image to be optimized for use on the web.

What You Do	How You Do It
1. **Specify the image settings.**	a. **Choose File→Save For Web.**
	b. In the Save For Web-Powered By ImageReady dialog box, **select the 2-Up tab.**
	c. From the Zoom Level drop-down list, **select 50%.**
	d. **Select the 4-Up tab.**
	e. **Select the bottom-left preview.**
	f. From the Optimized File Format drop-down list, **select JPEG format.**
	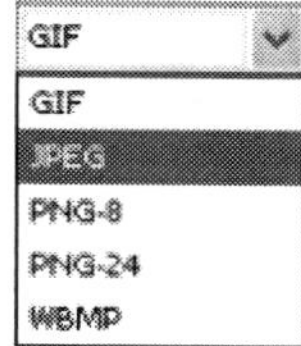
	g. From the Compression Quality drop-down list, **select Medium.**
	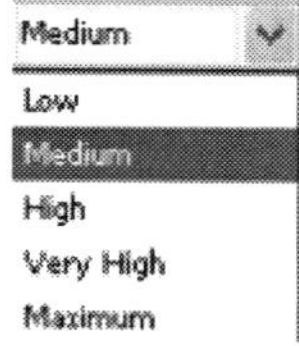
	h. In the Quality Field drop-down list, **drag the slider to a value of 50.**

2. **Specify the image size settings and save the file.**	a. In the Save For Web-Powered By ImageReady dialog box, in the 4-Up panel, **select the ImageSize tab.**

b. In the Width text box, **double-click, type *500* and click Apply.**

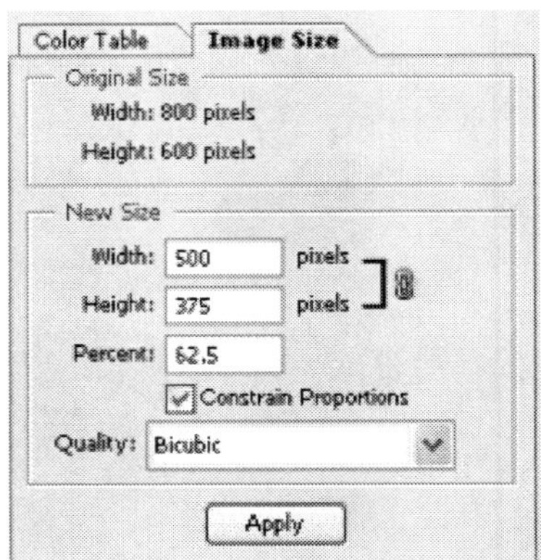

c. Verify that the JPEG optimized image preview at the bottom left is selected and **click Save.**

d. In the Save Optimized As dialog box, in the File Name text box, **type *thisnthat***

e. If necessary, **Navigate to the C:\084563Data\Saving Completed Images\Activity 2\Starter** folder.

f. **Click Save.**

g. **Choose File→Close.**

TOPIC C

Save Images as PDF

You have saved images for use in print applications, and for the web. Photoshop CS2 has new options that enable working with PDF files. In this topic, you will open, place, and save a PDF document in Photoshop. You will also manage PDF presets to make handling PDF documents easier and more efficient.

There may be times when you need to use content from a PDF within a Photoshop project. Having the ability to open, place, and save a PDF document within Photoshop saves you from having to work between two open applications.

The Adobe PDF Preset Command

PDF presets are a group of settings that are used to create consistent PDF files by balancing file size and quality, based on how the files will be used.

Preset	Description
High Quality Print	Creates PDF files for printing on desktop printers and proofers. Compatible with Acrobat and Adobe Reader 5.0 and later.
PDF/X-1a:2001	Creates PDF files that conform to the PDF/X-1a:2001 ISO standard. Compatible with Acrobat and Adobe Reader 4.0 and later.
PDF/X-3:2002	Creates PDF files that conform to the PDF/X-3:2002 ISO standard. Compatible with Acrobat and Adobe Reader 4.0 and later.
Press Quality	Creates PDF files for high-quality printing. Compatible with Acrobat and Adobe Reader 5.0 and later.
Smallest File Size	Creates PDF files for use on screen, in email, and on the Internet. Compatible with Acrobat and Adobe Reader 5.0 and later.

Each PDF preset includes options for modifying General, Compression, Output, and Security settings.

For more information about ISO standards for graphic content exchange, see the Adobe Acrobat User Guide.

How to Save a PDF in Photoshop

Procedure Reference: Open a PDF Document in Photoshop

To open a PDF document in Photoshop:

1. Choose File→Open.

2. Select the desired PDF document and click Open.
3. If necessary, edit the PDF document in Photoshop.

Procedure Reference: Place a PDF Document in Photoshop

To place a PDF document in Photoshop:

1. Open the desired image in Photoshop.
2. Choose File→Place.
3. In the Place PDF dialog box, select Page or Image and click OK.
4. Double-click within the Transform handles to place the image.

Procedure Reference: Save a PDF Document in Photoshop

To save a PDF document in Photoshop:

1. Choose File→Save As.
2. In the Save As dialog box, in the Format drop-down list, select Photoshop PDF.
3. Click Save.

Procedure Reference: Manage PDF Presets

To manage PDF presets:

1. Choose Edit→Adobe PDF Presets.
2. In the Adobe PDF Presets dialog box, in the Presets area, select the desired preset.
    - Select High Quality Print to create Adobe PDF documents for quality printing on desktop printers and proofers. These PDF documents can be opened with Acrobat and Adobe Reader 5.0 and later.
    - Select PDF/X1a:2001 to create PDF documents that must conform to PDF/X1a:2001, an ISO standard for graphic content exchange.
    - Select Press Quality to create Adobe PDF documents best suited for high-quality press printing. These PDF documents can be opened with Acrobat and Adobe Reader 5.0 and later.
3. Click Done.

ACTIVITY 10-3

Saving Images as a PDF Document in Photoshop

Data Files:

- Roof_design.pdf
- Magazine.psd

Scenario:

As a graphic designer for a design firm, you are involved in the creation of a magazine cover for a commercial publication. The client has already selected the artwork to be included and sent everything to you as a PDF file. You will open the PDF files in Photoshop to view them and then place them in the Photoshop file you created, which has the correct dimensions and requirements for the magazine. You will also be saving the file as a PDF for the client to view and print it.

What You Do	How You Do It
1. **Open a PDF file in Photoshop.**	a. From the C:\084563Data\Saving Completed Images\Activity 3\Starter folder, **open the Roof_design.pdf file.** b. In the Import PDF dialog box, **press Ctrl, select the second thumbnail, and click OK.** c. **View the Roof_design-2 file and click the Close button** to close the file. d. In the Adobe Photoshop message box, **click No.** e. **View the Roof_design-1 file and click the Close button.** f. In the Adobe Photoshop message box, **click No.**
2. **Place a PDF file in a Photoshop file.**	a. **Choose File→Open and double-click Magazine.psd.** b. **Choose File→Place and double-click Roof_design.pdf.** c. In the Place PDF dialog box, **click OK.**

d. On the image in the Magazine.psd file, **click the transform handle at the top-left corner and drag it to the right until the black bar is exposed.**

e. **Double-click within the transform boundaries of the Roof_design image.**

f. **Choose File→Place and double-click Roof_design.pdf.**

g. In the Place PDF dialog box, **click the second thumbnail and click OK.**

h. On the image in the Magazine.psd file, **drag the transform handle to the left and double-click within its transform boundaries.**

3. **Save the image as a PDF.**	a. **Choose File→Save As.**
	b. **Type *MyMagazine*, select Photoshop PDF as the format, and click Save.**
	c. In the Save Adobe PDF dialog box, **verify that the Preserve Photoshop Editing Capabilities check box is checked.**
	d. **Check the View PDF After Saving check box.**
	e. **Click Save PDF and click Yes.**
	f. In Adobe Reader, **click the Close button.**
	g. **Close all open files.**

ACTIVITY 10-4

Managing PDF Presets

Data Files:

- MyMagazine.pdf

Scenario:

You just finished the composition of the magazine cover and you are now ready to send it to the client for review. You will adjust the PDF presets and apply them to your image. You will also save the desired presets for future use.

What You Do	How You Do It
1. **Adjust the PDF presets.**	a. **Choose Edit→Adobe PDF Presets.**
	b. In the Adobe PDF Presets dialog box, in the Presets area, **select [Press Quality] and click Save As.**
	c. **Navigate to the C:\084563Data\Saving Completed Images\Activity 4\Starter folder.**
	d. In the File Name text box, **type *My_PDFsettings* and click Save.**
	e. In the Adobe PDF Presets dialog box, **click Done.**

2. **Apply PDF presets and save the file.**

a. **Choose File→Open.**

b. From the C:\084563Data\Saving Completed Images\Activity 4\Starter folder **open the MyMagazine.pdf file.**

c. **Choose Edit→Adobe PDF Presets.**

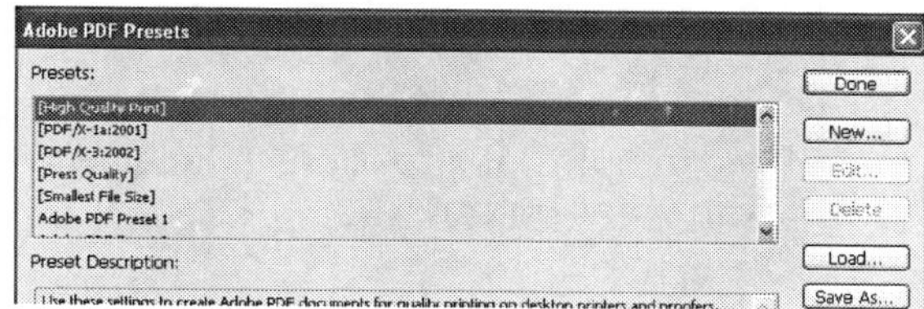

d. **Click Load.**

e. **Navigate to the C:\084563Data\Saving Completed Images\Activity 4\Starter folder.**

f. **Double-click My_PDFsettings.joboptions.**

g. **Click Done.**

h. **Choose File→Save As.**

i. **Navigate to the C:\084563Data\Saving Completed Images\Activity 4\Starter folder.**

j. If necessary, in the Save As dialog box, from the Format drop-down list, **select Photoshop PDF.**

k. **Click Save and click Yes.**

l. In the Save Adobe PDF dialog box, from the Adobe PDF Preset drop-down list, **select My_PDFsettings.**

m. **Click Save PDF.**

n. In the Save Adobe PDF message box, **click Yes.**

o. **Close all open files and exit Adobe Photoshop CS2.**

Lesson 10 Follow-up

In this lesson, you saved completed images for printed applications and for the web. In addition, you also saved the images as PDF documents.

1. **How do you make use of the new PDF presets when handling PDF files in Photoshop?**

2. **Give examples of situations in your workplace, when specific file formats were chosen for different outputs.**

Follow-up

In this course, you explored the Photoshop interface and used several tools for selecting parts of images, and moved, duplicated, and resized images. You also learnt to use layers, and to apply layer effects and filters to create special effects. Additionally, you used painting tools and blending modes to create shading effects, and performed adjustments to contrast and color balance. Finally, you saved images in formats for print and web use.

1. **How does customizing the Photoshop workspace environment help you?**

2. **How important is the role of color modes while working with images in Photoshop?**

3. **What are the factors that you need to consider while saving images for web and print applications?**

What's Next?

Adobe® Photoshop CS2 Level 1 Second Edition is the first course in this series. Adobe Photoshop® CS2 – Level 2 Second Edition is the next course.

Notes

APPENDIX A
Adobe Certified Expert (ACE) Objectives Mapping

The Adobe Certified Expert (ACE) Program is for graphic designers, web designers, developers, systems integrators, value-added resellers, and business professionals who seek recognition for their expertise with specific Adobe products. Certification candidates must pass a product proficiency exam in order to become an Adobe Certified Expert.

Selected Element K courseware addresses product-specific exam objectives. The following table indicates where Photoshop® CS2 exam objectives are covered in the Element K Adobe® Photoshop® CS2: Level 1 (Second Edition) course, Adobe® Photoshop® CS2: Level 2 (Second Edition) course, Adobe® Photoshop® CS2: Web Production course, and Adobe® Photoshop® CS2: Photo Printing and Color course.

Exam Objectives	Adobe® Photoshop® CS2: Level 1 (Second Edition)	Adobe® Photoshop® CS2: Level 2 (Second Edition)	Adobe® Photoshop® CS2: Web Production	Adobe® Photoshop® CS2: Photo Printing and Color
1.0 Working with the Photoshop UI				
1.1 Describe the advantages of saving workspaces.	1C			
1.2 Given a view in Adobe Bridge, explain when you would use that view.	1F			
1.3 Describe the basic functionality provided by the Preset Manager, and explain how to use the Preset Manager to manage libraries.	1C			

Exam Objectives	Adobe® Photoshop® CS2: Level 1 (Second Edition)	Adobe® Photoshop® CS2: Level 2 (Second Edition)	Adobe® Photoshop® CS2: Web Production	Adobe® Photoshop® CS2: Photo Printing and Color
1.4 Customize menus and keyboard shortcuts by selecting options in the Keyboard Shortcuts and Menus dialog box.	1E			
2.0 Painting and retouching				
2.1 Given a tool, paint an object by using that tool. (tools include: Brush Tool, Pencil Tool, Eraser)	7B and 4B			
2.2 Given a tool, retouch an image by using that tool. (tools include: Healing Brush, Patch Tool, Color Replacement Tool, Red Eye tool)		4E		
2.3 Adjust the tonal range of an image by selecting to proper options and using a levels adjustment layer.		4E		
2.4 Adjust the tonal range of an image by selecting the proper options and using a curves adjustment layer.		4E		
2.5 Explain how blending modes are used to control how pixels are effected when using a painting or editing tool	Appendix-C,5B			
2.6 Create and use patterns.		3C		
2.7 Create and use gradients.		3B		
2.8 Given a setting in the Exposure dialog box, explain how that setting affects an image.		4E		
2.9 Create and edit a custom brush.		4F		
3.0 Creating and using layers				
3.1 Create and arrange layers and groups.	4J, 4D, and 4G			
3.2 Explain the purpose of layer comps and when you would use a layer comp.		4C		
3.3 Explain how or why you would use a clipping group.		1F		
3.4 Explain how or why you would use a layer mask.		1D		

Exam Objectives	Adobe® Photoshop® CS2: Level 1 (Second Edition)	Adobe® Photoshop® CS2: Level 2 (Second Edition)	Adobe® Photoshop® CS2: Web Production	Adobe® Photoshop® CS2: Photo Printing and Color
3.5 Create and save a layer style.			4D	
3.6 Select and work with multiple layers in an image.	4D, 4F, 4G, and 4I			
3.7 Given a scenario, edit layer properties.	4D and 7B			
3.8 Create and use Smart objects.	4E			
4.0 Working with selections				
4.1 Create and modify selections by using the appropriate selection tool.	3A,3B,3C,3D,3E, and 3F			
4.2 Save and load selections.	3C and 4I			
4.3 Explain how to create and modify a temporary mask by using the Quick mask command.		1B		
4.4 Create and modify selections by using the Channels palette.	3C	1C		
5.0 Supporting video				
5.1 Explain the purpose of Video Preview.				3C
5.2 Describe the purpose of pixel aspect ratio correction.				3C
6.0 Understanding file properties				
6.1 Given a scenario, select the appropriate color mode for an image. (Scenarios include for Web, for Video, for Print)			3C	2B
6.2 Add metadata for an image in Adobe Photoshop.	1G			
6.3 Explain the functionality provided by High Dynamic Range (HDR) images and describe the workflow for HDR files.				3A
6.4 Explain the advantages of working with 16-bit images versus 8-bit images.				4B
7.0 Working with vector tools				

Exam Objectives	Adobe® Photoshop® CS2: Level 1 (Second Edition)	Adobe® Photoshop® CS2: Level 2 (Second Edition)	Adobe® Photoshop® CS2: Web Production	Adobe® Photoshop® CS2: Photo Printing and Color
7.1 Create shape layers and paths by using the Pen and Shape tools.		2A		
7.2 Explain the advantages of using vector drawing tools versus using raster drawing tools.		2A		
7.3 Given a scenario, alter the properties of type.	8A			
7.4 Create and edit paths by using the Paths palette.		2B		
8.0 Working with automation				
8.1 Create and use actions.		5A		
8.2 Create and use batches.		5A		
8.3 List and describe the automation features available in Adobe Photoshop.		5A		
8.4 Describe the difference between scripting and actions and when you would use one over the other.		5A		
9.0 Working with filters				
9.1 Given a scenario, select the appropriate settings and use the Reduce Noise filter.	8C			
9.2 Given a scenario, select the appropriate settings and use the Smart Sharpen filter.	8C			
9.3 Describe the functionality of the Filter Gallery.	8C			
10.0 Managing assets with Bridge				
10.1 List and describe the functionality Adobe Bridge provides for viewing assets.	1F			
10.2 Explain how to apply metadata and keywords to assets in Adobe Bridge.	1G			
10.3 List and describe the functionality and set the appropriate options for Camera RAW preferences, and the Apply Camera RAW Settings menu options.				3B
11.0 Using Camera RAW				

Exam Objectives	Adobe® Photoshop® CS2: Level 1 (Second Edition)	Adobe® Photoshop® CS2: Level 2 (Second Edition)	Adobe® Photoshop® CS2: Web Production	Adobe® Photoshop® CS2: Photo Printing and Color
11.1 Describe advantages of the RAW camera format.				3B
11.2 Given an adjustment setting, explain the purpose of that setting.				3B
11.3 Explain the purpose of and functionality provided by the Open, Save, and Done buttons in the Camera RAW dialog box.				3B
11.4 Describe how to use the Digital Negative converter and explain the importance of the DNG format.				3B
12.0 Outputting to print				
12.1 Given a color handling method in the Print with Preview dialog box, explain when you would use that method.				2D
12.2 Given a scenario, select and explain when to use a specific Print command (Print commands include: Print One Copy, Print Preview, Print)				2D
12.3 Explain the differences between monitor, images, and device resolution.	2A		1A	2A
13.0 Managing color				
13.1 Discuss the color management workflow process that is used in Adobe Photoshop. (topics include: ICC profiles, color management engine, color numbers)				1B and 2D
13.2 Describe the difference between assigning and converting to ICC profiles.				2D
13.3 Configure color settings by using the Color Settings dialog box.				2B
13.4 Explain the purpose of and how to use the Proof Setup command.				2D

Exam Objectives	Adobe® Photoshop® CS2: Level 1 (Second Edition)	Adobe® Photoshop® CS2: Level 2 (Second Edition)	Adobe® Photoshop® CS2: Web Production	Adobe® Photoshop® CS2: Photo Printing and Color
13.5 Discuss the relationship between color gamut and rendering intents.				7C
14.0 Preparing and Outputting images for the Web				
14.1 Given a scenario, choose the appropriate file format to optimize images for the Web.			1A and 2A	
14.2 Create transparent and matted images by using the Save for Web command.			2A	
14.3 Explain the purpose of and how to use Variables.		5A		
14.4 Explain how slices can be used to optimize images for the Web. (options include: layer based, user based, linking slices for optimization)			5A	
14.5 Explain the use of layers when creating an animation in Photoshop.			6A	

APPENDIX B

Adobe® Photoshop® CS2: New Features Mapping

The following table lists the new features of Adobe® Photoshop® CS2 covered in the Element K Adobe® Photoshop® CS2: Level 1 (Second Edition) course, Adobe® Photoshop® CS2: Level 2 (Second Edition) course, Adobe® Photoshop® CS2: Web Production course, and Adobe® Photoshop® CS2: Photo Printing and Color course.

New Features in Phtshop CS2	Photoshop CS2 Level-1	Photoshop CS2 Level-2	Photoshop CS2 Web Production	Photoshop CS2 Photo Printing_Color
Workspace Presets	1C			
Customize Menus- The Menus Dialog Box	1E			
The Red Eye Tool				5C
The Spot Healing Brush		4E		
The Exposure Dialog box		4E		
Edit Multiple Layers (Multiple layer control with smart guides)	4I			
Smart Objects	4E			
Image Warp		4B		
Vanishing point	8C			
Smart Sharpen	8C			
Advanced Noise Reduction	8C	4E		
Optical Lens Correction	8C			
Adobe Bridge	1F			

Appendix B

New Features in Photshop CS2	Photoshop CS2 Level-1	Photoshop CS2 Level-2	Photoshop CS2 Web Production	Photoshop CS2 Photo Printing_Color
Metadata and Keywords	1G			
Camera Raw				3B
Digital Negative Converter				3B
HDR Image (Includes 32 bit HDR)				3A
Video Preview				3C
Color Handling				2D
Variables		5A		
Animation			6A	
PDF Preset command	10C			
WYSIWYG Font Menus	8A			
Enhanced 16-bit Filter support				4B

Appendix C
Blending Modes

The following table lists each of Photoshop's blending modes, along with a brief description of each one's effect in an image.

Blending Mode	Effect
Normal	The default mode—no special effect.
Dissolve	Randomly replaces pixels with the blend color or the color below. The result depends on the opacity at the pixel location.
Darken	Uses whichever color is darker between the blend color and the color below. Lighter colors are covered up by darker colors.
Multiply	Multiplies the color of the blending object with the color of the object below. The result is always a darker color than either of the original colors. Any color blended with black is black. Any color blended with white is unchanged.
Color Burn	Darkens the blend color with the color beneath by increasing the contrast, but doesn't lighten. Using white as the blend color produces no change.
Linear Burn	Similar to Color Burn, but Linear Burn darkens the color beneath by decreasing brightness. The result is usually darker than Color Burn.
Lighten	Uses whichever color is lighter between the blend color and the color below. Darker colors are covered up by lighter colors.
Screen	Multiplies the inverse of the colors being blended. The result is always a lighter color than either of the original colors. Screening with a black color does not change the color beneath. Screening with white produces white. The effect is similar to projecting multiple photographic slides on top of each other.

Blending Mode	Effect
Color Dodge	Opposite of Color Burn—brightens the color below to match the blending color by decreasing the contrast. Using black with Color Dodge produces no change.
Linear Dodge	Similar to Color Dodge, but Linear Dodge brightens the color below to match the blending color by increasing the brightness. The result is usually brighter than Color Dodge.
Overlay	Multiplies or screens the colors based on the color below. The highlights or shadows of the objects below show through, but mid-range colors and patterns are blended like the Multiply mode.
Soft Light	Darkens or lightens depending on the color being blended. If the blend color is lighter than 50% gray, the image is lightened. If the blend color is darker than 50% gray, then the image is darkened. The effect is to make the shadows and highlights more pronounced, as if a diffuse spotlight were cast on the image.
Hard Light	Essentially the same as Soft Light but with a more extreme, pronounced effect, as if you're shining a harsh spotlight.
Vivid Light	Lightens the image by increasing the contrast, if the blend color is lighter than 50% gray. If the blend color is darker than 50% gray, the image is darkened by decreasing the contrast. It has a pronounced effect on the shadows and highlights in the image.
Linear Light	Similar to Vivid Light, except Linear Light lightens or darkens an image by increasing or decreasing the brightness.
Pin Light	Replaces colors, depending on the blend color. If the blend color is lighter than 50% gray, pixels darker than the blend color are replaced, and the lighter pixels do not change. If the blend color is darker than 50% gray, the pixels lighter than the blend color are replaced, and the darker pixels do not change. This can be used for adding special effects to an image.
Hard Mix	Darkens the dark pixels in an image, lightens the bright pixels in an image when layers are blended together.
Difference	Subtracts whichever is the brighter color from the darker color. Blending with white inverts the color below.
Exclusion	Creates a similar effect as Difference but with less contrast.

Blending Mode	Effect
Hue	Uses the luminance and saturation of the object below and the hue of the blending color. If the blending object is solid color, the Hue blending mode acts to colorize the underlying image, although the effect may be weak if the underlying object isn't deeply saturated.
Saturation	Uses the luminance and color of the object below and the saturation of the blending color.
Color	Uses the luminance of the object below and the saturation and color of the blending color. If the blending object is solid color, the Color blending mode acts to colorize the underlying image, usually in a more pronounced way than the Hue blending mode.
Luminosity	Uses the saturation and color of the object below and the luminance of the blending color.

Notes

Lesson Labs

Due to classroom setup constraints, some labs cannot be keyed in sequence immediately following their associated lesson. Your instructor will tell you whether your labs can be practiced immediately following the lesson or whether they require separate setup from the main lesson content.

Lesson 1 Lab 1

Customizing the Photoshop Environment

Objective:

Customize the Photoshop environment.

Data Files:

- enus_084563_01_lab.zip

Scenario:

The following questions will test your knowledge on customizing the Photoshop environment.

---

1. **Typically, which image type requires more memory and storage to manipulate—raster or vector?**

---

2. **Which image type (raster or vector) does Photoshop use? Why?**

---

3. **How do you hide all the Photoshop elements (menu bar, window controls, palettes, and so forth), so that you can view only the image?**

---

4. **Why do you rearrange the palettes in Photoshop?**

5. **How do you customize the menus in Photoshop?**

6. **Name at least two features that can be used to change the image magnification in Photoshop.**

7. **Which are some of the benefits of using the Navigator palette?**

LESSON 2 LAB 1

Controlling the Size and Resolution of Images

Objective:

Control the size and resolution of images.

Data Files:

- enus_084563_02_lab.zip

Scenario:

The following questions will test your knowledge on controlling the size and resolution of images.

1. **What are five Photoshop options that provide information on an images size?**

2. **What is the relationship between image resolution and linescreen?**

3. When do you crop an image?

4. How do you cancel a crop?

LESSON 3 LAB 1

Making Precise Selections

Objective:

Make precise selections.

Data Files:

- Kid Stuff.psd

Scenario:

You have explored the various selection tools and the techniques. You want to edit a few photographs in Photoshop and before you start work, you would like to practise selecting images in Photoshop so that you can make accurate selections.

1. **Open the Kid Stuff.psd file in Photoshop CS2.**
2. **Select the block with the letter O.**
3. **Rotate the selection to fit the block.**
4. **Save the selection with the default settings.**
5. **Load the selection and name the alpha channel with the selection as O Block Selection.**
6. **Select the letter O.**
7. **Set a higher tolerance value and then subtract the inner white portion of the letter O from the selection.**

8. Save the selection as O Selection.

LESSON 4 LAB 1

Selecting Images and Working with Layers

Objective:

Work with layers and image selections.

Data Files:

- enus_084563_04_lab.zip
- enus_084563_04_lab_solutions.zip

Scenario:

The following questions will test your knowledge of selecting images and working with layers.

1. When you deselect a floating selection, what happens to the image pixels below the selection?

2. What happens to the image pixels below a selection after you move it?

3. Which are some of the tools and commands you can use to undo previous steps?

4. How do you return a part of an image to a prior state without affecting recent changes you have made to other areas of the image?

5. How do you use the Move tool to duplicate a selected image area?

6. How do you edit images created in other Adobe applications in Photoshop, without affecting the source data?

7. Why do you duplicate a selected image area?

8. What are the benefits of using layers?

9. Name two methods of creating a new layer from an existing selection.

10. Why do you transform a layer or selection?

11. How do you rotate a selection using the Free Transform command?

12. Why do you copy layers between images?

13. Describe two techniques for moving a layer to another image window.

14. Name two graphic file formats that are typically used for print graphics.

15. Name two graphic file formats that are typically used for web graphics.

16. How does stacking order affect the appearance of the image?

17. **Describe two benefits of using layer sets.**

Lesson 5 Lab 1

Blending Layers and Selections

Objective:

blend layers and selections

Data Files:

- enus_084563_05_lab.zip

Scenario:

The following questions will test your knowledge of blending layers and selections.

1. **What does the Defringe command do?**

2. **How do you make a layer appear transparent?**

3. **How do you create a realistic transparency effect?**

4. **Name the two techniques used for creating a feathered selection.**

5. **After creating a feathered selection, name at least one command or action that will cause the feathered edge to become apparent.**

LESSON 6 LAB 1

Identifying Image Modes

Objective:

Identify image modes.

Data Files:

- enus_084563_06_lab.zip

Scenario:

The following questions will test your knowledge on identifying image modes.

1. **Describe the differences between Indexed color and RGB color.**

2. **When is Lab color used?**

3. **Which are the two characteristics that differentiate between Photoshop's image modes?**

4. **What does pixel depth determine?**

5. **What are the differences between Grayscale and Bitmap images?**

6. What are the differences between Grayscale and Duotone images?

7. What is the most typical use for images saved in RGB Color mode?

8. What is the most typical use for images saved in CMYK Color mode?

LESSON 7 LAB 1

Applying Colors

Objective:
Apply colors.

Data Files:
- enus_084563_07_lab.zip

Scenario:
The following questions will test your knowledge of applying colors.

1. How do you select a background color using the Color palette?

2. How do you use the Eyedropper tool to select color with precision?

3. Why is it better to paint shadows in a blank layer, rather than in the layer containing the artwork to which you are adding the shadows?

4. **What does the Airbrush option for the Brush tool control?**

5. **When do you use the Clone Stamp tool?**

6. **How do you sample part of an image with the Clone Stamp tool?**

LESSON 8 LAB 1

Enhancing Images

Objective:

Enhance images.

Data Files:

- enus_084563_08_lab.zip

Scenario:

The following questions will test your knowledge of enhancing images with text and special effects.

1. **How do you add text to a Photoshop image?**

2. **What is the difference between point text and paragraph text?**

3. **When do you use layer effects?**

4. How do you open the Layer Style dialog box to choose layer effects?

5. When do you use a filter? Which aspects of a filter's effects can the Fade command adjust?

6. Why do you merge layers in an image?

7. Describe two techniques for merging image layers.

LESSON 9 LAB 1

Adjusting Images

Objective:

Adjust images.

Data Files:

- enus_084563_09_lab.zip

Scenario:

The following questions will test your knowledge on adjusting images.

1. What is the advantage of using an adjustment layer?

2. What is the difference between the output levels controls and the input levels controls in the Levels dialog box?

3. Why do you use the toning tools instead of the Levels command?

4. What is the benefit of using the Burn tool to darken an image?

5. True or False? You can quickly replace a specific image color with a new color.

 ___ True

 ___ False

Lesson 10 Lab 1

Saving Images

Objective:

Save images.

Data Files:

- enus_084563_10_lab.zip
- enus_084563_10_lab_solutions.zip

Scenario:

The following questions will test your knowledge of saving images.

1. Why do you need to save a Photoshop image in a different format?

2. When saving a copy of a Photoshop image in a different format, why is it a good idea to keep the original image in Photoshop format as well?

3. When do you use the JPEG format instead of the GIF format?

4. What is the primary benefit of using the Save for Web command to save an image in a web format?

SOLUTIONS

Lesson 1

Activity 1-1

1. **True or False? Raster graphics require less memory and storage to manipulate them.**

   __ True

   ✓ False

2. **Which statements about raster graphics are true?**

   ✓ a) Raster graphics are composed of a grid of pixels.

   b) Raster graphics are composed of lines defined by a set of mathematical instructions.

   ✓ c) Raster graphics can be created using the Photoshop application.

   d) Raster graphics are composed of curves and geometrical shapes.

3. **True or False? Vector graphics are composed of mathematically defined shapes.**

   ✓ True

   __ False

Activity 1-9

1. **True or False? Adobe Bridge allows you to create and edit images from one central location.**

   __ True

   ✓ False

2. **Which tasks can be performed using Adobe Bridge?**

   ✓ a) Browse non-Adobe application files.

   b) Color correct Adobe Photoshop files.

   ✓ c) Run batch commands.

   d) Apply Photoshop filters to only flattened images.

3. **True or False? Adobe Bridge can be used to add and edit keywords and metadata to files.**

   ✓ True

   __ False

Lesson 1 Follow-up

Lesson 1 Lab 1

1. **Typically, which image type requires more memory and storage to manipulate—raster or vector?**

   Raster images typically require much more memory and storage to manipulate, since they are comprised of many pixels, which correlates to a lot of data. Vector graphics typically have much less information, because they are comprised of discrete objects.

2. **Which image type (raster or vector) does Photoshop use? Why?**

   Photoshop images are raster images. Raster images are comprised of a grid of pixels, and each pixel can be of a different color. This allows for a wide variation of color.

3. **How do you hide all the Photoshop elements (menu bar, window controls, palettes, and so forth), so that you can view only the image?**

   Click the Full Screen Mode icon at the bottom of the toolbox to hide the menu bar and window elements. Press Tab to hide all palettes.

4. **Why do you rearrange the palettes in Photoshop?**

   You might rearrange Photoshop's palettes so that they are organized in a way that allows you to work most efficiently. You can display just the palettes you use frequently, and close others that you don't use.

5. **How do you customize the menus in Photoshop?**

   You can customize the menus in Photoshop through the Menus tab in the Keyboard Shortcuts And Menus dialog box.

6. **Name at least two features that can be used to change the image magnification in Photoshop.**

   Answers include: The Zoom tool, the Zoom In and Zoom Out commands, the Fit On Screen and Actual Pixels commands, and the Navigator palette.

7. **Which are some of the benefits of using the Navigator palette?**

   Instead of switching tools, or scrolling through an image, you can use the Navigator palette to quickly navigate a document. You can easily zoom in or out using the slider, or the zoom icons.

Lesson 2 Follow-up

Lesson 2 Lab 1

1. **What are five Photoshop options that provide information on an images size?**

   The File Information box, the File Browser, the Rulers option, the Print Size command, and the Image Size command.

2. **What is the relationship between image resolution and linescreen?**

   Image resolution in ppi should be set to between $1^1/_2$ to 2 times the linescreen in lpi.

3. **When do you crop an image?**

   You might crop an image if you do not need to use the entire image, or to trim the background areas of an image. By cropping an image, you can change the focus of the image. For example, you may crop an image to show a person's head, instead of his/her entire body. An added benefit of cropping an image is that it reduces the file size.

4. **How do you cancel a crop?**

   If you have already pressed Enter to perform a crop, you can choose Edit→Undo Crop to undo the crop. If you have established a cropping marquee, but have not yet pressed Enter to perform the crop, you can press Esc to remove the cropping marquee so that the image is unchanged.

Lesson 4

Activity 4-11

2. **Which is not a valid Photoshop file format?**

   a) .EPS

   b) .PDD

   ✓ c) .HTM

   d) .PSD

Lesson 4 Follow-up

Lesson 4 Lab 1

1. **When you deselect a floating selection, what happens to the image pixels below the selection?**

   Once the floating selection is deselected, it becomes fixed and replaces the pixels below it.

2. **What happens to the image pixels below a selection after you move it?**

   The area the selection occupied will be filled with the background color.

3. **Which are some of the tools and commands you can use to undo previous steps?**

   Use the Eraser tool to erase pixels in the active layer. Use the Undo command to undo the most recent step. Use the History palette to undo multiple steps, or use the History Brush tool to return specific areas of an image to a prior state.

4. **How do you return a part of an image to a prior state without affecting recent changes you have made to other areas of the image?**

   Click the empty square to the left of History palette step that represents the image appearance you would like to return to, and drag with the History Brush tool over the area of the image that you want to revert.

5. **How do you use the Move tool to duplicate a selected image area?**

   Hold down Alt as you drag the selected image area with the Move tool to move a copy, rather than the original selection.

6. **How do you edit images created in other Adobe applications in Photoshop, without affecting the source data?**

   When you import an image created in other Adobe applications into Photoshop, it becomes a Smart Object. A Smart Object stores a copy of the source data within a Photoshop project and allows you to manipulate it without affecting the source.

7. **Why do you duplicate a selected image area?**

   You might want to repeat image areas throughout a composite.

8. **What are the benefits of using layers?**

   Placing only a specific part of an image in its own layer makes it much easier to work with that image area later. The part of the image you place in its own layer will not replace pixels on the Background layer when it overlaps those pixels.

9. **Name two methods of creating a new layer from an existing selection.**

   The New Layer Via Cut and the New Layer Via Copy commands.

10. **Why do you transform a layer or selection?**

    You might need to straighten the image area. You might also need to resize a layer or selection so the size is comparable with the rest of the image. You can also use the Free Transform command to create perspective.

11. **How do you rotate a selection using the Free Transform command?**

    Position the mouse pointer outside the transformation box and drag to rotate the selection.

12. **Why do you copy layers between images?**

    Copying layers between images is useful when creating composites.

13. **Describe two techniques for moving a layer to another image window.**

    To move a layer to another image, you can use the Move tool to drag the pixels within the selected layer to the other image window, or you can drag the layer name from the Layers palette to the other image window.

14. **Name two graphic file formats that are typically used for print graphics.**

    TIFF and EPS are two formats typically used for print graphics.

15. **Name two graphic file formats that are typically used for web graphics.**

    GIF and JPEG are typically used for web graphics.

16. **How does stacking order affect the appearance of the image?**

    Layers that appear higher on the Layers palette are higher in the stacking order. The pixels in layers that are higher in the stacking order will appear in front of the pixels in layers that are lower in the stacking order.

17. **Describe two benefits of using layer sets.**

    Answers may vary, but include: Layer sets allow you to organize layers into groups that can be collapsed or expanded on the Layers palette; they allow you to move the pixels within multiple layers as a unit. Layer sets allow you to hide or show all the layers within the set together.

Lesson 5 Follow-up

Lesson 5 Lab 1

1. **What does the Defringe command do?**

   The Defringe command changes the color of the pixels along the current layer's edge to a color from within the layer.

2. **How do you make a layer appear transparent?**

   Select the layer you want to adjust on the Layers palette, and set an opacity amount using the Opacity field.

3. **How do you create a realistic transparency effect?**

   In some cases, a more realistic transparency effect can be achieved by using layer blending modes. Blending modes can be used to create a variety of effects by blending the pixels in a layer or set of layers with the pixels in layers lower in the stacking order.

4. **Name the two techniques used for creating a feathered selection.**

   The first technique is to select a Marquee or Lasso tool and specify a feather amount in the Feather field on the Tool Options bar. Then create the selection. The second technique is to select an image area using any selection tool, and then choose Select→Feather. Type a value in the Feather Radius field in the dialog box that appears, and click OK.

5. **After creating a feathered selection, name at least one command or action that will cause the feathered edge to become apparent.**

   Answers may vary but include: Choose the Cut command, choose the Copy command; move the selection; and fill the selection.

Lesson 6

Activity 6-1

1. **What does pixel depth determine?**

   ✓ a) The total number of shades of brightness an image can utilize.

   ✓ b) The accuracy of the image.

   c) The way the image is printed.

   ✓ d) The file size.

2. **True or False? Photoshop uses channels to divide color images into components.**

   ✓ True

   __ False

3. **How many channels does a grayscale image require?**

   ✓ a) One

   b) Two

   c) Three

   d) Four

Activity 6-2

2. **Which image does not contain any gray level?**

   ✓ a) BMP

   b) JPEG

   c) PNG

   d) GIF

3. **True or False? Duotone is a one-channel 8-bit image.**

   ✓ True

   __ False

Activity 6-3

1. **Which color mode has three 8-bit channels?**

   a) Indexed

   ✓ b) RGB

   c) CMYK

   d) Lab

2. **Which color mode defines colors mathematically?**

   a) Indexed

   b) RGB

   c) CMYK

   ✓ d) Lab

3. **True or False? Color separation is the process of converting an image to CMYK by printers that use the PostScript printing language.**

   _✓_ True

   ___ False

Lesson 6 Follow-up

Lesson 6 Lab 1

1. **Describe the differences between Indexed color and RGB color.**

   Indexed color only has an 8-bit depth, which means it can only store up to 256 colors. RGB color has 24-bit depth, storing up to 16,777,216 colors.

2. **When is Lab color used?**

   Lab color is used internally by Photoshop when editing colors between image modes. It is used by color management software that modify images automatically to appear the same on different printers and monitors. Lab color is also useful for editing image lightness without modifying the color.

3. **Which are the two characteristics that differentiate between Photoshop's image modes?**

   The number of channels and the bit depth of each channel.

4. **What does pixel depth determine?**

   The pixel depth, measured in bits, determines the total number of colors or shades of brightness an image can utilize. The greater the pixel depth, the more accurately the image is represented.

5. **What are the differences between Grayscale and Bitmap images?**

   Grayscale images have an 8-bit channel, and bitmap images have a 1-bit channel.

6. **What are the differences between Grayscale and Duotone images?**

   Grayscale and Duotone images have 8-bit channels. Grayscale and Duotone images differ in their printed output. Grayscale images are printed using only black ink, while Duotone images can be printed with two, three, or four inks.

7. **What is the most typical use for images saved in RGB Color mode?**

   RGB Color mode is most typically used for images that will be displayed on screen, such as images used on the World Wide Web.

8. **What is the most typical use for images saved in CMYK Color mode?**

   CMYK Color mode is most typically used for images that will be printed.

Lesson 7 Follow-up

Lesson 7 Lab 1

1. **How do you select a background color using the Color palette?**

   Hold down Alt and click the Color palette's color ramp.

2. **How do you use the Eyedropper tool to select color with precision?**

   Drag the Eyedropper tool over the image and view the Info palette and/or the Foreground Color icon so you will know when the mouse pointer is positioned on a pixel that uses the exact color you want.

3. **Why is it better to paint shadows in a blank layer, rather than in the layer containing the artwork to which you are adding the shadows?**

   It is best to create shadows on a separate layer so that no pixels in the rest of the image are replaced by the shadows you draw. This allows you to be much more creative and experimental with your painting.

4. **What does the Airbrush option for the Brush tool control?**

   When the Airbrush option is enabled, it controls how quickly the paint builds up as you drag the Brush tool.

5. **When do you use the Clone Stamp tool?**

   The Clone Stamp tool is useful for duplicating parts of an image.

6. **How do you sample part of an image with the Clone Stamp tool?**

   Position the Clone Stamp tool over the part of the image you want to sample, hold down Alt, and click to sample the image.

Lesson 8 Follow-up

Lesson 8 Lab 1

1. **How do you add text to a Photoshop image?**

   Use the Type tool to click or drag, which automatically creates a type layer within the image. Type to add text, and then press Enter on the numeric keypad or click the Commit Any Current Edits button on the Tool Options bar.

2. **What is the difference between point text and paragraph text?**

   The text that wraps within a bounding box is called paragraph text, while text that does not wrap within a bounding box is called point text. Point text is useful when you want each line of text to flow independently of other lines. Paragraph text is useful when you want the text to flow within a specified bounding box. You can resize the bounding box for paragraph text at any time.

3. **When do you use layer effects?**

   Layer effects are a quick way to apply shadows to an image, as well as embossing, beveling, cutouts, glows, or color fills.

4. **How do you open the Layer Style dialog box to choose layer effects?**

   Double-click a layer on the Layers palette, or choose a specific layer effect from the Layer Style submenu of the Layer menu.

5. **When do you use a filter? Which aspects of a filter's effects can the Fade command adjust?**

   Filters can be used to create original textures and effects, or to alter existing images or artwork. You can make your image look hand painted or like glass using a filter. After applying a filter, you can use the Fade command in the Edit menu to adjust the opacity and blending mode of the filter.

6. **Why do you merge layers in an image?**

   Merging layers helps reduce the file size. You must first merge the layers into a single layer if you want to apply a filter to multiple layers.

7. **Describe two techniques for merging image layers.**

   Answers mat vary but include: To merge linked layers, select any one of the linked layers, and select Merge Linked from the Layers palette drop-down list; to merge layers within a layer set, select the layer set's name, and select Merge Layer Set from the Layers palette drop-down list; to merge all visible layers, select Merge Visible from the Layers palette drop-down list; to merge a selected layer with the layer below it, select Merge Down from the Layers palette drop-down list; and to merge all layers, select Flatten Image from the Layers palette drop-down list.

Lesson 9

Activity 9-3

1. **True or False? The Hue/Saturation command allows you to change specific hues within a layer.**

   ✓ True

   __ False

Lesson 9 Follow-up

Lesson 9 Lab 1

1. **What is the advantage of using an adjustment layer?**

   It allows you to experiment with brightness, contrast, and color modifications without permanently modifying pixel values in the image.

2. **What is the difference between the output levels controls and the input levels controls in the Levels dialog box?**

   The output levels controls allow you to reduce image contrast, and the input levels controls allow you to increase image contrast. Also, the input levels controls allow you to adjust image midtones, while output levels controls do not.

3. **Why do you use the toning tools instead of the Levels command?**

   The toning tools create results similar to those generated by the Levels command. However, since you paint directly in the image with the toning tools, they can be used to very selectively darken or lighten specific areas of an image.

4. **What is the benefit of using the Burn tool to darken an image?**

   The Burn tool allows you to darken specific areas of an image using painting techniques.

5. **True or False? You can quickly replace a specific image color with a new color.**

   ✓ True

   __ False

Lesson 10

Activity 10-1

2. **In which formats do you save Photoshop images designed for print?**

   ✓ a) TIFF

   ✓ b) EPS

   c) PSB

   d) PICT

3. **True or False? The Byte Order allows you to specify the platform on which the file will be read.**

   ✓ True

   __ False

Lesson 10 Follow-up

Lesson 10 Lab 1

1. **Why do you need to save a Photoshop image in a different format?**

   Photoshop images that will be imported into documents designed for print are typically saved in either TIFF or EPS formats because not all applications can use native Photoshop files. Also, some applications don't support the use of layers in images, so it is important to save the image in a compatible format.

2. **When saving a copy of a Photoshop image in a different format, why is it a good idea to keep the original image in Photoshop format as well?**

   Most formats don't support multiple layers. Saving an image in the TIFF format, for example, will ordinarily flatten the image, combining all layers into one. Keeping the original image in Photoshop format is important so that you can return to the original image with all the layers intact, and make adjustments if needed.

3. **When do you use the JPEG format instead of the GIF format?**

   Use the JPEG format for photographs and other continuous tone images since JPEG images can contain millions of colors and shades. The GIF format supports only 256 colors.

4. **What is the primary benefit of using the Save for Web command to save an image in a web format?**

   The Save For Web command allows you to preview several versions of an image to see how the image will appear when exported using a variety of web formats and format options. This allows you to choose the format and format options that provide the best balance between small file size and image quality.

Notes

GLOSSARY

adjustment layer
A special type of layer used for making adjustments to tonality of an image without changing the pixels in any existing layers.

Adobe Bridge
A next generation file browser that lets you view, sort, and manage both Adobe and non-Adobe application files from a central location.

alpha channel
A channel that consists of additional information stored with an image, in the form of a grayscale image, and is typically used to store selections.

Anti-aliasing
A feature that enables you to smoothen jagged edges by placing light pixels around the outside of a selected object.

bitmap images
Images that use either black or white color to represent the pixels in the image. In this mode, each pixel occupies 1 bit.

blending modes
Options that determine which pixels blend with each other to create a special effect and how well they do so.

Brush tool
A tool that applies foreground color as you drag within an image, in the form of freehand lines that can have soft or hard edges.

Clone Stamp tool
A tool that is used for duplicating parts of an image, and for correcting blemishes or mistakes.

CMYK color
Assigns each pixel a percentage value for each process ink. The lightest colors are assigned small percentages, whereas the darker colors are assigned high percentages of process ink colors. This is the commonly used color mode in the printing industry.

color palette
A palette that is used to select an available color from the color ramp.

cropping
The process of removing parts of the image that you do not need.

cross hair cursor
A cursor that replaces the Lasso tool cursor on pressing the Caps Lock key.

Defringe command
A command used to remove unwanted pixels from around the edge of a selection.

duotone images
One-channel, 8-bit images that assign two, three, or four inks namely duotone, tritone, or quadtone, to print certain tones of the image in different colors.

Eraser tool
A tool used to erase pixels in an image.

Fade command
A command that is used to change the opacity and blending mode of the filter.

feathering
An effect that creates a blurred transition between the selection edge and the surrounding pixels, and allows you to specify the width of the feathered edge.

File Information box
Displays information on the physical and storage size of the displayed Photoshop image.

filters
Features in Photoshop that allow you to change the appearance of images.

fixed selection
Refers to a selected group of pixels that are moved to another spot and deselected.

floating selection
Refers to a selected group of pixels that are moved from their original spot.

grayscale images
One channel images resulting in 256 brightness levels ranging from 0 or pure black to 255 or pure white.

halftone screen
A dot pattern used to print varying brightness levels of a base ink color; for example, a halftone screen of black ink produces varying gray levels.

History Brush tool
A tool used to revert to part of an image if necessary.

History palette
A palette that keeps tracks of all your previous menu choices and menu movements.

indexed color
Single-channel mode, where the bit depth ranges from 1 to 8 bits, and each pixel is a color.

keywords
Words that allow you to identify files from content.

Lab color mode
Describes a color as the result of a lightness component (L), and two chromatic components: (a: green to red), and (b: blue to yellow). In Photoshop, this mode is used as an intermediate format for color conversions.

layers
Transparent pieces of an image, stacked on top of one another to create one image.

Layers palette
A palette that is used to create and name layers, and apply layer effects.

linescreen
The number of rows of dots in one inch, and it is measured in lines per inch.

Magic Wand tool
Makes selections based on pixels that fall within a specified color and its brightness range.

metadata
Text that describes a file using keywords, author, resolution, color space, and other file properties.

New Layer Via Cut command
A command that removes the selected group of pixels from their original layer, and places them in a new layer.

opacity
The amount of transparency in a layer.

paragraph text
Text that wraps within a bounding box.

PDF presets
A group of settings that are used to create consistent PDF files by balancing file size and quality, based on how the files will be used.

Pencil tool
A tool that applies foreground color as you drag within an image, creating freehand lines that are always hard edged.

Photoshop workspace
A work area that contains the Photoshop environment elements.

pixel depth
Determines the total number of colors or shades of brightness an image can utilize.

pixels
A colored, black and white, or transparent squares that are positioned adjacent to each other vertically and horizontally.

point text
Text that does not wrap within a bounding box.

Preset Manager
Allows you to choose your own workspace customizations from the library of preset palettes.

printer resolution
The number of dots in a given distance produced by a printing device; usually measured in dots per inch (dpi).

raster graphics
Image formats composed of a grid or raster, which is an array of small squares called pixels.

resampling
Determines whether or not to change the pixel dimensions of the image.

Revert command
A command to return to the version of the image saved on your hard disk.

RGB color
Comprise of red, blue, or green color components that use 256 shades of brightness.

Smart Object
An object imported into or created within Photoshop, and it stores a copy of the object's source data within a Photoshop project.

Tolerance
Refers to Magic Wand tool's sensitivity to color differences. If the tolerance is low, it means that the Magic Wand tool has less tolerance for color differences, and vice versa.

toolbox
Used to select, move, edit, paint, and view images.

transform
The scaling, rotating, distorting, shearing, or perspective applied to an image or selected areas in the image.

Undo command
A command used to undo the most recent changes that you have made.

vector graphics
Image formats composed of lines, curves, and geometric shapes that are defined by a set of mathematical instructions. They are not pixelated.

Workspace presets
Used to customize and organize menu items.

Zoom tool
A tool used to change the magnification of an image.

Notes

INDEX

Notes